March of America Facsimile Series

Number 71

Commerce of the Prairies

VOLUME II

Josiah Gregg

Commerce
of the Prairies

VOLUME II

by Josiah Gregg

ANN ARBOR

UNIVERSITY MICROFILMS, INC.

A Subsidiary of Xerox Corporation

Commerce of the Prairies

VOLUME II

F. Didier

A. L. Dick.

INDIAN ALARM ON THE CIMARRON RIVER.

New York. Henry G. Langley, 8 Astor House.

Vol. 1 page 74.

COMMERCE OF THE PRAIRIES:

OR THE

Journal of a Santa Fé Trader,

DURING

EIGHT EXPEDITIONS ACROSS

THE GREAT WESTERN PRAIRIES,

AND

A RESIDENCE OF NEARLY NINE YEARS

IN

NORTHERN MEXICO.

Illustrated with Maps and Engravings.

BY JOSIAH GREGG.

IN TWO VOLUMES.

VOL. II.

NEW YORK:

HENRY G. LANGLEY, 8 ASTOR HOUSE.

M DCCC XLIV.

S. W. BENEDICT & CO.,
STEREOTYPERS AND PRINTERS, 16 Spruce st.

CONTENTS OF VOL. II.

~~~~~~

CHAPTER III.

CHAPTER IV.

CHAPTER V.

CHAPTER VI.

CHAPTER VII.

CHAPTER VIII.

CHAPTER IX.

CONCLUSION OF THE SANTA FE TRADE.

CHAPTER X.

GEOGRAPHY OF THE PRAIRIES.

CHAPTER XI.

ANIMALS OF THE PRAIRIES.

CHAPTER XV.

INDIANS OF THE PRAIRIES.

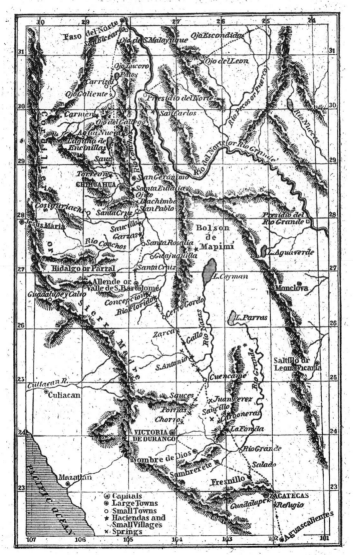

COMMERCE OF THE PRAIRIES.

CHAPTER I.

A Return to Prairie Life—Abandonment of the regular Route —The Start—A Suicide—Arrest of a Mulatto for Debt— Cherokee 'Bankrupt Law'—Chuly, the Creek Indian—The Muster and the Introduction—An ' *Olla Podrida*'—Adventure of a 'Down-Easter'—Arrival of U. S. Dragoons—Camp Holmes, and the Road—A Visit from a Party of Comanches —Tabba-quena, a noted Chief—His extraordinary Geographical Talent—Indians set out for the 'Capitan Grande,' and we through an Unexplored Region—Rejoined by Tabba-quena and his ' *suite* '—Spring Valley—The Buffalo Fever—The Chase—A Green-horn Scamper—Prairie Fuel.

AN unconquerable propensity to return to prairie life inclined me to embark in a fresh enterprise. The blockade of the Mexican ports by the French also offered strong inducements for undertaking such an expedition in the spring of 1839; for as Chihuahua is supplied principally through the sea-ports, it was now evident that the place must be suffering from great scarcity of goods. Being anxious to reach the market before the ports of the Gulf were reopened, we deemed it expedient to abandon the regular route from

Missouri for one wholly untried, from the borders of Arkansas, where the pasturage springs up nearly a month earlier. It is true, that such an attempt to convey heavily laden wagons through an unexplored region was attended with considerable risk; but as I was familiar with the general character of the plains contiguous to the north, I felt little or no apprehension of serious difficulties, except from what might be occasioned by regions of sandy soil. I have often been asked since, why we did not steer directly for Chihuahua, as our trade was chiefly destined for that place, instead of taking the circuitous route *via* Santa Fé. I answer, that we dreaded a journey across the southern prairies on account of the reputed aridity of the country in that direction, and I had no great desire to venture directly into a southern port in the present state of uncertainty as to the conditions of entry.

Suitable arrangements having been made, and a choice stock of about $25,000 worth of goods shipped to Van Buren on the Arkansas river, we started on the evening of the 21st of April, but made very little progress for the first eight days. While we were yet but ten or fifteen miles from Van Buren, an incident occurred which was attended with very melancholy results. A young man named Hays, who had driven a wagon for me for several months through the interior of Mexico, and thence to the United States in 1838, having heard that this expedition was projected, was desirous of engaging again in the same employ. I was equally desirous to secure his services, as he was well-tried, and had proved himself an excellent fellow on those perilous journeys. But soon after our outset, and without any apparent reason, he expressed an inclination to abandon the trip. I earnestly strove to dissuade him from his purpose, and supposed I had succeeded. What was my surprise, then, upon my return after a few hours' absence in advance of the company, to learn that he had secretly absconded! I was now led to reflect upon some of his eccentricities, and bethought me of several evident indications of slight mental derangement. We were, however, but a few miles from the settlements of the whites, and in the midst of the civilized Cherokees, where there was little or no danger of his suffering; therefore, there seemed but little occasion for serious uneasiness on his account. As it was believed he had shaped his course back to Van Buren, I immediately wrote to our friends there, to have search made for him. However, nothing could be found of him till the next day, when his hat and coat were discovered upon the bank of the Arkansas, near Van Buren, which were the last traces ever had of the unfortunate Hays! Whether intentionally or accidentally, he was evidently drowned.

On the 28th of April we crossed the Arkansas river a few miles above the mouth of the Canadian fork. We had only proceeded

a short distance beyond when a Cherokee shop-keeper came up to us with an attachment for debt against a free mulatto,
whom we had engaged as teamster.   The
poor fellow had no alternative but to return
with the importunate creditor, who committed him at once to the care of 'Judge Lynch'
for trial.   We ascertained afterwards that he
had been sentenced to 'take the benefit of
the bankrupt law' after the manner of the
Cherokees of that neighborhood.   This is
done by stripping and tying the victim to a
tree; when each creditor, with a good cow-
hide or hickory switch in his hand, scores the
amount of the bill due upon his bare back.
One stripe for every dollar due is the usual
process of 'whitewashing,' and as the appli-
cation of the lash is accompanied by all sorts
of quaint remarks, the exhibition affords no
small merriment to those present, with the
exception, no doubt, of the delinquent himself.   After the ordeal is over, the creditors
declare themselves perfectly satisfied: nor
could they, as is said, ever be persuaded there-
after to receive one red cent of the amount
due, even if it were offered to them.   As the
poor mulatto was also in our debt, and was
perhaps apprehensive that we might exact
payment in the same currency, he never
showed himself again.

On the 2d of May we crossed the North
Fork of the Canadian about a mile from its
confluence with the main stream.   A little
westward of this there is a small village of

Creek Indians, and a shop or two kept by American traders. An Indian who had quarrelled with his wife, came out and proposed to join us, and, to our great surprise, carried his proposal into execution. The next morning his repentant consort came to our camp, and set up a most dismal weeping and howling after her truant husband, who, notwithstanding, was neither to be caught by tears nor softened by entreaties, but persisted in his determination to see foreign countries. His name was Echú-eleh-hadjó (or *Crazy-deer-foot*), but, for brevity's sake, we always called him *Chuly*. He was industrious, and possessed many clever qualities, though somewhat disposed to commit excesses whenever he could procure liquor, which fortunately did not occur until our arrival at Santa Fé. He proved to be a good and willing hand on the way, but as he spoke no English, our communication with him was somewhat troublesome. I may as well add here, that, while in Santa Fé, he took another freak and joined a volunteer corps, chiefly of Americans, organized under one James Kirker to fight the Navajó and Apache Indians; the government of Chihuahua having guarantied to them all the spoils they should take. With these our Creek found a few of his 'red brethren'— Shawnees and Delawares, who had wandered thus far from the frontier of Missouri. After this little army was disbanded, Chuly returned home, as I have been informed, with a small party who crossed the plains directly from Chihuahua..

We had never considered ourselves as perfectly *en chemin* till after crossing the Arkansas river; and as our little party experienced no further change, I may now be permitted to introduce them collectively to the reader. It consisted of thirty-four men, including my brother John Gregg and myself. These men had all been hired by us except three, two of whom were Eastern-bred boys—a tailor and a silversmith—good-natured, clever little fellows, who had thought themselves at the 'jumping-off place' when they reached Van Buren, but now seemed nothing loth to extend their peregrinations a thousand miles or so further, in the hope of 'doing' the 'Spaniards,' as the Mexicans are generally styled in the West, out of a little surplus of specie. The other was a German peddler, who somewhat resembled the Dutchman's horse, "put him as you vant, and he ish alvays tere;" for he did nothing during the whole journey but descant on the value of a chest of trumperies which he carried, and with which he calculated, as he expressed it, to "py a plenty of te Shpanish tollar." The trip across the Prairies cost these men absolutely nothing, inasmuch as we furnished them with all the necessaries for the journey, in consideration of the additional strength they brought to our company.

It is seldom that such a variety of ingredients are found mixed up in so small a compass. Here were the representatives of seven distinct nations, each speaking his own native language, which produced at times a very respectable jumble of discordant sounds. There was one Frenchman whose volubility of tongue and curious gesticulations, contrasted very strangely with the frigidity of two phlegmatic wanderers from Germany; while the calm eccentricity of two Polish exiles, the stoical look of two sons of the desert (the Creek already spoken of, and a Chickasaw), and the pantomimic gestures of sundry loquacious Mexicans, contributed in no small degree to heighten the effects of the picture. The Americans were mostly backwoodsmen, who could handle the rifle far better than the whip, but who nevertheless officiated as wagoners.

We had fourteen road wagons, half drawn by mules, the others by oxen (eight of each to the team); besides a carriage and a Jersey wagon. Then we had two swivels mounted upon one pair of wheels; but one of them was attached to a movable truckle, so that, upon stopping, it could be transferred to the other side of the wagons. One of these was a long brass piece made to order, with a calibre of but an inch and a quarter, yet of sufficient metal to throw a leaden ball to the distance of a mile with surprising accuracy. The other was of iron, and a little larger. Besides these, our party was well supplied with small arms. The Americans mostly had their rifles and a musket in addition, which

they carried in their wagons, always well
charged with ball and buckshot Then my
brother and myself were each provided with
one of Colt's repeating rifles, and a pair of
pistols of the same, so that we could, if necessary, carry thirty-six ready-loaded shots apiece;
which alone constituted a capacity of defence
rarely matched even on the Prairies.

Previous to our departure we had received
a promise from the war department of an escort of U. S. Dragoons, as far as the borders
of the Mexican territory; but, upon sending
an express to Gen. Arbuckle at Fort Gibson to
that effect, we were informed that in consequence of some fresh troubles among the
Cherokees, it was doubtful whether the force
could be spared in time. This was certainly
no very agreeable news, inasmuch as the escort would have been very serviceable in as-
sisting to search out a track over the unexplored wilderness we had to pass. It was
too late, however, to recede; and so we resolved at all hazards to pursue our journey.

We had advanced beyond the furthest
settlements of the Creeks and Seminoles,
and pitched our camp on a bright balmy evening, in the border of a delightful prairie, when
some of the young men, attracted by the prospect of game, shouldered their rifles and
wended their steps through the dense forest
which lay contiguous to our encampment.
Among those that went forth, there was one
of the 'down-easters' already mentioned, who
was much more familiar with the interior of

a city than of a wilderness forest. As the shades of evening were beginning to descend and all the hunters had returned except him, several muskets and even our little field-pieces were fired, but without effect. The night passed away, and the morning dawned upon the encampment, and still he was absent. The firing was then renewed; but soon after he was seen approaching, very sullen and dejected. He came with a tale of perilous adventures and 'hair-breadth 'scapes' upon his lips, which somewhat abated the storm of ridicule by which he was at first assailed. It seemed that he had heard our firing on the previous evening, but believed it to proceed from a contrary direction—a very common mistake with persons who have become bewildered and lost. Thus deceived and stimulated by the fear of Indians (from a party of whom he supposed the firing to proceed), he continued his pathless wanderings till dark, when, to render his situation still more critical, he was attacked by a 'painter'—*anglice*, panther—which he actually succeeded in beating off with the breech of his gun, and then betook himself to the topmost extremity of a tree, where, in order to avoid a similar intrusion, he passed the remainder of the night. From a peculiar odor with which the shattered gun was still redolent, however, it was strongly suspected that the 'terrific painter' was not many degrees removed, in affinity, from a——polecat.

We had just reached the extreme edge of

2*

the far famed 'Cross-Timbers' when we were gratified by the arrival of forty dragoons, under the command of Lieut. Bowman, who had orders to accompany us to the supposed boundary of the United States. On the same evening we had the pleasure of encamping together at a place known as Camp Holmes, a wild romantic spot in latitude 35° 5', and but a mile north of the Canadian river. Just at hand there was a beautiful spring where, in 1835, Colonel Mason with a force of U. S. troops, had a 'big talk' and still bigger 'smoke' with a party of Comanche and Witchita Indians. Upon the same site Col. Chouteau had also caused to be erected not long after, a little stockade fort, where a considerable trade was subsequently carried on with the Comanches and other tribes of the southwestern prairies. The place had now been abandoned, however, since the preceding winter.

From the Arkansas river to Chouteau's Fort, our route presented an unbroken succession of grassy plains and fertile glades, intersected here and there with woody belts and numerous rivulets, most of which, however, are generally dry except during the rainy season. As far as Camp Holmes, we had a passable wagon road, which was opened upon the occasion of the Indian treaty before alluded to, and was afterwards kept open by the Indian traders. Yet, notwithstanding the road, this stretch gave us more trouble—presented more rugged passes, miry ravines and steep ascents—than all the rest of our journey put together.

We had not been long at the Fort, before we received a visit from a party of Comanches, who having heard of our approach came to greet us a welcome, on the supposition that it was their friend Chouteau returning to the fort with fresh supplies of merchandise. Great was their grief when we informed them that their favorite trader had died at Fort Gibson, the previous winter. On visiting their wigwams and inquiring for their *capitan*,* we were introduced to a corpulent, squint-eyed old fellow, who certainly had nothing in his personal appearance indicative of rank or dignity. This was Tábba-quena (or the Big Eagle), a name familiar to all the Comanche traders. As we had frequently heard that he spoke Spanish fluently, we at once prepared ourselves for a social chit-chat; but, on accosting him in that tongue and inquiring whether he could talk Spanish, he merely replied ' *Poquito*,' putting at the same time his forefinger to his ear, to signify that he merely understood a little—which proved true to a degree, for our communication was chiefly by signs. We were now about to launch upon an unknown region—our route lay henceforth across that unexplored wilderness, of which I have so frequently spoken, without either pilot or trail to guide us for nearly 500 miles. We had to depend entirely upon

* Most of the prairie Indians seem to have learned this Spanish word, by which, when talking with the whites, all their chiefs are designated.

our knowledge of the geographical position
of the country for which we were steering,
and the indications of a compass and sextant.
This was emphatically a pioneer trip; such a
one also as had, perhaps, never before been
undertaken—to convey heavily laden wagons
through a country almost wholly untrod by
civilized man, and of which *we*, at least, knew
nothing. We were therefore extremely anxious to acquire any information our visitors
might be able to give us; but Tábba-quena
being by no means experienced in wagon
tactics, could only make us understand, by
gestures, mixed with a little wretched Spanish, that the route up the Canadian presented
no obstacles according to *his* mode of travelling. He appeared, however, very well acquainted with the whole Mexican frontier,
from Santa Fé to Chihuahua, and even to the
Gulf, as well as with all the Prairies. During
the consultation he seemed occasionally to
ask the opinions of other chiefs who had hud-
dled around him. Finally, we handed him a
sheet of paper and a pencil, signifying at the
same time a desire that he would draw us a
map of the Prairies. This he very promptly
executed; and although the draft was somewhat rough, it bore, much to our astonishment, quite a map-like appearance, with a far
more accurate delineation of all the principal
rivers of the plains—the road from Missouri
to Santa Fé, and the different Mexican settlements, than is to be found in many of the en-
graved maps of those regions.

Tabba-quena's party consisted of about sixty persons, including several squaws and papooses, with a few Kiawa chiefs and warriors, who, although of a tribe so entirely distinct, are frequently found domiciled among the Comanches. As we were about to break up the camp they all started for Fort Gibson, for the purpose, as they informed us, of paying a visit to the 'Capitan Grande'—a Spanish phrase used by many prairie tribes, and applied, in their confused notions of rank and power, not only to the President of the United States himself, but to the seat of the federal government. These they are again apt to confound with Fort Gibson and the commanding officer of that station.

On the 18th of May, we set out from Chouteau's fort. From this forward our wagons were marched in two lines, and regularly 'formed' at every camp, so as to constitute a fortification and a *corral* for the stock. This is different from the 'forming' of the large caravans. The two front wagons are driven up side by side, with their 'tails' a little inclined outward. About half of the rest are drawn up in the same manner, but each stopped with the fore-wheel a little back of the hindwheel of the next ahead. The remainder are similarly brought up, but inclined inward behind, so as nearly to close again at the rear of the pen; leaving a gap through which to introduce the stock. Thus the *corral* remains of an ovate form. After the drivers become expert the whole is performed in a very short time.

On the following day we were again joined
by old Tabba-quena, and another Comanche
chief, with five or six warriors, and as many
squaws, including Tab's wife and infant son.
As we were jogging along in the afternoon, I
held quite a long conversation in our semi-
mute language with the squinting old chief.
He gave me to understand, as well as he could,
that his comrades* had proceeded on their
journey to see the Capitan Grande, but that
he had concluded to return home for better horses. He boasted in no measured terms
of his friendship for the Americans, and pro-
mised to exert his influence to prevent the
turbulent and unruly spirits of his nation from
molesting us. But he could not disguise his
fears in regard to the Pawnees and Osages,
who, he said, would be sure to run off with
our stock while we were asleep at night.
When I informed him that we kept a strict
night-watch, he said, "*Está bueno*" (that's
good), and allowed that our chances for safety
were not so bad after all.

These friendly Indians encamped with us
that night, and on the following morning the
old chief informed us that some of his party
had a few "mulas para *swap*" (mules to trade;
for having learned the word *swap* of some
American traders, he very ingeniously tacked
it at the tail of his little stock of Spanish).
A barter for five mules was immediately con-

---

* Some of these (principally Kiawas, as I afterwards learned),
reached Fort Gibson, and received a handsome reward of government presents for their visit.

cluded upon, much to our advantage, as our
teams were rather in a weak condition. Old
Tab and his party then left us to join his band,
which, he said, was located on the Faux
Ouachittâ river, and we never saw aught of
them more.

After leaving the Fort we generally kept on
the ridge between the Canadian and the
North Fork, crossing sometimes the tributary
brooks of the one and sometimes those of
the others. Having travelled in this manner
for about eighty miles, we entered one of the
most charming prairie vales that I have ever
beheld, and which in the plenitude of our enthusiasm, we named 'Spring Valley,' on account of the numerous spring-fed rills and
gurgling rivulets that greeted the sight in
every direction; in whose limpid pools
swarms of trout and perch were carelessly
playing. Much of the country, indeed, over
which we had passed was somewhat of a
similar character—yet nowhere quite so beautiful. I must premise, however, that westward of this, it is only the valleys immediately
bordering the streams that are at all fit for
cultivation: the high plains are too dry and
sandy. But here the soil was dark and mel-
low, and the rich vegetation with which it was
clothed plainly indicated its fertility. 'Spring
Valley' gently inclines towards the North
Fork, which was at the distance of about five
miles from our present route. It was somewhere along the border of this enchanting
vale that a little picket fort was erected in

1822 by an unfortunate trader named Mc-Knight, who was afterwards betrayed and murdered by the faithless Comanches. The landscape is beautifully variegated with stripes and fringes of timber: while the little herds of buffalo that were scattered about in fantastic groups imparted a degree of life and picturesqueness to the scene, which it was truly delightful to contemplate.

It was three days previous that we had first met with these 'prairie cattle.' I have often heard backwoodsmen speak of the 'buck ague,' but commend me to the 'buffalo fever' of the Prairies for novelty and amusement. Very few of our party had ever seen a buffalo before in its wild state; therefore at the first sight of these noble animals the excitement surpassed anything I had ever witnessed before. Some of our dragoons, in their eagerness for sport, had managed to frighten away a small herd that were quietly feeding at some distance, before our 'still hunters,' who had crawled towards them, had been able to get within rifle-shot of them. No sooner were the movements of our mounted men perceived, than the whole extent of country, as far as the eye could reach, became perfectly animate with living objects, fleeing and scampering in every direction. From the surrounding valleys sprang up numerous herds of these animals which had hitherto been unobserved, many of which, in their indiscriminate flight, passed so near the wagons, that the drivers, carried away by the contagious excitement of the moment, would leave the teams and keep up a running fire after them. I had the good fortune to witness the exploits of one of our Northern greenhorns, who, mounted upon a sluggish mule, and without any kind of weapon, amused himself by chasing every buffalo that came scudding along, as if he expected tc capture him by laying hold of his tail. Plying spur and whip, he would gallop after one division till he was left far behind : and then turn to another and another with the same earnestness of purpose, until they had all passed out of sight. He finally came back disheartened and sullen, with his head hanging down like one conscious of having done something supremely ridiculous; but still cursing his lazy mule, which, he said, might have caught the buffalo, if it had had a mind to.

The next day the buffalo being still more numerous, the chase was renewed with greater zest. In the midst of the general hurly-burly which ensued, three persons on foot were perceived afar off, chasing one herd of buffalo and then another, until they completely disappeared. These were two of our cooks, the one armed with a pistol, the other with a musket, accompanied by Chuly (the Creek), who was happily provided with a rifle. We travelled several miles without hearing or seeing anything of them. At last, when we had almost given them up for lost, Frank, the French cook, came trudging in, and his rueful countenance was no bad index of the doleful tale he had to relate. Although he had been chasing and shooting all day, he had, as he expressed it, "no killet one," till eventually he happened to stumble upon a wounded calf, which he boldly attacked; but as ill luck would have it, the youngster took it into his head to give him battle. "Foutre de varment! he butt me down," exclaimed the exasperated Frenchman,—"Sacré! me plentee scart; but me kill him for all." Chuly and the other cook came in soon after, in equally dejected spirits; for, in addition to his ill luck in hunting, the latter had been lost. The Indian had perhaps killed buffalo with his rifle, but he was in no humor to be communicative in his language of signs; so nothing was ever known of his adventures. One thing seemed pretty certain, that they were all cured of the 'buffalo fever.'

On the night after the first buffalo scamper, we encamped upon a woodless ravine, and were obliged to resort to 'buffalo chips' (dry ordure) for fuel. It is amusing to witness the bustle which generally takes place in collecting this offal. In dry weather it is an excellent substitute for wood, than which it even makes a hotter fire; but when moistened by rain, the smouldering pile will smoke for hours before it condescends to burn, if it does at all. The buffalo meat which the hunter roasts or broils upon this fire, he accounts more savory than the steaks dressed by the most delicate cooks in civilized life.

CHAPTER II.

As it now appeared that we had been forced at least two points north of the course we had originally intended to steer, by the northern bearing of the Canadian, we made an effort to cross a ridge of timber to the south, which, after considerable labor, proved successful. Here we found a multitude of gravelly, bright-flowing streams, with rich bottoms, lined all along with stately white oak, black-walnut, mulberry, and other similar growths, that yielded us excellent materials for wagon repairs, of which the route from Missouri, after passing Council Grove, is absolutely in want.

Although we found the buffalo extremely
scarce westward of Spring Valley, yet there
was no lack of game; for every nook and
glade swarmed with deer and wild turkeys,
partridges and grouse.   We had also occasion
to become acquainted with another species
of prairie-tenant whose visits generally produced impressions that were anything but
agreeable.   I allude to a small black insect
generally known to prairie travellers as the
'buffalo-gnat.' It not only attacks the face
and hands, but even contrives to insinuate itself into those parts which one is most careful to guard against intrusion.   Here it fastens
itself and luxuriates, until completely satisfied.
Its bite is so poisonous as to give the face, neck,
and hands, or any other part of the person upon which its affectionate caresses have been
bestowed, the appearance of a pustulated varioloid.   The buffalo-gnat is in fact a much
more annoying insect than the mosquito, and
also much more frequently met with on the
Prairies.

We now continued our line of march between the Canadian and the timbered ridge
with very little difficulty. Having stopped to
'noon' in a bordering valley, we were quite
surprised by the appearance of an Indian
with no other protection than his squaw.
From what we could gather by their signs,
they had been the victims of a 'love scrape.'
The fellow, whom I found to be a Kiawa,
had, according to his own account, stolen the
wife of another, and then fled to the thickets,

where he purposed to lead a lonely life, in hopes of escaping the vengeance of his incensed predecessor. From this, it would appear that affairs of gallantry are not evils exclusively confined to civilization. Plausible, however, as the Indian's story seemed to be, we had strong suspicions that others of his band were not far off; and that he, with his 'better half,' had only been skulking about in hopes of exercising their 'acquisitiveness' at our expense; when, on finding themselves discovered, they deemed it the best policy fearlessly to approach us. This singular visit afforded a specimen of that confidence with which civilization inspires even the most untutored savages. They remained with us, in the utmost nonchalance, till the following morning.

Shortly after the arrival of the visitors, we were terribly alarmed at a sudden prairie conflagration. The old grass of the valley in which we were encamped had not been burned off, and one of our cooks having unwittingly kindled a fire in the midst of it, it spread at once with wonderful rapidity, and a brisk wind springing up at the time, the flames were carried over the valley, in spite of every effort we could make to check them. Fortunately for us, the fire had broken out to the leeward of our wagons, and therefore occasioned us no damage; but the accident itself was a forcible illustration of the danger that might be incurred by pitching a camp in the midst of dry grass, and the advantages

3*

that might be taken by hostile savages in such a locality.

After the fire had raged with great violence for a few hours, a cloud suddenly obscured the horizon, which was almost immediately followed by a refreshing shower of rain: a phenomenon often witnessed upon the Prairies after an extensive conflagration; and affording a practical exemplification of Professor Espy's celebrated theory of artificial showers.

We now continued our journey without further trouble, except that of being still forced out of our proper latitude by the northern bearing of the Canadian. On the 30th of May, however, we succeeded in 'doubling' the spur of the Great North Bend. Upon ascending the dividing ridge again, which at this point was entirely destitute of timber, a 'prairie expanse' once more greeted our view. This and the following day, our route lay through a region that abounded in gypsum, from the finest quality down to ordinary plaster. On the night of the 31st we encamped on a tributary of the North Fork, which we called Gypsum creek, in consequence of its being surrounded with vast quantities of that substance.

Being compelled to keep a reckoning of our latitude, by which our travel was partly governed, and the sun being now too high at noon for the use of the artificial horizon, we had to be guided entirely by observations of the meridian altitude of the moon, planets, or

fixed stars. At Gypsum creek our latitude
was 36° 10'—being the utmost northing we
had made. As we were now about thirty
miles north of the parallel of Santa Fé, we
had to steer, henceforth, a few degrees south
of west in order to bring up on our direct
course.

The following night we encamped in a region covered with sandy hillocks, where there
was not a drop of water to be found : in fact,
an immense sand-plain was now opening
before us, somewhat variegated in appearance, being entirely barren of vegetation in
some places, while others were completely
covered with an extraordinarily diminutive
growth which has been called *shin-oak*, and
a curious plum-bush of equally dwarfish stature. These singular-looking plants (undistinguishable at a distance from the grass of
the prairies) were heavily laden with acorns
and plums, which, when ripe, are of considerable size, although the trunks of either
were seldom thicker than oat-straws, and frequently not a foot high. We also met with
the same in many other places on the Prairies.

Still the most indispensable requisite, water, was nowhere to be found, and symptoms
of alarm were beginning to spread far and
wide among us. When we had last seen the
Canadian and the North Fork, they appeared
to separate in their course almost at right
angles, therefore it was impossible to tell at
what distance we were from either. At last

my brother and myself, who had been scour-
ing the plains during the morning without
success, finally perceived a deep hollow leading in the direction of the Canadian, where
we found a fine pool of water, and our wagons 'made port' again before mid-day; thus
quieting all alarm.

Although we had encountered but very
few buffalo since we left Spring Valley, they
now began to make their appearance again,
though not in very large droves; together
with the deer and the fleet antelope, which
latter struck me as being much more tame in
this wild section of the Prairies than I had
seen it elsewhere. The graceful and majes-
tic mustang would also now and then sweep
across the naked country, or come curvetting
and capering in the vicinity of our little caravan, just as the humor prompted them. But
what attracted our attention most were the
little dog settlements, or, as they are more
technically called, 'dog towns,' so often alluded to by prairie travellers. As we were passing through their 'streets,' multitudes of the
diminutive inhabitants were to be seen among
the numerous little hillocks which marked
their dwellings, where they frisked about, or
sat perched at their doors, yelping defiance,
to our great amusement—heedless of the danger that often awaited them from the rifles of
our party; for they had perhaps never seen
such deadly weapons before.

On the 5th of June, we found ourselves
once more travelling on a firm rolling prairie,

about the region, as we supposed,* of the boundary between the United States and Mexico; when Lieut. Bowman, in pursuance of his instructions, began to talk seriously of returning. While the wagons were stopped at noon, a small party of us, including a few dragoons, advanced a few miles ahead to take a survey of the route. We had just ascended the highest point of a ridge to get a prospect of the country beyond, when we descried a herd of buffalo in motion and two or three horsemen in hot pursuit. "Mexican Ciboleros!" we all exclaimed at once; for we supposed we might now be within the range of the buffalo hunters of New Mexico. Clapping spurs to our horses, we set off towards them at full speed. As we might have expected, our precipitate approach frightened them away and we soon lost sight of them altogether. On reaching the spot where they had last been seen, we found a horse and two mules saddled, all tied to the carcass of a slain buffalo which was partly skinned. We made diligent search in some copses of small growth, and among the adjacent ravines, but could discover no further traces of the fugitives. The Indian rigging of the animals, however, satisfied us that they were not Mexicans.

We were just about giving up the pursuit, when a solitary Indian horseman was espied upon a ridge about a mile from us. My

---

* From subsequent observations, this point appears to have been some miles west of the 100th degree of longitude.

brother and myself set out towards him, but
on seeing us approach, he began to manifest
some fear, and therefore my brother advanced
alone. As soon as he was near enough he
cried out "*Amigo!*" to which the Indian replied "*Comantz!*" and giving himself a thump
upon the breast he made a graceful circuit,
and came up at full speed, presenting his
hand in token of friendship. Nothing, however, could induce him to return to his animals with us, where the rest of our party had
remained. He evidently feared treachery and
foul play. Therefore we retraced our steps to
the wagons, leaving the Indian's property just
as we had found it, which, we subsequently
discovered, was taken away after our departure.

In the afternoon of the same day, five more
Indians (including a squaw), made their appearance, and having been induced by friendly tokens to approach us, they spent the night
at our encampment. The next morning, we
expressed a desire, by signs, to be conducted
to the nearest point on our route where good
pasturage and water might be found. A
sprightly young chief, armed only with his
bow and arrows, at once undertook the task,
while his comrades still travelled along in our
company. We had not progressed far before
we found ourselves in the very midst of another large 'dog-town.'

The task of describing the social and domestic habits of these eccentric little brutes,
has been so graphically and amusingly exe-

cuted by the racy and popular pen of G.
Wilkins Kendall, that any attempt by me
would be idle; and I feel that the most agreeable service I can do my readers is to borrow
a paragraph from his alluring " Narrative,"
describing a scene presented by one of these
prairie commonwealths.

"In their habits they are clannish, social,
and extremely convivial, never living alone
like other animals, but, on the contrary, always found in villages or large settlements.
They are a wild, frolicsome, madcap set of
fellows when undisturbed, uneasy and ever
on the move, and appear to take especial delight in chattering away the time, and visiting
from hole to hole to gosip and talk over each
other's affairs—at least so their actions would
indicate. . . . . . . On several occasions I crept
close to their villages, without being observed,
to watch their movements. Directly in the
centre of one of them I particularly noticed a
very large dog, sitting in front of the door or
entrance to his burrow, and by his own actions
and those of his neighbors it really seemed as
though he was the president, mayor, or chief—
at all events, he was the 'big dog' of the place.
For at least an hour I secretly watched the operations in this community. During that time
the large dog I have mentioned received at
least a dozen visits from his fellow-dogs, which
would stop and chat with him a few moments,
and then run off to their domicils. All this
while he never left his post for a moment, and
I thought I could discover a gravity in his de-

portment not discernible in those by which he was surrounded. Far is it from me to say that the visits he received were upon business, or had anything to do with the local government of the village; but it certainly appeared so. If any animal has a system of laws regulating the body politic, it is certainly the prairie dog."

As we sat on our horses, looking at these 'village transactions,' our Comanche guide drew an arrow for the purpose of cutting short the career of a little citizen that sat yelping most doggedly in the mouth of his hole, forty or fifty paces distant. The animal was almost entirely concealed behind the hillock which encompassed the entrance of his apartment, so that the dart could not reach it in a direct line; but the Indian had resort to a manœuvre which caused the arrow to descend with a curve, and in an instant it quivered in the body of the poor little quadruped. The slayer only smiled at his feat, while we were perfectly astounded. There is nothing strange in the rifleman's being able to hit his mark with his fine-sighted barrel; but the accuracy with which these savages learn to shoot their feathered missiles, with such random aim, is almost incomprehensible. I had at the same time drawn one of Colt's repeating pistols, with a view of paying a similar compliment to another dog; when, finding that it excited the curiosity of the chief, I fired a few shots in quick succession, as an explanation of its virtues. He seemed to comprehend the secret instantly, and, drawing his bow once more, he discharged a number of arrows with the same rapidity, as a palpable intimation that he could shoot as fast with his instrument as we could with our patent fire-arms. This was not merely a vain show: there was more of reality than of romance in his demonstration.

Shortly after this we reached a fresh brook, a tributary of the North fork, which wound its silent course in the midst of a picturesque valley, surrounded by romantic hills and craggy knobs. Here we pitched our camp: when three of our visitors left us for the purpose of going to bring all the 'capitanes' of their tribe, who were said to be encamped at no great distance from us.

Our encampment, which we designated as ' Camp Comanche,' was only five or six miles from the North Fork, while, to the southward, the main Canadian was but a little more distant.

After waiting anxiously for the arrival of the Comanche chiefs, until our patience was well nigh exhausted, I ascended a high knoll just behind our camp, in company with the younger of the two chiefs who had remained with us, to see if anything could be discovered. By and by, the Comanche pointed anxiously towards the northwest, where he espied a party of his people, though at such a great distance, that it was some time before I could discern them. With what acuteness of vision are these savages endowed! As we

tomed to the open plains, and like the eagle
to look out for their prey at immense distances, their optical perception is scarcely excelled by that of the king of birds.

The party, having approached still nearer,
assembled upon an eminence as if for the
purpose of reconnoitring; but our chief upon
the knoll hoisting his blanket, which seemed
to say, 'come ahead,' they advanced slowly
and deliberately—very unlike the customary
mode of approach among all the prairie tribes.

The party consisted of about sixty warriors,
at the head of whom rode an Indian of small
stature and agreeable countenance, verging
on the age of fifty. He wore the usual Comanche dress, but instead of moccasins, he
had on a pair of long white cotton hose,
while upon his bare head waved a tall red
plume,—a mark of distinction which pro-
claimed him at once the *capitan mayor*, or
principal chief. We addressed them in Spanish, inquiring if they had brought an interpreter, when a lank-jawed, grum-looking savage announced his readiness to officiate in
that capacity. "*Sabes hablar en Español,
amigo?*" (can you talk Spanish, friend?) I
inquired. "*Si*" (yes), he gruffly replied.
"Where are your people?" "Encamped just
above on yonder creek." "How many of you
are there?" "Oh, a great many—nearly all
the Comanche nation; for we are *en junta* to
go and fight the Pawnees." "Well, can you
tell us how far it is to Santa Fé?"—But the
surly savage cut short my inquiries by observ-

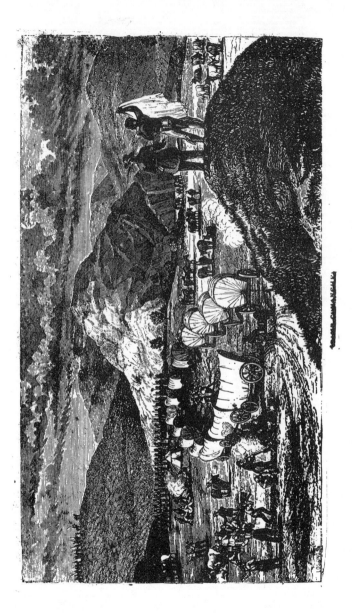

ing—" *Ahí platicarémos despues*"—" We will
talk about that hereafter."

We then showed them a spot a few rods
from us, where they might encamp so as not
to intermix their animals with ours; after
which all the *capitanes* were invited to our
camp to hold a 'big talk.' In a very short
time we had ten chiefs seated in a circle within our tent, when the pipe, the Indian token
of peace, was produced: but, doubting perhaps the sincerity of our professions, they at
first refused to smoke. The interpreter, however, remarked as an excuse for their conduct,
that it was not their custom to smoke until
they had received some presents: but a few
Mexican *cigarritos* being produced, most of
them took a whiff, as if under the impression
that to smoke cigars was no pledge of friendship.

Lieut. Bowman now desired us to broach
the subject of peace and amity betwixt the
Comanches and our people, and to invite
them to visit the ' Capitan Grande' at Washington, and enter into a perpetual treaty to
that effect; but they would not then converse
on the subject. In fact, the interpreter inquired, " Are we not at war?—how can we
go to see the Capitan Grande?" We knew
they held themselves at war with Mexico and
Texas, and probably had mistaken us for Texans, which had no doubt caused the interpreter to speak so emphatically of their immense
numbers. Upon this we explained to them
that the United States was a distinct govern-

ment and at peace with the Comanches. As an earnest of our friendly disposition, we then produced some scarlet cloth, with a small quantity of vermilion, tobacco, beads, etc., which being distributed among them, they very soon settled down into a state of placidness and contentment. Indeed, it will be found, that, with wild Indians, presents are always the corner-stone of friendship. "We are rejoiced," at last said the elder chief with a ceremonious air, "our hearts are glad that you have arrived among us: it makes our eyes laugh to see Americans walk in our land. We will notify our old and young men —our boys and our maidens—our women and children,—that they may come to trade with you. We hope you will speak well of us to your people, that more of them may hunt the way to our country, for we like to trade with the white man." This was delivered in Comanche, but translated into Spanish by the interpreter, who, although a full Indian, had lived several years among the Mexicans and spoke that language tolerably well. Our 'big talk' lasted several hours, after which the Indians retired to sleep. The next morning, after renewing their protestations of friendship, they took their departure, the principal chief saying, "Tell the Capitan Grande that when he pleases to call us we are all ready to go to see him."

The project of bringing some of the chiefs of these wild prairie tribes to Washington city, has been entertained, but never yet carried into effect. The few who have penetrated as far as Fort Gibson, or perhaps to a frontier village, have probably left with more unfavorable impressions than they had before. Believing the former to be our great Capital, and the most insignificant among the latter, our largest cities, they have naturally come to the conclusion that they surpass us in numbers and power, if not in wealth and grandeur. I have no doubt that the chiefs of the Comanches and other prairie tribes, if rightly managed, might be induced to visit our veritable 'Capitan Grande,' and our large cities, which would doubtless have a far better effect than all the treaties of peace that could be concluded with them for an age to come. They would then 'see with their own eyes and hear with their own ears' the magnificence and power of the whites, which would inspire them at once with respect and fear.

This was on the 7th of June. About noon, Lieut. Bowman and his command finally took leave of us, and at the same time we resumed our forward march. This separation was truly painful: not so much on account of the loss we were about to experience, in regard to the protection afforded us by the troops (which, to say the truth, was more needed now than it had ever been before), as for the necessity of parting with a friend, who had endeared himself to us all by his affable deportment, his social manners and accommodating disposition. Ah! little did we think then that we should never see that gallant officer more!

So young, so robust, and so healthy, little did we suspect that the sound of that voice which shouted so vigorously in responding to our parting salute in the desert, would never greet our ears again! But such was Fate's decree! Although he arrived safely at Fort Gibson, in a few short weeks he fell a victim to disease.

There were perhaps a few timid hearts that longed to return with the dragoons, and ever and anon a wistful glance would be cast back at the receding figures in the distance. The idea of a handful of thirty-four men having to travel without guide or protection through a dreary wilderness, peopled by thousands of savages who were just as likely to be hostile as friendly, was certainly very little calculated to produce agreeable impressions. Much to the credit of our men, however, the escort was no sooner out of sight than the timorous regained confidence, and all seemed bound together by stronger ties than before. All we feared were ambuscades or surprise; to guard against which, it was only necessary to redouble our vigilance.

On the following day, while we were enjoying our noon's rest upon a ravine of the Canadian, several parties of Indians, amounting altogether to about three hundred souls, including women and children, made their appearance. They belonged to the same band of Comanches with whom we had had so agreeable an intercourse, and had brought several mules in the expectation of driving a trade with us. The squaws and papooses were so anxious to gratify their curiosity, and so very soon began to give such striking manifestations of their pilfering propensities, that, at the request of the chiefs, we carried some goods at a little distance, where a trade was opened in hopes of attracting their attention. One woman, I observed, still lingered among the wagons, who, from certain peculiarities of features, struck me very forcibly as not being an Indian. In accordance with this impression I addressed her in Spanish, and was soon confirmed in all my suspicions. She was from the neighborhood of Matamoros, and had been married to a Comanche since her captivity. She did not entertain the least desire of returning to her own people.

Similar instances of voluntary captivity have frequently occurred. Dr. Sibley, in a communication to the War Department, in 1805, relates an affecting case, which shows how a sensitive female will often prefer remaining with her masters, rather than encounter the horrible ordeal of ill-natured remarks to which she would inevitably be exposed on being restored to civilized life. The Comanches, some twenty years previous, having kidnapped the daughter of the Governor-General of Chihuahua, the latter transmitted $1000 to a trader to procure her ransom. This was soon effected, but to the astonishment of all concerned, the unfortunate girl refused to leave the Indians. She sent word to her father, that they had disfigured her by tattooing; that she was married and perhaps *en-*

ceinte ; and that she would be more unhappy by returning to her father under these circumstances than by remaining where she was.

My attention was next attracted by a sprightly lad, ten or twelve years old, whose nationality could scarcely be detected under his Indian guise. But, though quite 'Indianized,' he was exceedingly polite. I inquired of him in Spanish, "Are you not a Mexican?" "Yes, sir,—I once was." "What is your name?" "Bernardino Saenz, sir, at your service." "When and where were you taken?" "About four years ago, at the Hacienda de las Animas, near Parral." "Shan't we buy you and take you to your people?—we are going thither." At this he hesitated a little, and then answered in an affecting tone, *"No, señor ; ya soy demasiado bruto para vivir entre los Cristianos"* (O, no, sir; I am now too much of a brute to live among Christians); adding that his owner was not there, and that he knew the Indian in whose charge he came would not sell him.

The Hacienda de las Animas is in the department of Chihuahua, some fifteen miles from the city of Parral, a much larger place than Santa Fé. Notwithstanding this, about three hundred Comanches made a bold inroad into the very heart of the settlements— laid waste the unfortunate hacienda, killing and capturing a considerable number—and remained several days in the neighborhood, committing all sorts of outrages. This occurred in 1835. I happened to be in Chihuahua at the time, and very well remember the bustle and consternation that prevailed. A thousand volunteers were raised, commanded by the governor himself, who 'hotly pursued' the enemy during their tardy retreat; but returned with the usual report—"*No les pudimos alcanzar*,"—we could not overtake them.

Out of half a dozen Mexican captives that happened to be with our new visitors, we only met with one who manifested the slightest inclination to abandon Indian life. This was a stupid boy about fifteen years of age, who had probably been roughly treated on account of his laziness. We very soon struck a bargain with his owner, paying about the price of a mule for the little outcast, whom I sent to his family as soon as we reached Chihuahua. Notwithstanding the inherent stupidity of my *protégé*, I found him abundantly grateful—much to his credit be it spoken—for the little service I had been able to render him.

We succeeded in purchasing several mules, which cost us between ten and twenty dollars worth of goods apiece. In Comanche trade the main trouble consists in fixing the price of the first animal. This being settled by the chiefs, it often happens that mule after mule is led up and the price received without further cavil. Each owner usually wants a general assortment; therefore the price must consist of several items, as a blanket, a looking-glass, an awl, a flint, a little tobacco, vermillion, beads, etc.

Our trade with the new batch of Comanches being over, they now began to depart as they had come, in small parties, without bidding us adieu, or even informing us of their intention, it being the usual mode of taking leave among Indians, to depart *sans cérémonie*, and as silently as possible.

The Santa Fé caravans have generally avoided every manner of trade with the wild Indians, for fear of being treacherously dealt with during the familiar intercourse which necessarily ensues. This I am convinced is an erroneous impression; for I have always found, that savages are much less hostile to those with whom they trade, than to any other people. They are emphatically fond of traffic, and, being anxious to encourage the whites to come among them, instead of committing depredations upon those with whom they trade, they are generally ready to defend them against every enemy.

CHAPTER III.

THE Comanches having all disappeared, we resumed our march, and soon emerged into an open plain or *mesa* which was one of the most monotonous I had ever seen, there being not a break, not a hill nor valley, nor even a shrub to obstruct the view. The only thing which served to turn us from a direct course pursued by the compass, was the innumerable ponds which bespeckled the plain, and which kept us at least well supplied with water. Many of these ponds seem to have grown out of 'buffalo wallows,'—a term used on the Prairies to designate a sink made by the buffalo's pawing the earth for the purpose of obtaining a smooth dusty surface to roll upon.

After three or four days of weary travel over this level plain, the picturesque valley of the Canadian burst once more upon our view, presenting one of the most magnificent sights I had ever beheld. Here rose a perpendicular cliff, in all the majesty and sublimity of its desolation;—there another sprang forward as in the very act of losing its balance and about to precipitate itself upon the vale below. A little further on a pillar with crevices and cornices so curiously formed as easily to be mistaken for the work of art; while a thousand other objects grotesquely and fantastically arranged, and all shaded in the sky-bound perspective by the blue ridge-like brow of the *mesa* far beyond the Canadian, constituted a kind of chaotic space where nature seemed to have indulged in her wildest caprices. Such was the confusion of ground-swells and eccentric cavities, that it was altogether impossible to determine whereabouts the channel of the Canadian wound its way among them.

It would seem that these mesas might once have extended up to the margin of the stream, leaving a *cañon* or chasm through which the river flowed, as is still the case in some other places. But the basis of the plain not having been sufficiently firm to resist the action of the waters, these have washed and cut the bordering *cejas* or brows into all the shapes they now present. The buffalo and other animals have no doubt assisted in these transmutations. Their deep-worn paths over the brows of the plains, form channels for the descending rains; which are soon washed into the size of ravines—and even considerable creeks. The beds of these continue to be worn down until veins of lasting water are opened, and constant-flowing streams thus established. Numerous were the embryo rivulets which might be observed forming in this way along the borders of those streams. The frequent isolated benches and mounds, whose tabular summits are on a level with the adjacent plains, and appear entirely of a similar formation, indicate that the intermediate earth has been washed away, or removed by some other process of nature—all seeming to give plausibility to our theory.

It was somewhere in this vicinity that a small party of Americans experienced a terrible calamity in the winter of 1832-3, on their way home; and as the incident had the tendency to call into play the most prominent features of the Indian character, I will digress so far here as to relate the facts.

The party consisted of twelve men, chiefly citizens of Missouri. Their baggage and about ten thousand dollars in specie were packed upon mules. They took the route of the Canadian river, fearing to venture on the northern prairies at that season of the year. Having left Santa Fé in December, they had proceeded without accident thus far, when a large body of Comanches and Kiawas were seen advancing towards them. Being well acquainted with the treacherous and pusillanimous disposition of those races, the traders prepared at once for defence; but the savages having made a halt at some distance, began to approach one by one, or in small parties, making a great show of friendship all the while, until most of them had collected on the spot. Finding themselves surrounded in every direction, the travellers now began to move on, in hopes of getting rid of the intruders: but the latter were equally ready for the start; and, mounting their horses, kept jogging on in the same direction. The first act of hostility perpetrated by the Indians proved fatal to one of the American traders named Pratt, who was shot dead while attempting to secure two mules which had become separated from the rest. Upon this, the companions of the slain man immediately dismounted and commenced a fire upon the Indians, which was warmly returned, whereby another man of the name of Mitchell was killed.

By this time the traders had taken off their packs and piled them around for protection; and now falling to work with their hands, they very soon scratched out a trench deep enough to protect them from the shot of the enemy. The latter made several desperate charges, but they seemed too careful of their own personal safety, notwithstanding the enormous superiority of their numbers, to venture too near the rifles of the Americans. In a few hours all the animals of the traders were either killed or wounded, but no personal damage was done to the remaining ten men, with the exception of a wound in the thigh received by one, which was not at the time considered dangerous.

During the siege, the Americans were in great danger of perishing from thirst, as the Indians had complete command of all the water within reach. Starvation was not so much to be dreaded; because, in case of necessity, they could live on the flesh of their slain animals, some of which lay stretched close around them. After being pent up for thirty-six hours in this horrible hole, during which time they had seldom ventured to raise their heads above the surface without being shot at, they resolved to make a bold *sortie* in the night, as any death was preferable to the fate which awaited them there. As there was not an animal left that was at all in a condition to travel, the proprietors of the money gave permission to all to take and appropriate to themselves whatever amount each man could safely undertake to carry. In this way a few hundred dollars were started with, of which, however, but little ever reached the United States. The remainder was buried deep in the sand, in hopes that it might escape the cupidity of the savages; but to very little purpose, for they were afterwards seen by some Mexican traders making a great display of specie, which was without doubt taken from this unfortunate *cache*.

With every prospect of being discovered, overtaken, and butchered, but resolved to sell their lives as dearly as possible, they at last

emerged from their hiding-place, and moved
on silently and slowly until they found themselves beyond the purlieus of the Indian
camps.   Often did they look back in the direction where from three to five hundred savages were supposed to watch their movements, but, much to their astonishment, no
one appeared to be in pursuit.   The Indians,
believing no doubt that the property of the
traders would come into their hands, and having no amateur predilection for taking scalps
at the risk of losing their own, appeared willing enough to let the spoliated adventurers
depart without further molestation.

The destitute travellers having run themselves short of provisions, and being no longer
able to kill game for want of materials to
load their rifles with, they were very soon reduced to the necessity of sustaining life upon
the roots and the tender bark of trees.   After
travelling for several days in this desperate
condition, with lacerated feet, and utter pros-
tration of mind and body, they began to disa-
gree among themselves about the route to be
pursued, and eventually separated into two
distinct parties.   Five of these unhappy men
steered a westward course, and after a succession of sufferings and privations which
almost surpassed belief, they reached the settlements of the Creek Indians, near the Arkansas river, where they were treated with
great kindness and hospitality.   The other
five wandered about in the greatest state of
distress and bewilderment, and only two

finally succeeded in getting out of the mazes of the wilderness. Among those who were abandoned to their fate, and left to perish thus miserably, was a Mr. Schenck, the same individual who had been shot in the thigh; a gentleman of talent and excellent family connections, who was a brother, as I am informed, of the Hon. Mr. Schenck, at present a member of Congress from Ohio.

But let us resume our journey. We had for some days, while travelling along the course of the Canadian, been in anxious expectation of reaching a point from whence there was a cart-road to Santa Fé, made by the Ciboleros; but being constantly baffled and disappointed in this hope, serious apprehensions began to be entertained by some of the party that we might after all be utterly lost. In this emergency, one of our Mexicans who pretended to be a great deal wiser than the rest, insisted that we were pursuing a wrong direction, and that every day's march only took us further from Santa Fé. There appeared to be so much plausibility in his assertion, as he professed a perfect knowledge of all the country around, that many of our men were almost ready to mutiny,—to take the command from the hands of my brother and myself and lead us southward in search of the Colorado, into the fearful *Llano Estacado*, where we would probably have perished. But our observations of the latitude, which we took very frequently, as well as the course we were pursuing, completely contradicted the

5*

Mexican wiseacre.   A few days afterwards
we were overtaken by a party of *Comancheros*, or Mexican Comanche traders, when we
had the satisfaction of learning that we were
in the right track.

These men had been trading with the band
of Comanches we had lately met, and learning from them that we had passed on, they had
hastened to overtake us, so as to obtain our
protection against the savages, who, after selling their animals to the Mexicans, very frequently take forcible possession of them
again, before the purchasers have been able to
reach their homes.   These parties of *Comancheros* are usually composed of the indigent
and rude classes of the frontier villages, who
collect together, several times a year, and
launch upon the plains with a few trinkets
and trumperies of all kinds, and perhaps a
bag of bread and may-be another of *pinole*,
which they barter away to the savages for
horses and mules.   The entire stock of an
individual trader very seldom exceeds the
value of twenty dollars, with which he is content to wander about for several months, and
glad to return home with a mule or two, as the
proceeds of his traffic.

These Mexican traders had much to tell us
about the Comanches: saying, that they were
four or five thousand in number, with perhaps a thousand warriors, and that the fiery
young men had once determined to follow
and attack us; but that the chiefs and sages
had deterred them, by stating that our can-

nons could kill to the distance of many miles, and shoot through hills and rocks and destroy everything that happened to be within their range. The main object of our visitors, however, seemed to be to raise themselves into importance by exaggerating the perils we had escaped from. That they had considered themselves in great jeopardy, there could be no doubt whatever, for, in their anxiety to overtake us, they came very near killing their animals.

It was a war-party of this band of Comanches that paid the 'flying visit' to Bent's Fort on the Arkansas river, to which Mr. Farnham alludes in his trip to Oregon. A band of the same Indians also fell in with the caravan from Missouri, with whom they were for a while upon the verge of hostilities.

The next day we passed the afternoon upon a ravine where we found abundance of water, but to our great surprise our animals refused to drink. Upon tasting the water, we found it exceedingly nauseous and bitter; far more repugnant to some palates than a solution of Epsom salts. It is true that the water had been a little impregnated with the same loathsome substance for several days; but we had never found it so bad before. The salinous compound which imparts this savor, is found in great abundance in the vicinity of the table-plain streams of New Mexico, and is known to the natives by the name of *salitre*.* We

* Literally *saltpetre;* but the *salitre* of New Mexico is a compound of several other salts beside nitre.

had the good fortune to find in the valley, a few sinks filled by recent rains, so that actually we experienced no great inconvenience from the want of fresh water. As far as our own personal necessities were concerned, we were abundantly supplied; it being an unfailing rule with us to carry in each wagon a five-gallon keg always filled with water, in order to guard against those frightful contingencies which so frequently occur on the Prairies. In truth upon leaving one watering place, we never knew where we would find the next.

On the 20th of June we pitched our camp upon the north bank of the Canadian or Colorado, in latitude 35° 24' according to a meridian altitude of Saturn. On the following day, I left the caravan, accompanied by three Comancheros, and proceeded at a more rapid pace towards Santa Fé. This was rather a hazardous journey, inasmuch as we were still within the range of the Pawnee and Comanche war-parties, and my companions were men in whom I could not repose the slightest confidence, except for pilotage; being fully convinced that in case of meeting with an enemy, they would either forsake or deliver me up, just as it might seem most conducive to their own interest and safety. All I had to depend upon were my fire-arms, which could hardly fail to produce an impression in my favor; for, thanks to Mr. Colt's invention, I carried thirty-six charges ready-loaded, which I could easily fire at the rate of a dozen per minute. I do not believe that any band of those timorous savages of the western prairies would venture to approach even a single man, under such circumstances. If, according to an old story of the frontier, an Indian supposed that a white man fired both with his tomahawk and scalping knife, to account for the execution done by a brace of pistols, thirty-six shots discharged in quick succession would certainly overawe them as being the effect of some great medicine.

As we jogged merrily along, I often endeavored to while away the time by catechising my three companions in relation to the topography of the wild region we were traversing; but I soon found, that, like the Indians, these ignorant rancheros have no ideas of distances, except as compared with time or with some other distance. They will tell you that you may arrive at a given place by the time the sun reaches a certain point: otherwise, whether it be but half a mile or half a day's ride to the place inquired for, they are as apt to apply *está cerquita* (it is close by), or *está lejos* (it is far off), to the one as to the other, just as the impression happens to strike them, when compared with some other point more or less distant. This often proves a source of great annoyance to foreign travellers, as I had an opportunity of experiencing before my arrival. In giving directions, these people—in fact, the lower classes of Mexicans generally—are also in the habit of using very odd gesticulations, altogether peculiar to themselves. Instead of pointing with their hands and fingers, they generally employ the mouth, which is done by thrusting out the lips in the direction of the spot, or object, which the inquirer wishes to find out—accompanied by *aquí* or *allí está*. This habit of substituting labial gestures for the usual mode of indicating, has grown from the use of the *sarape*, which keeps their hands and arms perpetually confined.

From the place where we left the wagons, till we reached the *Angostura*, or narrows (a distance of 60 miles), we had followed a plain cart-road, which seemed everywhere passable for wagons. Here, however, we found the point of a table plain projecting abruptly against the river, so as to render it impossible for wagons to pass without great risk. The huge masses of solid rock, which occur in this place, and the rugged cliffs or brows of the table lands which rise above them, appear to have been mistaken by a detachment of the Texan Santa Fé expedition, for spurs of the Rocky Mountains; an error which was rational enough, as they not unfrequently tower to the height of two thousand feet above the valley, and are often as rocky and rough as the rudest heaps of trap-rock can make them. By ascending the main summit of these craggy promontories, however, the eastern ridge of the veritable Rocky Mountains may be seen, still very far off in the western horizon, with a wide-spread and apparently level table plain, intervening and extending in every direction, as far as the eye can reach; for even the deep-cut chasms of the intersecting rivers are rarely visible except one be upon their very brink.

Upon expressing my fears that our wagons would not be able to pass the *Angostura* in safety, my comrades informed me that there was an excellent route, of which no previous mention had been made, passing near the *Cerro de Tucumcari*, a round mound plainly visible to the southward. After several vain efforts to induce some of the party to carry a note back to my brother, and to pilot the cara-van through the Tucumcari route, one of them, known as Tio Baca, finally proposed to undertake the errand for a bounty of ten dol-lars, besides high wages till they should reach the frontier. His conditions being accepted, he set out after breakfast, not, however, with-out previously recommending himself to the Virgin Guadalupe, and all the saints in the calendar, and desiring us to remember him in our prayers. Notwithstanding his fears, however, he arrived in perfect safety, and I had the satisfaction of learning afterward that my brother found the new route everything he could have desired.

I continued my journey westward with my two remaining companions; but, owing to their being provided with a relay of horses, they very soon left me to make the balance of the travel alone—though yet in a region haunted by hostile savages. On the follow-ing day, about the hour of twelve, as I was pursuing a horse-path along the course of the

Rio Pecos, near the frontier settlements, I met with a shepherd, of whom I anxiously inquired the distance to San Miguel. "O, it is just there," responded the man of sheep. "Don't you see that point of mesa yonder? It is just beyond that." This welcome information cheered me greatly; for, owing to the extraordinary transparency of the atmosphere, it appeared to me that the distance could not exceed two or three miles. "*Está cerquita,*" exclaimed the shepherd as I rode off; "*ahora está V. allá*"—"it is close by; you will soon be there."

I set off at as lively a pace as my jaded steed could carry me, confident of taking dinner in San Miguel. Every ridge I turned I thought must be the last, and thus I jogged on, hoping and anticipating my future comforts till the shades of evening began to appear; when I descended into the valley of the Pecos, which, although narrow, is exceedingly fertile and beautifully lined with verdant fields, among which stood a great variety of mud cabins. About eight o'clock, I called at one of these cottages and again inquired the distance to San Miguel; when a swarthy-looking ranchero once more saluted mine ears with "*Está cerquita; ahora está V. allá.*" Although the distance was designated in precisely the same words used by the shepherd eight hours before, I had the consolation at least of believing that I was something nearer. After spurring on for a couple of miles over a rugged road, I at last reached the long-sought village.

The next day, I hired a Mexican to carry some flour back to meet the wagons; for our party was by this time running short of provisions. In fact, we should long before have been in danger of starvation, had it not been for our oxen; for we had not seen a buffalo since the day we first met with the Comanches. Some of our cattle being in good plight, and able, as we were, to spare a few from our teams, we made beef of them when urged by necessity: an extra advantage in ox-teams on these perilous expeditions.

On the 25th of June I arrived safely at Santa Fé,—but again rode back to meet the wagons, which did not reach the capital till the 4th of July. We did not encounter a very favorable reception from 'his majesty,' Gov. Armijo. He had just established his arbitrary impost of $500 per wagon, which bore rather heavily upon us; for we had an overstock of coarse articles which we had merely brought along for the purpose of increasing the strength of our company, by adding to the number of our wagons.

But these little troubles in a business way, were entirely drowned in the joyful sensations arising from our safe arrival, after so long and so perilous an expedition. Considering the character and our ignorance of the country over which we had travelled, we had been exceedingly successful. Instances are certainly rare of heavily-laden wagons' having been conducted, without a guide, through an unexplored desert; and yet we performed the trip without any important accident—without encountering any very difficult passes—without suffering for food or for water.

We had hoped that at least a few days of rest and quiet recreation might have been allowed us after our arrival; for relaxation was sorely needed at the end of so long a journey and its concomitant privations: but it was ordered otherwise. We had scarcely quartered ourselves within the town before a grand 'flare-up' took place between Gov. Armijo and the foreigners* in Santa Fé, which, for a little while, bid fair to result in open hostilities. It originated in the following circumstances.

In the winter of 1837–8, a worthy young American, named Daley, was murdered at the Gold Mines, by a couple of villains, solely for plunder. The assassins were arrested, when they confessed their guilt; but, in a short time, they were permitted to run at large again, in violation of every principle of justice or humanity. About this time they were once more apprehended, however, by the interposition of foreigners: and, at the solicitation of the friends of the deceased, a memorial from the Americans in Santa Fé was presented to Armijo, representing the injustice of permitting the murderers of their countrymen to go unpunished; and praying that the culprits might

---

* Among the New Mexicans, the terms *foreigner* and *American* are synonymous: indeed, the few citizens of other nations to be found there identify themselves with those of the United States. All foreigners are known there as *Americanos ;* but south of Chihuahua they are indiscriminately called *Los Ingleses*, the English.

be dealt with according to law. But the governor affected to consider the affair as a conspiracy; and, collecting his ragamuffin militia, attempted to intimidate the petitioners. The foreigners were now constrained to look to their defence, as they saw that no justice was to be expected. Had Armijo persisted, serious consequences might have ensued; but seeing the 'conspirators' firm, he sent an apology, affecting to have misconstrued their motives, and promising that the laws should be duly executed upon the murderers.

Besides the incentives of justice and humanity, foreigners felt a deep interest in the execution of this promise. But a few years previous, another person had been assassinated and robbed at the same place; yet the authorities having taken no interest in the matter, the felons were never discovered: and now, should these assassins escape the merited forfeit of their atrocious crime, it was evident there would be no future security for our lives and property. But the governor's *due execution of the laws* consisted in retaining them a year or two in nominal imprisonment, when they were again set at liberty: yet by far the greater portion of this time they were merely the *criados sin sueldo* (servants without hire) of the governor, laboring for him as a remuneration for both the life and liberty which he granted them. Besides these, other foreigners have been murdered in New Mexico, and all with the same impunity.

CHAPTER IV.

AFTER passing the custom-house ordeal, and exchanging some of our merchandise for 'Eagle Dollars'—an operation which occupied us several weeks, I prepared to set out for the Chihuahua market, whither a portion of our stock had been designed. Upon this expedition I was obliged to depart without my brother, who was laboring under the 'home fever,' and anxious to return to his family. "He that hath wife and children," says Lord Bacon, "hath given hostages to fortune; for they are impediments to great enterprises, either of virtue or mischief." Men under such bonds are peculiarly unfitted for the chequered life of a Santa Fé trader. The domestic hearth, with all its sacred and most endearing recollections, is sure to haunt them in the hour of trial, and almost every step of their journey is apt to be attended by melancholy reflections of home and domestic dependencies.

Before starting on this new journey I deem it proper to make a few observations relative to the general character of the *Chihuahua Trade.* I have already remarked, that much surprise has frequently been expressed by those who are unacquainted with all the bearings of the case, that the Missouri traders should take the circuitous route to Santa Fé, instead of steering direct for Chihuahua, inasmuch as the greatest portion of their goods is destined for the latter city. But as Chihuahua never had any port of entry for foreign goods till the last six or eight years, the market of that department had to be supplied in a great measure from Santa Fé. By opening the ports of El Paso and Presidio del Norte, the commercial interest was so little affected, that when Santa Anna's decree for closing them again was issued, the loss was scarcely felt at all.

The mode of transmitting merchandise from the ports to the interior, is very different from what it is in the United States. It is not enough to have to pass the tedious ordeal of custom-houses on the frontier ;—we have not only to submit to a supervision and repayment of duty on arriving at our point of destination, but our cargo is subject to scrutiny at every town we have to pass through on our

journey. Nor would it be advisable to forsake the main route in order to avoid this ty-
rannical system of taxation; because, according
to the laws of the country, every *cargamento*
which is found out of the regular track (except in cases of unavoidable necessity), is subject to confiscation, although accompanied
by the necessary custom-house documents.

There are also other risks and contingencies very little dreamed of in the philosophy
of the inexperienced trader. Before setting
out, the entire bill of merchandise has to be
translated into Spanish; when, duplicates of
the translation being presented to the custom-
house, one is retained, while the other, accompanied by the *guia* (a sort of clearance
or mercantile passport), is carried along with
the cargo by the conductor. The trader can
have three points of destination named in his
guia, to either of which he may direct his
course, but to no others: while in the drawing up of the *factura*, or invoice, the greatest
care is requisite, as the slightest mistake,
even an accidental slip of the pen, might, according to the terms of the law, subject the
goods to confiscation.*

The *guia* is not only required on leaving
the ports for the interior, but is indispensable
to the safe conveyance of goods from one department of the republic to another: nay, the

---

* In confirmation of this, it is only necessary to quote the following from the *Pauta de Comisos*, Cap. II., Art. 22 : "Ni las
guias, ni las facturas, ni los pases, en todos los casos de que trata
este decreto, han de contener enmendatura, raspadura, ni entreren-
glonadura alguna"—and this under penalty of confiscation.

simple transfer of property from town to town, and from village to village, in the same department, is attended by precisely the same proportion of risk, and requires the same punctilious accuracy in the accompanying documents. Even the produce and manufactures of the country are equally subject to these embarrassing regulations. New Mexico has no internal custom-houses, and is therefore exempt from this rigorous provision; but from Chihuahua south every village has its revenue officers; so that the same stock of merchandise sometimes pays the internal duty at least half-a-dozen times before the sale is completed.

Now, to procure this same *guia*, which is the cause of so much difficulty and anxiety in the end, is no small affair. Before the authorities condescend to draw a single line on paper, the merchant must produce an endorser for the *tornaguía*, which is a certificate from the custom-house to which the cargo goes directed, showing that the goods have been legally entered there. A failure in the return of this document within a prescribed limit of time, subjects the endorser to a forfeiture equal to the amount of the impost. Much inconvenience and not a little risk are also occasioned on this score by the irregularity—I may say, insecurity of the mails.

Speaking of mails, I beg leave to observe, that there are no conveniences of this kind in New Mexico, except on the route from Santa Fé to Chihuahua, and these are very irregular and uncertain. Before the Indians had obtained such complete possession of the highways through the wilderness, the mails between these two cities were carried semi-monthly; but now they are much less frequent, being mere expresses, in fact, dispatched only when an occasion offers. There are other causes, however, besides the dread of marauding savages, which render the transportation of the mails in New Mexico very insecure: I mean the dishonesty of those employed in superintending them. Persons known to be inimical to the post-master, or to the 'powers that be,' and wishing to forward any communication to the South, most generally either wait for a private conveyance, or send their letters to a post-office (the only one besides that of Santa Fé in all New Mexico) some eighty miles on the way; thus avoiding an overhauling at the capital. Moreover, as the post-rider often carries the key of the mail-bag (for want of a supply at the different offices), he not unfrequently permits whomsoever will pay him a trifling *douceur*, to examine the correspondence. I was once witness to a case of this kind in the Jornada del Muerto, where the entire mail was tumbled out upon the grass, that an individual might search for letters, for which luxury he was charged by the accommodating carrier the moderate price of one dollar.

The *derecho de consumo* (the internal or consumption duty) is an impost averaging nearly twenty per cent. on the United States cost of the bill. It supplies the place of a direct tax for the support of the departmental government, and is decidedly the most troublesome, if not the most oppressive revenue system that ever was devised for internal purposes. It operates at once as a drawback upon the commercial prosperity of the country, and as a potent incentive to fraudulent practices. The country people especially have resort to every species of clandestine intercourse, to escape this galling burden; for, every article of consumption they carry to market, whether fish, flesh or fowl, as well as fruit and vegetables, is taxed more or less; while another impost is levied upon the goods they purchase with the proceeds of their sales. This system, so beautifully entangled with corruptions, is supported on the ground that it supersedes direct taxation, which, in itself, is an evil that the 'free and independent' people of Mexico would never submit to. Besides the petty annoyances incidental upon the laxity of custom-house regulations, no one can travel through the country without a passport, which, to free-born Americans, is a truly insupportable nuisance.

Having at last gone through with all the vexatious preparations necessary for our journey, on the 22d of August we started for Chihuahua. I fitted out myself but six wagons for this market, yet joining in company with several other traders, our little caravan again amounted to fourteen wagons, with about forty men. Though our route lay through

the interior of Northern Mexico, yet, on account of the hostile savages which infest most
of the country through which we had to pass,
it was necessary to unite in caravans of respectable strength, and to spare few of those
precautions for safety which are required on
the Prairies.

The road we travelled passes down through
the settlements of New Mexico for the first
hundred and thirty miles, on the east side of
the Rio del Norte.   Nevertheless, as there
was not an inn of any kind to be found upon
the whole route, we were constrained to put
up with very primitive accommodations.   Being furnished from the outset, therefore, with
blankets and buffalo rugs for bedding, we
were prepared to bivouac, even in the suburbs of the villages, in the open air; for in this
dry and salubrious atmosphere it is seldom
that travellers go to the trouble of pitching
tents.*   When travelling alone, however, or
with but a comrade or two, I have always experienced a great deal of hospitality from the
rancheros and villageois of the country. Whatever sins these ignorant people may have to
answer for, we must accord to them at least
two glowing virtues—gratitude and hospitality.
I have suffered like others, however, from
one very disagreeable custom which prevails

* How scant soever our outfit of ' camp comforts' might appear,
our Mexican muleteers were much more sparely supplied.   The
exposure endured by this hardy race is really surprising.   Even in
the coldest winter weather, they rarely carry more than one blan
ket apiece—the *sarape*, which serves as a cloak during the day,
and at night is their only ' bed and bedding.'

among them. Instead of fixing a price for the services they bestow upon travellers, they are apt to answer, " *Lo que guste,*" or " *Lo que le dé la gana*" (whatever you please, or have a mind to give), expecting, of course, that the liberal foreigner will give more than their consciences would permit them to exact.

In about ten days' drive we passed the southernmost settlements of New Mexico, and twenty or thirty miles further down the river we came to the ruins of Valverde. This village was founded about twenty years ago, in one of the most fertile valleys of the Rio del Norte. It increased rapidly in population, until it was invaded by the Navajoes, when the inhabitants were obliged to abandon the place after considerable loss, and it has never since been repeopled. The bottoms of the valley, many of which are of rich alluvial loam, have lain fallow ever since, and will perhaps continue to be neglected until the genius of civilization shall have spread its beneficent influences over the land. This soil is the more valuable for cultivation on account of the facilities for irrigation which the river affords; as it too frequently happens that the best lands of the settlements remain unfruitful for want of water.

Our next camping place deserving of mention was *Fray Cristóbal,* which, like many others on the route, is neither town nor village, but a simple isolated point on the river-bank—a mere *parage,* or camping-ground. We had already passed San Pascual, El Con-

tadero, and many others, and we could hear
Aleman, Robledo, and a dozen such spoken of
on the way, leading the stranger to imagine
that the route was lined with flourishing villages. The arriero will tell one to hasten—
"we must reach San Diego before sleeping."
We spur on perhaps with redoubled vigor, in
hopes to rest at a town; but lo! upon arriving, we find only a mere watering-place, without open ground enough to graze the *caballada*. Thus every point along these wilderness
highways used as a camping-site, has received
a distinctive name, well known to every muleteer who travels them. Many of these *pa-
rages*, without the slightest vestige of human
improvement, figure upon most of the current
maps of the day as towns and villages. Yet
there is not a single settlement (except of very
recent establishment) from those before mentioned to the vicinity of El Paso, a distance
of near two hundred miles.

We arrived at Fray Cristóbal in the evening, but this being the threshold of the famous *Jornada del Muerto*, we deemed it prudent to let our animals rest here until the
following afternoon. The road over which
we had hitherto been travelling, though it
sometimes traverses upland ridges and undulating sections, runs generally near the border
of the river, and for the most part in its immediate valley: but here it leaves the river
and passes for nearly eighty miles over a
table-plain to the eastward of a small ledge
of mountains, whose western base is hugged

by the circuitous channel of the Rio del Norte. The craggy cliffs which project from these mountains render the eastern bank of the river altogether impassable. As the direct route over the plain is entirely destitute of water, we took the precaution to fill all our kegs at Fray Cristóbal, and late in the afternoon we finally set out. We generally find a great advantage in travelling through these arid tracts of land in the freshness of the evening, as the mules suffer less from thirst, and move on in better spirits—particularly in the season of warm weather.

Early the next morning we found ourselves at the *Laguna del Muerto*, or 'Dead Man's Lake,' where there was not even a vestige of water. This *lake* is but a sink in the plain of a few rods in diameter, and only filled with water during the rainy season. The *marshes*, which are said by some historians to be in this vicinity, are nowhere to be found : nothing but the firmest and driest table land is to be seen in every direction. To procure water for our thirsty animals, it is often necessary to make a halt here, and drive them to the *Ojo del Muerto* (Dead Man's Spring), five or six miles to the westward, in the very heart of the mountain ridge that lay between us and the river. This region is one of the favorite resorts of the Apaches, where many a poor arriero has met with an untimely end. The route which leads to the spring winds for two or three miles down a narrow cañon or gorge, overhung on either side by abrupt precipices, while the various clefts and crags, which project their gloomy brows over the abyss below, seem to invite the murderous savage to deeds of horror and blood.

There is a tradition among the arrieros from which it would appear that the only road known in ancient time about the region of the *Jornada,* wound its circuitous course on the western side of the river. To save distance, an intrepid traveller undertook to traverse this desolate tract of land in one day, but having perished in the attempt, it has ever after borne the name of *La Jornada del Muerto,* 'the Dead Man's Journey,' or, more strictly, 'the Day's Journey of the Dead Man.' One thing appears very certain, that this dangerous pass has cost the life of many travellers in days of yore; and when we at last reached Robledo, a camping-site upon the river, where we found abundance of wood and water, we felt truly grateful that the arid *Jornada* had not been productive of more serious consequences to our party. We now found ourselves within the department of Chihuahua, as the boundary betwixt it and New Mexico passes not far from Robledo.

We were still some sixty miles above Paso del Norte, but the balance of the road now led down the river valley or over the low bordering hills. During our journey between this and El Paso we passed the ruins of several settlements, which had formerly been the seat of opulence and prosperity, but which have since been abandoned in consequence of the marauding incursions of the Apaches.

On the 12th of September we reached the usual ford of the Rio del Norte, six miles above El Paso; but the river being somewhat flushed we found it impossible to cross over with our wagons. The reader will no doubt be surprised to learn that there is not a single ferry on this 'Great River of the North' till we approach the mouth. But how do people cross it? Why, during three-fourths of the year it is everywhere fordable, and when the freshet season comes on; each has to remain on his own side or swim, for canoes even are very rare. But as we could neither swim our wagons and merchandise, nor very comfortably wait for the falling of the waters, our only alternative was to unload the vehicles, and ferry the goods over in a little 'dug-out' about thirty feet long and two feet wide, of which we were fortunate enough to obtain possession.

We succeeded in finding a place shallow enough to haul our empty wagons across: but for this good fortune we should have been under the necessity of taking them to pieces (as I had before done), and of ferrying them on the 'small craft' before mentioned. Half of a wagon may thus be crossed at a time, by carefully balancing it upon the canoe, yet there is of course no little danger of capsizing during the passage.

This river even when fordable often occasions a great deal of trouble, being, like the Arkansas, embarrassed with many quicksand mires.   In some places, if a wagon is permitted to stop in the river but for a moment, it sinks to the very body.   Instances have occurred where it became necessary not only to drag out the mules by the ears and to carry out the loading package by package, but to haul out the wagon piece by piece—wheel by wheel.

On the 14th we made our entrance into the town of *El Paso del Norte*,* which is the northernmost settlement in the department of Chihuahua.   Here our cargo had to be examined by a stern, surly officer, who, it was feared, would lay an embargo on our goods upon the slightest appearance of irregularity in our papers; but notwithstanding our gloomy forebodings, we passed the ordeal without any difficulty.

The valley of El Paso is supposed to contain a population of about four thousand inhabitants, scattered over the western bottom of the Rio del Norte to the length of ten or twelve miles.   These settlements are so thickly interspersed with vineyards, orchards, and cornfields, as to present more the appearance of a series of plantations than of a town: in fact, only a small portion at the head of the valley, where the *plaza pública* and parochial church are located, would seem to merit this title.

---

* This place is often known among Americans as ‘ *The Pass*.’ It has been suggested in another place, that it took its name from the *passing* thither of the refugees from the massacre of 1680; yet many persons very rationally derive it from the *passing* of the river (*el paso del Rio del Norte*) between two points of mountains which project against it from each side, just above the town.

Two or three miles above the *plaza* there is a dam of stone and brush across the river, the purpose of which is to turn the current into a dike or canal, which conveys nearly half the water of the stream, during a low stage, through this well cultivated valley, for the irrigation of the soil. Here we were regaled with the finest fruits of the season : the grapes especially were of the most exquisite flavor. From these the inhabitants manufacture a very pleasant wine, somewhat resembling Malaga. A species of *aguardiente* (brandy) is also distilled from the same fruit, which, although weak, is of very agreeable flavor. These liquors are known among Americans as 'Pass wine' and 'Pass whiskey,' and constitute a profitable article of trade, supplying the markets of Chihuahua and New Mexico.*

As I have said before, the road ftom Santa Fé to El Paso leads partly along the margin of the Rio del Norte, or across the bordering hills and plains; but the *sierra* which separates the waters of this river and those of the Rio Pecos was always visible on our left. In some places it is cut up into detached ridges, one of which is known as *Sierra Blanca*, in consequence of its summit's being covered with snow till late in the spring, and having all

* There is very little wine or legitimate *aguardiente* manufactured in New Mexico. There was not a distillery, indeed, in all the province until established by Americans some fifteen or twenty years ago. Since that period, considerable quantities of whiskey have been made there, particularly in the vicinity of Taos,—distilled mainly from wheat, as this is the cheapest grain the country affords.

the appearance of a glittering white cloud. There is another still more picturesque ridge further south, called *Los Organos*, consisting of an immense cliff of basaltic pillars, which bear some resemblance to the pipes of an *organ*, whence the mountain derived its name. Both these sierras are famous as being the strongholds of the much-dreaded Apaches.

The mountains from El Paso northward are mostly clothed with pine, cedar, and a dwarfish species of oak. The valleys are timbered with cottonwood, and occasionally with *mezquite*, which, however, is rarely found higher up than the lower settlements of New Mexico. In the immediate vicinity of El Paso there is another small growth called *tornillo* (or screw-wood), so denominated from a spiral pericarp, which, though different in shape, resembles that of the mezquite in flavor. The plains and highlands generally are of a prairie character, and do not differ materially from those of all Northern Mexico, which are almost everywhere completely void of timber.

One of the most useful plants to the people of El Paso is the *lechuguilla*, which abounds on the hills and mountain sides of that vicinity, as well as in many other places from thence southward. Its blades, which resemble those of the palmilla, being mashed, scraped and washed, afford very strong fibres like the common Manilla sea-grass, and equally serviceable for the manufacture of ropes, and other purposes.

After leaving El Paso, our road branched off at an angle of about two points to the westward of the river, the city of Chihuahua being situated nearly a hundred miles to the west of it. At the distance of about thirty miles we reached *Los Médanos*, a stupendous ledge of sand-hills, across which the road passes for about six miles. As teams are never able to haul the loaded wagons over this region of loose sand, we engaged an *atajo* of mules at El Paso, upon which to convey our goods across. These Médanos consist of huge hillocks and ridges of pure sand, in many places without a vestige of vegetation. Through the lowest gaps between the hills, the road winds its way.

What renders this portion of the route still more unpleasant and fatiguing, is the great scarcity of water. All that is to be found on the road for the distance of more than sixty miles after leaving El Paso, consists in two fetid springs or pools, whose water is only rendered tolerable by necessity. A little further on, however, we very unexpectedly encountered, this time, quite a superabundance of this necessary element. Just as we passed Lake Patos, we were struck with astonishment at finding the road ahead of us literally overflowed by an immense body of water, with a brisk current, as if some great river had suddenly been conjured into existence by the aid of supernatural arts. A considerable time elapsed before we could unravel the mystery. At last we discovered that a freshet had lately occurred in the streams that fed Lake Patos, and caused it to overflow its banks, which accounted for this unwelcome visitation. We had to flounder through the mud and water for several hours, before we succeeded in getting across.

The following day we reached the *acequia* below Carrizal, a small village with only three or four hundred inhabitants, but somewhat remarkable as being the site of a *presidio* (fort), at which is stationed a company of troops to protect the country against the ravages of the Apaches, who, notwithstanding, continue to lay waste the ranchos in the vicinity, and to depredate at will within the very sight of the fort.

About twelve miles south of Carrizal there is one of the most charming warm springs called Ojo Caliente, where we arrived the next day. It forms a basin some thirty feet long by about half that width, and just deep and warm enough for a most delightful bath at all seasons of the year. Were this spring (whose outlet forms a bold little rivulet) anywhere within the United States, it would doubtless soon be converted into a place of fashionable resort. There appears to be a somewhat curious phenomenon connected with this spring. It proceeds, no doubt, from the little river of Cármen which passes within half a mile, and finally discharges itself into the small lake of Patos before mentioned. All the water of this stream disappears in the sand several miles above the spring; and what medium it traverses in its subterranean passage to impart to it so high a temperature, before breaking out in this fountain, would afford to the geologist an interesting subject of inquiry.

After fording the Rio Cármen, which, though usually without a drop of water in its channel, we now found a very turbulent stream, we did not meet with any object particularly worthy of remark, until we reached the *Laguna de Encinillas*. This lake is ten or twelve miles long by two or three in width, and seems to have no outlet even during the greatest freshets, though fed by several small constant-flowing streams from the surrounding mountains. The water of this lake during the dry season is so strongly impregnated with nauseous and bitter salts, as to render it wholly unpalatable to man and beast. The most predominant of these noxious substances is a species of alkali, known there by the title of *tequesquite*. It is often seen oozing out from the surface of marshy grounds, about the table plains of all Northern Mexico, forming a grayish crust, and is extensively used in the manufacture of soap, and sometimes by the bakers even for raising bread. Here we had another evidence of the alarming effects of the recent flood, the road for several miles along the margin of the lake being completely inundated. It was, however, in the city of Chihuahua itself that the disastrous consequences of the freshet were most severely felt. Some inferior houses of *adobe* were so much soaked by the rains, that they tumbled to the ground, occasioning the loss of several lives.

The valley of Encinillas is very extensive and fertile, and is the locale of one of those princely estates which are so abundant further south, and known by the name of *Haciendas*. It abounds in excellent pasturage, and in cattle of all descriptions. In former times, before the Apachés had so completely devastated the country, the herds which grazed in this beautiful valley presented much the appearance of the buffalo of the plains, being almost as wild and generally of dark color. Many of the proprietors of these princely haciendas pride themselves in maintaining a uniformity in the color of their cattle: thus some are found stocked with black, others red, others white—or whatsoever shade the owner may have taken a fancy to.

As we drew near to Chihuahua, our party had more the appearance of a funeral procession than of a band of adventurers about to enter into the full fruition of 'dancing hopes,' and the realization of 'golden dreams.' Every one was uneasy as to what might be the treatment of the revenue officers. For my own part, I had not quite forgotten sundry annoyances and trials of temper I had been made to experience in the season of 1837, on a similar occasion. Much to our surprise, however, as well as delight, we were handled with a degree of leniency by the custom-house deities, on our arrival, that was almost incomprehensible. But the charm which operated in our favor, when understood, was very simple. A caravan had left Chihuahua direct for the United States the spring previous, and was daily expected back. The officers of the custom-house were already compromised by certain cogent arguments to receive the proprietors of this caravan with striking marks of favor, and the *Señor Administrador de Rentas*, Zuloaga himself, was expecting an *ancheta* of goods. Therefore, had they treated us with their wonted severity, the contrast would have been altogether too glaring.

We arrived at Chihuahua on the first of October, after a trip of forty days, with wagons much more heavily laden than when we started from the United States. The whole distance from Santa Fé to Chihuahua is about 550 miles,—being reckoned 320 to Paso del Norte, and 230 from thence to Chihuahua. The road from El Paso south is mostly firm and beautiful, with the exception of the sand-hills before spoken of; and is only rendered disagreeable by the scarcity and occasional ill-savor of the water. The route winds over an elevated plain among numerous detached ridges of low mountains—spurs, as it were, of the main Cordilleras, which lie at a considerable distance to the westward. Most of these extensive intermediate plains, though in many places of fertile looking soil, must remain wholly unavailable for agricultural purposes, on account of their natural aridity and a total lack of water for irrigation.

CHAPTER V.

THE patient reader who may have accompanied me thus far, without murmuring at
the dryness of some of the details, will perhaps pardon me for presenting here a brief
account of a trip which I made to *Aguascalientes*, in the interior of Northern Mexico, in
the year 1835, and which the arrangement I
have adopted has prevented me from intro-
ducing before, in its chronological order.

The trade to the South constitutes a very
important branch of the commerce of the
country, in which foreigners, as well as na-

tives, are constantly embarking. It is customary for most of those who maintain mercantile establishments in Chihuahua, to procure assortments of Mexican fabrics from the manufactories of Leon, Aguascalientes, and other places of the same character in the more southern districts of the republic. At certain seasons of the year, there are held regular *ferias*, at which the people assemble in great numbers, as well of sellers as of purchasers. There are some eight or ten of these annual fairs held in the republic, each of which usually lasts a week or more. It was about as much, however, from a desire to behold the sunny districts of the South, as for commercial purposes, that I undertook this expedition in 1835; and as my engagements have not permitted me to revisit this section since, the few notes of interest I was then able to collect, seem to come more appropriately in this part of my work than in any other place that I could readily select.

I set out from Chihuahua on the 26th of February, 1835. My party consisted of four men (including myself) and two empty wagons—not a very formidable escort to protect our persons as well as specie and bullion (the only transmissible currency of the country) against the bands of robbers which at all times infest that portion of our route that lay south of Durango. From Chihuahua to that city the road was rendered still more perilous by the constant hostilities of the Indians. On the 7th of March, however, we arrived, without accident, at the town of Cerro Gordo, the northernmost settlement in the department of Durango ; and the following day we reached La Zarca, which is the principal village of one of the most extensive haciendas in the North. So immense is the amount of cattle on this estate, that, as it was rumored, the proprietor once offered to sell the whole hacienda, stock, etc., for the consideration alone of fifty cents for each head of cattle found on the estate ; but that no person has ever yet been able or willing to muster sufficient capital to take up the offer. It is very likely, however, that if such a proposition was ever made, the proprietor intended to include all his stock of rats and mice, reptiles and insects—in short, every genus of ' small cattle' on his premises. This estate covers a territory of perhaps a hundred miles in length, which comprises several flourishing villages.

In two days more, we reached Rio Nazas, a beautiful little river that empties itself into Lake Cayman. * Rio Nazas has been celebrated for the growth of cotton, which, owing to the mildness of the climate, is sometimes planted fresh only every three or four years. The light frosts of winter seldom destroy more than the upper portion of the stalk, so that

---

* The numerous little lakes throughout the interior of Mexico, without outlet, yet into which rivers are continually flowing, present a phenomenon which seems quite singular to the inhabitants of our humid climates. But the wastage in the sand, and still greater by evaporation in those elevated dry regions, is such that there are no important rises in the lakes except during unusual freshets.

the root is almost perennial. About twenty-five miles further, we stopped at the mining village of La Noria, where we were obliged to purchase water for our mules—a novel expense to the American traveller, but scarcely to be complained of, inasmuch as the water had to be drawn from wells with a great deal of labor. It is not unusual, also, for the proprietors of haciendas to demand remuneration for the pasturage on the open plains, consumed by the animals of travellers—a species of exaction which one never hears of in the North of Mexico.

Our next stopping-place was Cuencamé, which may well be called the Village of Churches: for, although possessing a very small population, there are five or six edifices of this description. As I had business to transact at Durango, which is situated forty or fifty miles westward of the main Southern road, I now pursued a direct route for that city, where I arrived on the 16th of March.

Durango is one of the handsomest cities in the North, with a population of about 20,000. It is situated in a level plain, surrounded in every direction by low mountains. It presents two or three handsome squares, with many fine edifices and some really splendid churches. The town is supplied with water for irrigating the gardens, and for many other ordinary purposes, by several open aqueducts, which lead through the streets, from a large spring, a mile or two distant; but as these are kept filthy by the offal that is thrown into them, the inhabitants who are able to buy it, procure most of their water for drinking and culinary purposes, from the *aguadores,* who pack it, on asses, usually in large jars, from the spring.

This is the first Northern city in which there is to be found any evidence of that variety of tropical fruits, for which Southern Mexico is so justly famed. Although it was rather out of season, yet the market actually teemed with all that is most rich and exquisite in this kind of produce. The *maguey,* from which is extracted the popular beverage called *pulque,* * is not only cultivated extensively in the fields, but grows wild every where upon the plains. This being the height of the pulque season, a hundred shanties might be seen loaded with jugs and goblets filled with this favorite liquor, from its sweetest unfermented state to the grade of 'hard cider;' while the incessant cries of "Pulque! pulque dulce! pulque bueno!" added to the shrill and discordant notes of the fruit venders, created a confusion of

---

* Also, from the *Pulque* is distilled a spiritous liquor called *mezcal.* The *maguey* (*Agave Americana*) is besides much used for hedging. It here performs the double purpose of a cheap and substantial fence, and of being equally valuable for *pulque.* When no longer serviceable in these capacities, the pulpy stalk is converted, by roasting, into a pleasant item of food, while the fibrous blades, being suitably dressed, are still more useful. They are manufactured into ropes, bags, etc., which resemble those made of the common sea-grass, though the fibres are finer. There is one species (which does not produce pulque, however), whose fibres, known in that country as *pita,* are nearly as fine as dressed hemp, and are generally used for sewing shoes, saddery, and similar purposes

sounds amidst which it was impossible to hear oneself talk.

Durango is also celebrated as being the head-quarters, as it were, of the whole scorpion family. During the spring, especially, so much are the houses infested by these poisonous insects, that many people are obliged to have resort to a kind of mosquito-bar, in order to keep them out of their beds at night. As an expedient to deliver the city from this terrible pest, a society has actually been formed, which pays a reward of a *cuartilla* (three cents) for every *alacran* (or scorpion) that is brought to them. Stimulated by the desire of gain, the idle boys of the city are always on the look-out: so that, in the course of a year, immense numbers of this public enemy are captured and slaughtered. The body of this insect is of the bulk and cast of a medium spider, with a jointed tail one to two inches long, at the end of which is a sting whose wounds are so poisonous as often to prove fatal to children, and are very painful to adults.

The most extraordinary peculiarity of these scorpions is, that they are far less dangerous in the North than in the South, which in some manner accounts for the story told Capt. Pike, that even those of Durango lose most of their venom as soon as they are removed a few miles from the city.

Although we were exceedingly well armed, yet so many fearful stories of robberies said to be committed, almost daily, on the Southern roads, reached my ears, that before

leaving Durango, I resolved to add to my
weapons of defence' one of those peculiarly
terrible dogs which are sometimes to be found
in this country, and which are very serviceable to travellers situated as I was.   Having
made my wishes known to a free negro from
the United States, named George, he recom-
mended me to a custom-house officer, and a
very particular friend of his, as being possessed of the very article I was in search of.
I accordingly called at the house of that func-
tionary, in company with my sable informant,
and we were ushered into a handsome parlor,
where two or three well-dressed señoritas
sat discussing some of the fruitful topics of
the day.   One of them—the officer's wife, as
it appeared, and a very comely dame she
was—rose immediately, and, with a great deal
of ceremonious deference, saluted *Señor Don
Jorge*, inviting him at the same time to a
seat, while I was left to remain perfectly un-
noticed in my standing position.   George appeared considerably embarrassed, for he had
not quite forgotten the customs and manners
of his native country, and was even yet in the
habit of treating Americans not only with respect but with humility.   He therefore de-
clined the tendered distinction, and remarked
that '*el señor*' had only come to purchase their
dog.   Upon this, the lady pointed to a kennel
in a corner, when the very first glimpse of
the ferocious animal convinced me that he
was precisely the sort of a customer I wanted
for a companion.   Having therefore paid

down six dollars, the stipulated sum of purchase, I bowed myself out of the presence of the ladies, not a little impressed with my own insignificance, in the eyes of these fair *doñas*, contrasted with the grandeur of my sable companion. But the popularity of negroes in Northern Mexico has ceased to be a matter of surprise to the traveller.

With regard to *Don Jorge*, if I was surprised at the marks of attention paid him by a white lady, I had cause to be much more astonished shortly after. As the sooty don was lounging about my wagons, a clever-visaged youth approached and placed in his hands a satin stock, with the compliments of his sister (the officer's wife), hoping that he would receive that trifle, wrought by her own hand, as a token of her particular regard! But, notwithstanding these marks of distinction (to apply no harsher epithet), George was exceedingly anxious to engage in my employ, in whatsoever capacity I might choose to take him; for he had discovered that such honors were far from affording him a livelihood: yet I did not then need his services, and have never heard of him since.

On the 22d we left Durango, and after a few days' march found ourselves once more in the *camino real* that led from Chihuahua to Zacatecas. All the frightful stories I had heard about robbers now began to flash upon my memory, which made me regard every man I encountered on the road with a very suspicious eye. As all travellers go armed, it

is impossible to distinguish them from banditti ;* so that the unsuspecting traveller is very
frequently set upon by the very man he had
been consorting with in apparent good-fellow-
ship, and either murdered on the spot, or
dragged from his horse with the lazo, and
plundered of all that is valuable about him.

I have heard it asserted that there is a regular
bandit trade organized throughout the country,
in which some of the principal officers of state
(and particularly of the judicial corps) are not
unfrequently engaged.   A capital is made up
by shares, as for any other enterprise, bandits
are fitted out and instructed where to operate,
and at stated periods of the year a regular
dividend is paid to the stockholders.   The
impunity which these 'gentlemen of the order' almost everywhere enjoy in the country,
is therefore not to be marvelled at.   In Durango, during my sojourn there, a well dressed caballero was frequently in the habit of
entering our *meson*, whom mine host soon
pointed out to me as a notorious brigand.
" Beware of him," said the honest publican;
"he is prying into your affairs"—and so it
turned out; for my muleteer informed me
that the fellow had been trying to pump from
him all the particulars in regard to our condition and destination.   Yet this worthy was
not only suffered to prowl about unmolested

* Travellers on these public highways not only go ' armed to the
teeth,' but always carry their weapons exposed.   Even my wagoners carried their guns and pistols swung upon the pommels of their
saddles.   At night, as we generally camped out, they were laid under our heads, or close by our sides.

by the authorities, but appeared to be on familiar terms with many of the principal dignitaries of the city. Notwithstanding all our apprehensions, however, we arrived at our place of destination without even the novelty of an incident to swell our budget of gossip.

The city of Aguascalientes is beautifully situated in a level plain, and would appear to contain about twenty thousand inhabitants, who are principally engaged in the manufacture of *rebozos* and other textures mostly of cotton. As soon as I found myself sufficiently at leisure I visited the famous warm spring (*ojo caliente*) in the suburbs, from which the city derives its euphonious name. I followed up the *acequia* that led from the spring—a ditch four or five feet wide, through which flowed a stream three or four feet in depth. The water was precisely of that agreeable temperature to afford the luxury of a good bath, which I had hoped to enjoy; but every few paces I found men, women, and children, submerged in the acequia; and when I arrived at the basin, it was so choked up with girls and full-grown women, who were paddling about with all the nonchalance of a gang of ducks, that I was forced to relinquish my long-promised treat.

It had been originally my intention to continue on to Leon, another manufacturing town some seventy or eighty miles from Aguascalientes; but, hearing that Santa Anna had just arrived there with a large army, on his way to Zacatecas to quell an insurrection, I felt very little curiosity to extend my rambles further. Having, therefore, made all my pur chases in the shortest possible time, in a few days I was again in readiness to start for the North.

That my mules might be in condition for the hard travel before me, it was necessary to have them shod: a precaution, however, which is seldom used in the north of Mexico, either with mules or horses. Owing a little to the peculiar breed, but more still no doubt to the dryness of the climate, Mexican animals have unusually hard hoofs. Many will travel for weeks, and even months, over the firm* and often rocky roads of the interior (the pack-mules carrying their huge loads), without any protection whatever to the feet, save that which nature has provided. But most of mine being a little tender-footed, I engaged Mexican *herreros* to fit them out in their own peculiar style. Like almost everything else of their manufacturing, their mule-shoes are of a rather primitive model—broad thin plates, tacked on with large club-headed nails. But the expertness of the shoers compensated in some degree for the defects of the *herraduras.* It made but little odds how wild and vicious the mule—an assistant would draw up his foot in an instant, and soon place him *hors de combat;* and then fixing a nail, the shoer

---

* Some of these table-plain highways, though of but a dry sandy and clayey soil, are as firm as a brick pavement. In some places, for miles, I have remarked that the nail-heads of my shod animals would hardly leave any visible impression

would drive it to the head at a single stroke, standing usually at full arm's length, while the assistant held the foot. Thus in less than half the time I had ever witnessed the execution of a similar job before, they had completely shod more than twenty of the most unruly brutes—without once resorting to the expedient so usual in such cases, of throwing the animals upon the ground.

Just as the process of shoeing my mules had been completed, a person who proved to be a public officer entered the *corral*, and pointing to the mules, very politely informed me that they were wanted by the government to transport troops to Zacatecas. "They will be called for to-morrow afternoon," he continued; "let them not be removed!" I had of course to bow acquiescence to this imperative edict, well knowing that all remonstrance would be vain; yet fully determined to be a considerable distance on the road northward before that 'morrow' should be very far advanced.

But a new difficulty now presented itself. I must procure a *guia* or passport for my cargo of merchandise, with a *responsible endorser*, —an additional imposition I was wholly unprepared for, as I was then ignorant of any law to that effect being in force, and had not a single acquaintance in the city. I was utterly at a loss what to do: under any other circumstances I might have left the amount of the *derecho de consumo* in deposit, as others have been obliged to do on similar occasions; but unfortunately I had laid out the last dollar of my available means.

As I left the custom-house brooding over these perplexities, one of the principal clerks of the establishment slipped a piece of paper into my hand containing the following laconic notice :—" *Aguárdeme afuera*" (wait for me without);—an injunction I passively obeyed, although I had not the least idea of its purport. The clerk was soon with me, and remarked, "You are a stranger in the city, and ignorant of our severe revenue laws: meet me in an hour from this at my lodgings, and we will devise some remedy for your difficulties." It may be well supposed that I did not fail to be punctual. I met the obliging officer in his room with a handful of blank custom-house *pases*. It should be understood that a *pase* only differs from a *guia* in requiring no endorser, but they can only be extended for amounts of goods not exceeding fifty dollars. Taking my bill, he very soon filled me up a *pase* for every package, directing each to a different point in the North. "Now," observed my amiable friend, "if you are disposed to do a little smuggling, these will secure your safety, if you avoid the principal cities, till you reach the borders of Chihuahua: if not, you may have a friend on the way who will endorse your *guia*." I preferred the latter alternative. I had formed an acquaintance with a worthy German merchant in Durango, who, I felt convinced, would generously lend his signature to the required document.

As the revenue officers of Northern Mexico are not celebrated for liberality and disinterestedness, I took it for granted that my friend of the custom-house was actuated by selfish motives, and therefore proffered him a remuneration for the trouble he had taken on my account; but to my surprise, he positively refused accepting anything, observing that he held it the duty of every honest man to assist his fellow creatures in case of difficulty. It is truly a pleasant task to bear record of such instances of disinterestedness, in the midst of so many contaminating influences.

While speaking of *guias*, I may as well remark that they are also frequently required for specie and always for bullion. This is often very annoying to the traveller, not only because it is sometimes inconvenient to find an endorser, but because the robbers are thus enabled to obtain precise and timely information of the funds and route of every traveller; for they generally have their agents in all the principal cities, who are apt to collude with some of the custom-house clerks, and thus procure regular reports of the departures, with the amounts of valuables conveyed.

I was not long in taking leave of Aguascalentes, and heard nothing more of the impressment of my mules. It was not my good fortune, however, to remain for any length of time out of trouble. Being anxious to take the city of Zacatecas in my route without jeoparding my goods, I took passage by the *diligencia*, while my wagons continued on in

the *camino real* or main road. On my arrival at Zacatecas, I very soon discovered that
by leaving 'my bed and board' behind with
the wagons, I had doomed myself to no small
inconvenience and privation. It was with
the greatest difficulty I could obtain a place to
lie upon, and clean victuals with which to al-
lay my hunger.   I could get a room, it is true,
even for a *real* per day, in one of those great
barn-like *mesones* which are to be met with in
all these cities, but not one of them was at all
furnished. There is sometimes, in a corner,
a raised platform of mud, much resembling a
common blacksmith's hearth, which is to supply the place of a bedstead, upon which the
traveller may spread his blankets, if he hap-
pen to have any. On this occasion I succeeded in borrowing one or two of the stage-
driver who was a Yankee, and so made out
'pretty comfortably' in the sleeping way.
These *mesones* are equally ill-prepared to furnish food for the traveller, unless he is willing
to put up with a dish of *frijoles* and *chile gui-
sado* with *tortillas*, all served up in the most
filthy manner.   I therefore sought out a public *fonda* kept by an Italian, where I procured
an excellent supper. Fondas, however, are
mere *restaurants*, and consequently without
accommodations for lodging.

Strange as the fact may appear, one may travel fifteen hundred miles, and perhaps more,
on the main public highway through Northern
Mexico, without finding a single tavern with
general accommodations. This, however, may

be accounted for, by taking into consideration the peculiar mode of travelling of the country, which renders resorts of this kind almost unnecessary. *Arrieros* with their *atajos* of pack mules always camp out, being provided with their cooks and stock of provisions, which they carry with them. Ordinary travellers generally unite in little caravans, for security against robbers and marauders; and no caballero ever stirs abroad without a train of servants, and a pack-mule to carry his *cantinas* (a pair of large wallets or leathern boxes), filled with provisions, on the top of which is lashed a huge machine containing a mattrass and all the other 'fixings' for bed furniture. Thus equipped, the caballero snaps his fingers at all the *hotels garnis* of the universe, and is perfectly independent in every movement.

The city of Zacatecas, as my readers are doubtless aware, is celebrated for its mining interests. Like all other Mexican towns of the same class, it originated in small, insignificant settlements on the hillsides, in the immediate vicinity of the mines, until it gradually grew up to be a large and wealthy city, with a population of some 30,000 inhabitants. Its locale is a deep ravine formed among rugged mountain ridges; and as the houses are mostly built in rows, overtopping one another, along the hillsides, some portions of the city present all the appearance of a vast amphitheatre. Many of the streets are handsomely paved, and two of the squares are finely ornamented with curiously carved *jets-d'eau*, which are supplied with water raised by mule power, from wells among the adjacent hills. From these the city is chiefly furnished with water.

I have already mentioned, that General Santa Anna was at this time marching against Zacatecas with a large force. It may be remembered that after the General's accession to the supreme authority of Mexico (upon the establishment of *Centralismo*), he deemed it expedient to issue a decree abolishing the state militia, known as *Cívicos*, as being dangerous to the liberties of——the *dictador*. Zacatecas, so far from obeying this despotic mandate, publicly called on the Cívicos to defend their rights, and Santa Anna was now descending upon them with an army double that which the city could raise, to enforce their obedience. The *Zacatecanos*, however, were not idle. The militia was pouring in from the surrounding villages, and a degree of enthusiasm prevailed throughout the city, which seemed to be the presage of a successful defence. In fact, the city itself, besides being from its location almost impregnable, was completely protected by artificial fortifications. The only accessible point was by the main road, which led from the south immediately up the narrow valley of the ravine. Across this a strong wall had been erected some years before, and the road passed through a large gate, commanded by a bastion upon the hillside above, whence a hundred men well supplied with arms and ammunition, might easily cut off thousands upon thousands, as fast as they advanced. The city was therefore deemed impregnable, and being supplied with provisions for a lengthy siege, the patriots were in high spirits. A foreign engineer or two had been engaged to superintend the fortifications.

Santa Anna reached Zacatecas a few days after my departure. As he had no idea of testing the doubtful mettle of his army by an attempt to storm the place which presented so formidable an appearance, he very quietly squatted himself down at the village of Guadalupe, three miles below. From this point he commenced his operations by throwing 'missiles' into the city—not of lead, or cast iron, or any such cruel agents of warfare, but *bombs of paper*, which fell among the besieged, and burst with gentle overtures to their commanding officers. This novel ' artillery' of the dictator produced a perfectly electric effect; for the valor of the Commandant of the Cívicos rose to such a pitch, that he at once marched his forces out of the fortifications, to attack the besiegers in the open field—face to face, as true bravery required. But on the very first onset, this valiant officer, by some mysterious agency which could not be accounted for, was suddenly seized with a strange panic, and, with all his forces, made a precipitate retreat, fleeing helter-skelter, as if all the engines of destruction that were ever invented, had been brought to bear upon them; when the victorious army of Santa Anna marched into the city without further opposition.

9*

This affair is a pretty just sample of most of the successful battles of this 'great general.' The treacherous collusion of the principal Zacatecas officers was so apparent, that they deemed it prudent to fly the city for safety, lest the wrath of their incensed fellow-citizens should explode upon them. Meanwhile the soldiery amused themselves by sacking the city, and by perpetrating every species of outrage that their mercenary and licentious appetites could devise. Their savage propensities were particularly exercised against the few foreigners that were found in the place.

By this time I was journeying very leisurely towards Durango, where I arrived on the 21st of April. As the main wagon road to the north does not pass through that city, it was most convenient and still more prudent for me to leave my wagons at a distance : their entrance would have occasioned the confiscation of my goods, for the want of the 'necessary documents,' as already alluded to. But I now procured a *guia* without further difficulty ; which was indeed a principal object of my present visit to that city.

Before leaving Durango I witnessed one of those civil broils which are so common in Mexico. I was not even aware that any difficulty had been brewing, till I was waked on the morning of the 25th by a report of fire-arms. Stepping out to ascertain what was the matter, I perceived the *azotea* of the parochial church occupied by armed men, who seemed to be employed in amusing themselves by discharging their guns at random upon the people in the streets. These *bravos*, as I was afterwards informed, belonged to the bishop's party, or that of the *Escoceses*, which was openly at war with the liberalists, anti-hierarchists, or *Yorkinos*, and were resorting to this summary mode of proceeding, in order to bring about a change of affairs; for at this time the liberal party had the ascendency in the civil government of Durango.

Being somewhat curious to have a nearer view of what was going on, I walked down past the church, towards a crowd which was assembled in a *plaza* beyond. This movement on my part was rather inconsiderate: for foreigners were in extremely bad odor with the belligerents; nor had I mingled with the multitude many minutes, before a sober-looking citizen plucked me by the sleeve, and advised me, if I valued my two ears, and did not wish to have my career of usefulness cut short prematurely, to stay within doors. Of course I needed no further persuasion, and returned at once to my lodgings, where I made immediate preparations for a speedy departure. As I was proceeding through the streets soon afterward, with a cargo of goods, I received, just after leaving the custom-house, a very warm salutation from the belligerents, which made the dust start from almost under my very feet. The *cargadores* who were carrying my packages were no doubt as much frightened as myself. They supposed the reason of their shooting at us to be be-

cause they imagined we were carrying off
the *parque* (ammunition) of the government,
which was deposited in the building we had
just left.

We were soon under way, and very little
regret did I feel when I fairly lost sight of the
city of scorpions. But I was not yet wholly
beyond the pale of difficulties. Owing to the
fame of the Indian hostilities in the North, it
was almost impossible to procure the services
of Mexican muleteers for the expedition. One
I engaged, took the first convenient opportunity to escape at night, carrying away a gun
with which I had armed him ; yet I felt grateful that he did not also take a mule, as he had
the whole *caballada* under his exclusive charge:
and soon after, a Mexican wagoner was frightened back by the reports of savages.

After a succession of such difficulties, and
still greater risks from the Indians that infested
the route, I was of course delighted when I
reached Chihuahua, on the 14th of May, in
perfect safety.*

---

* The distance from Chihuahua to Durango is about five hundred miles, and from thence to Aguascalientes it is nearly three
hundred—upon the route we travelled, which was very circuitous.
All the intermediate country resembles, in its physical features,
that lying immediately north of Chihuahua, which has already
been described.

CHAPTER VI.

BEFORE resuming my regular narrative, I
trust the reader will pardon me for introduc-
ing here a brief account of an excursion which
I made in the fall of the year 1835, to the
mining town of Jesus-Maria, one of the most
important mineral districts in the department
of Chihuahua, situated about a hundred and
fifty miles west of the city, in the very heart
of the great Cordilleras.

I had long been desirous of visiting some
of the mining establishments of Mexico, and
seeing a favorable opportunity of embarking
in a profitable enterprise, I set out from Chihuahua on the 15th of October. My party
consisted of but one American comrade with

a Mexican muleteer—and three or four mules freighted with specie to be employed in the *silver trade:* a rather scanty convoy for a route subject to the inroads both of savages and robbers. For transportation, we generally pack our specie in sacks made of raw beef-hide, which shrinks upon drying, and thus presses the contents so closely as to prevent friction. A pair of these packages, usually containing between one and two thousand dollars each, constitutes an ordinary mule-load on the mountain routes.

The road in this direction leads through the roughest mountain passes; and, in some places, it winds so close along the borders of precipices, that by a single misstep an animal might be precipitated several hundred feet. Mules, however, are very sure-footed; and will often clamber along the most craggy cliffs with nearly as much security as the goat. I was shown the projecting edge of a rock over which the road had formerly passed. This shelf was perhaps thirty feet in length by only two or three in width. The road which leads into the town of Jesus-Maria from the west side of the mountain is also extremely perilous and steep, and seems almost to overhang the houses below. Heavily laden mules have sometimes slipped off the track, and tumbled headlong into the town. This place is even more pent up between ridges than Zacatecas: the valley is narrower and the mountains much higher; while, as is the case with that remarkable city, the houses are sometimes built in successive tiers, one above another; the *azoteas* of the lower ones forming the yard of those above.

The first mine I visited consisted of an immense horizontal shaft cut several hundred feet into a hill-side, a short distance below the town of Jesus-Maria, upon which the proprietors had already sunk, in the brief space of one year, the enormous sum of one hundred and twenty thousand dollars! Such is often the fate of the speculative miner, whose vocation is closely allied to gaming, and equally precarious.

The most important mine of Jesus-Maria at this time was one called Santa Juliana, which had been the means of alternately making and sinking several splendid fortunes. This mine had then reached a depth of between eight and nine hundred feet, and the operations were still tending downwards. The materials were drawn up by mule power applied to a windlass: but as the rope attached to it only extended half way down, another windlass had been erected at the distance of about four hundred feet from the mouth of the cavern, which was also worked by mules, and drew the ores, etc., from the bottom. On one occasion, as I was standing near the aperture of this great pit watching the ascent of the windlass-rope, expecting every moment the appearance of the large leathern bucket which they employ for drawing up the minerals as well as the rubbish and water* from the bot-

* Water has sometimes accumulated so rapidly in this mine as to stop operations for weeks together.

tom, what should greet my vision but a mule,
puffing and writhing, firmly bound to a huge
board constructed for the purpose, and looking
about as demure upon the whole as a sheep under the shears.   On being untied, the emanci-
pated brute suddenly sprang to his feet, and
looked around him at the bright scenes of the
upper world with as much astonishment as Rip
Van Winkle may be supposed to have felt
after waking up from his twenty years' sleep.

The ore which is obtained from these mines,
if sufficiently rich to justify the operation, is
transferred to the smelting furnaces, where
the pure metal is melted down and extracted
from the virgin fossil. ` If, on the contrary, the
ore is deemed of inferior quality, it is then
submitted to the process of amalgamation.

The *moliendas*, or crushing-mills (*arrastres*, as called at some mines), employed for the purpose of grinding the ores, are somewhat singular machines. A circular (or rather annular) cistern of some twenty or thirty feet in diameter is dug in the earth, and the sides as well as the bottom are lined with hewn stone of the hardest quality. Transversely through an upright post which turns upon its axis in the centre of the plan, passes a shaft of wood, at each end of which are attached by cords one or two grinding stones with smooth flat surfaces, which are dragged (by mules fastened to the extremities of the shaft) slowly around upon the bottom of the cistern, into which the ore is thrown after being pounded into small pieces. It is here ground, with the addition of water, into an impalpable mortar, by the constant friction of the dragging stones against the sides and bottom of the cistern. A suitable quantity of quicksilver is perfectly mixed with the mortar; to which are added some muriates, sulphates, and other chemical substances, to facilitate the amalgamation. The compound is then piled up in small heaps, and not disturbed again until this process is supposed to be complete, when it is transferred to the washing-machine. Those I have observed are very simple, consisting of a kind of stone tub, into which a stream of water is made to flow constantly, so as to carry off all the lighter matter, which is kept stirred up by an upright studded with pegs, that revolves in the centre, while the amalgamated metals sink to the bottom. Most of the quicksilver is then pressed out, and the silver submitted to a burning process, by which the remaining portion of mercury is expelled.

The silver which is taken from the furnace, generally contains an intermixture of gold, averaging from ten to thirty per cent.; but what is extracted by amalgamation is mostly separated in the washing. While in a liquid state, the gold, from its greater specific gravity, mostly settles to the bottom: yet it usually retains a considerable alloy of silver. The compound is distinguished by the name of *oroche*. The main portion of the silver generally retains too little gold to make it worth separating.

Every species of silver is moulded into *barras* or ingots, weighing from fifty to eighty pounds each, and usually worth between one and two thousand dollars. These are assayed by an authorized agent of the government and stamped with their weight and character, which enables the holder to calculate their value by a very simple rule. When the bullion is thus stamped, it constitutes a species of currency, which is much safer for remittances than coin. In case of robbery, the *barras* are easily identified, provided the robbers have not had time to mould them into some other form. For this reason, people of wealth frequently lay up their funds in ingots; and the cellars of some of the *ricos* of the South, are often found teeming with large quantities of them, presenting the appearance of a winter's supply of fuel.

As the charge for parting the gold and silver at the Mexican mints, is generally from one to two dollars, and coinage about fifty cents, per pound, this assayed bullion yields a profit upon its current value of nearly ten per cent. at the United States Mint; but, if unassayed, it generally produces an advance of about double that amount upon the usual cost at the mines. The exportation of bullion, however, is prohibited, except by special license from the general government. Still a large quantity is exported in this way, and considerable amounts smuggled out through some of the ports.

A constant and often profitable business in the 'silver trade' is carried on at these mines. As the miners rarely fail being in need of ready money, they are generally obliged to sell their bullion for coin, and that often at a great sacrifice, so as to procure available means to prosecute their mining operations. To profit by this trade, as is already mentioned, was a principal object of my present visit. Having concluded my business transactions, and partially gratified my curiosity, I returned to Chihuahua, where I arrived November 24, 1835, without being molested either by robbers or Indians, though the route is sometimes infested by both of these classes of independent gentry.

But, as it is now high time I should put an end to this digression, I will once more resume my narrative, where it was interrupted at my arrival in Chihuahua, on the first of October, 1839.

It is usual for each trader, upon his arrival in that city, to engage a store-room, and to open and exhibit his goods, as well for the purpose of disposing of them at wholesale as retail. His most profitable custom is that of the petty country merchants from the surrounding villages. Some traders, it is true, continue in the retail business for a season or more, yet the greater portion are transient dealers, selling off at wholesale as soon as a fair bargain is offered.

The usual mode of selling by the lot in Chihuahua is somewhat singular. All such cottons as calicoes and other prints, bleached, brown and blue domestics both plain and twilled, stripes, checks, etc., are rated at two or three *reales** per *vara*, without the least reference to quality or cost, and the 'general assortment' at 60 to 100 per cent. upon the bills of cost, according to the demand. The *varage* is usually estimated by adding eight per cent. to the yardage, but the *vara* being thirty-three inches (nearly), the actual difference is more than nine. In these sales, cloths—

---

* The Mexican money table is as follows: 12 *granos* make 1 *real ;* 8 *reales,* 1 *peso,* or dollar. These are the divisions used in computation, but instead of *granos,* the copper coins of Chihuahua and many other places, are the *claco* or *jola* (⅛ real) and the *cuartilla* (¼ real). The silver coins are the *medio* (6¼ cents), the *real* (12½ cents), the *peseta* (2 reales), the *toston* or half dollar, and the *peso* or dollar. The gold coins are the *doblon* or *onza* (doubloon), with the same subdivisions as the silver dollar, which are also precisely of the weight. The par value of the doubloon is sixteen dollars; but, as there is no kind of paper currency, gold, as the most convenient remittance, usually commands a high premium—sometimes so high, indeed, that the doubloon is valued in the North at from eighteen to twenty dollars.

indeed all measurable goods, except ribands and the like, sometimes enter at the *varage* rate. I have heard of some still more curious contracts in these measurement sales, particularly in Santa Fé, during the early periods of the American trade. Everything was sometimes rated by the vara—not only all textures, but even hats, cutlery, trinkets, and so on! In such cases, very singular disputes would frequently arise as to the mode of measuring some particular articles: for instance, whether pieces of riband should be measured in bulk, or unrolled, and yard by yard; looking-glasses, cross or lengthwise; pocket-knives, shut or open; writing-paper, in the ream, in the quire, or by the single sheet; and then, whether the longer or shorter way of the paper; and many others.

Before the end of October, 1839, I had an opportunity of selling out my stock of goods to a couple of English merchants, which relieved me from the delays, to say nothing of the inconveniences attending a retail trade: such, for, instance, as the accumulation of copper coin, which forms almost the exclusive currency in petty dealings. Some thousands of dollars' worth are frequently accumulated upon the hands of the merchant in this way, and as the copper of one department is worthless in another, except for its intrinsic value, which is seldom more than ten per cent. of the nominal value, the holders are subjected to a great deal of trouble and annoyance.

With regard to the city, there is but little to
10*

be said that is either very new or unusually interesting. When compared with Santa Fé and all the towns of the North, Chihuahua might indeed be pronounced a magnificent place; but, compared with the nobler cities of *tierra afuera*, it sinks into insignificance. According to Capt. Pike, the city of Chihuahua was founded in 1691. The ground-plan is much more regular than that of Santa Fé, while a much greater degree of elegance and classic taste has been exhibited in the style of the architecture of many buildings; for though the bodies be of *adobe*, all the best houses are cornered with hewn stone, and the doors and windows are framed in the same. The streets, however, remain nearly in the same state as Nature formed them, with the exception of a few roughly-paved side-walks. Although situated about a hundred miles east of the main chain of the Mexican Cordilleras, Chihuahua is surrounded on every side by detached ridges of mountains, but none of them of any great magnitude. The elevation of the city above the ocean is between four and five thousand feet; its latitude is 28° 36'; and its entire population numbers about ten thousand souls.

The most splendid edifice in Chihuahua is the principal church, which is said to equal in architectural grandeur anything of the sort in the republic. The steeples, of which there is one at each front corner, rise over a hundred feet above the azotea. They are composed of very fancifully-carved columns; and in appropriate niches of the frontispiece, which is also an elaborate piece of sculpture, are to be seen a number of statues, as large as life, the whole forming a complete representation of Christ and the twelve Apostles. This church was built about a century ago, by contributions levied upon the mines (particularly those of Santa Eulalia, fifteen or twenty miles from the city), which paid over a per centage on all the metal extracted therefrom ; a *medio*, I believe, being levied upon each *marco* of eight ounces. In this way, about a million of dollars was raised and expended in some thirty years, the time employed in the construction of the building. It is a curious fact, however, that, notwithstanding the enormous sums of money expended in outward embellishments, there is not a church from thence southward, perhaps, where the interior arrangements bear such striking marks of poverty and neglect. If, however, we are not dazzled by the sight of those costly decorations for which the churches of Southern Mexico are so much celebrated, we have the satisfaction of knowing that the turrets are well provided with bells, a fact of which every person who visits Chihuahua very soon obtains auricular demonstration. One, in particular, is so large and sonorous that it has frequently been heard, so I am informed, at the distance of twenty-five miles.

A little below the *Plaza Mayor* stands the ruins (as they may be called) of San Francisco—the mere skeleton of another great church

of hewn-stone, which was commenced by the
Jesuits previous to their expulsion in 1767,
but never finished. By the outlines still traceable amid the desolation which reigns around,
it would appear that the plan of this edifice
was conceived in a spirit of still greater magnificence than the Parroquia which I have
been describing. The abounding architectural treasures that are mouldering and ready
to tumble to the ground, bear sufficient evidence that the mind which had directed its
progress was at once bold, vigorous and comprehensive.

This dilapidated building has since been
converted into a sort of state prison, particularly for the incarceration of distinguished
prisoners. It was here that the principals of
the famous Texan Santa Fé Expedition were
confined, when they passed through the place,
on their way to the city of Mexico. This edifice has also acquired considerable celebrity
as having received within its gloomy embraces several of the most distinguished patriots,
who were taken prisoners during the first
infant struggles for Mexican independence.
Among these was the illustrious ecclesiastic,
Don Miguel Hidalgo y Costilla, who made
the first declaration at the village of Dolores,
September 16, 1810. He was taken prisoner
in March, 1811, some time after his total defeat at Guadalaxara; and being brought to
Chihuahua, he was shot on the 30th of July
following, in a little square back of the prison,
where a plain white monument of hewn stone

has been erected to his memory.   It consists
of an octagon base of about twenty-five feet
in diameter, upon which rises a square, un-
ornamented pyramid to the height of about
thirty feet.   The monument indeed is not an
unapt emblem of the purity and simplicity of
the curate's character.

Among the few remarkable objects which
attract the attention of the traveller is a row
of columns supporting a large number of stupendous arches which may be seen from the
heights, long before approaching the city from
the north.   This is an aqueduct of considerable magnitude which conveys water from the
little river of Chihuahua, to an eminence
above the town, whence it is passed through
a succession of pipes to the main public
square, where it empties itself into a large
stone cistern ; and by this method the city is
supplied with water.   This and other public
works to be met with in Chihuahua, and in
the southern cities, are glorious remnants of
the prosperous times of the Spanish empire.
No improvements on so exalted a scale have
ever been made under the republican government.   In fact, everything in this benighted
country now seems to be on the decline, and
the plain honest citizen of the old school is
not unfrequently heard giving vent to his feelings by ejaculating " *¡Ojalá por los dias felices
del Rey !*"—Oh, for the happy days of the
King !   In short, there can be no doubt, that
the common people enjoyed more ease—
more protection against the savages—more

security in their rights and property—more *liberty*, in truth, under the Spanish dynasty than at present.

No better evidence can be found of the extensive operations which have been carried on in this the greatest mining district of Northern Mexico, than in the little mountains of *scoria* which are found in the suburbs of the city. A great number of poor laborers make a regular business of hammering to pieces these metallic excrescences, from which they collect silver enough to buy their daily bread. An opinion has often been expressed by persons well acquainted with the subject, that a fair business might be done by working this same scoria over again. There are still in operation several furnaces in the city, where silver ores extracted from the mines of the surrounding mountains are smelted. There is also a rough mint in Chihuahua (as there is indeed in all the mining departments), yet most of its silver and all of its gold have been coined in the cities further south.

When I arrived at Chihuahua, in 1839, a great fête had just come off for the double purpose of celebrating the anniversary of the Emperor Iturbide's birth day (Sept. 27, 1783), and that of his triumphal entrance into the city of Mexico in 1821. It will be remembered, that, after Mexico had been struggling for independence several years, General Iturbide, who had remained a faithful officer of the crown, and an active agent in persecuting the champions of Mexican liberty, finding

himself, about the close of 1820, at the head of
a large division of the royal army sent against
the patriot Guerrero, suddenly turned over
his whole force to the support of the republican cause, and finally succeeded in destroying
the last vestige of Spanish authority in Mexico. How he was afterwards crowned emperor, and subsequently dethroned, outlawed by
a public decree and eventually executed, is all
matter of history. But it is not generally
known, I believe, that this unfortunate soldier
has since received the honors of the Father of
the Republic, a dignity to which he was probably as much entitled as any one else—absurd though the adoption of such a hero as
the 'champion of liberty,' may appear to 're-
publicans of the Jefferson school.' A *grande
fête d'hilarité* takes place annually, in honor
of his political canonization, which 'comes
off' at the date already mentioned. To this
great ball, however, no Americans were invited,
with the exception of a Mexicanized denizen
or two, whose invitation tickets informed the
honored party that the price of admission to
this famous feast,—a ball given by the governor and other magnates of the land, in honor
of the hero of independence,—was twenty-
five dollars.

Balls or reunions of this kind, however,
seem not as frequent in Chihuahua as in New
Mexico: and to those we hear of, claiming the
title of 'fashionable,' Americans are very rarely
invited. There is, in fact, but little social intercourse between foreigners and the natives,

except in a business way, or with a certain class of the former, at the gambling-table. This want of hospitable feelings is one of the worst traits in the character of the Chihua-hueños, and when placed in contrast with the kind and courteous treatment those who visit the United States invariably experience from the lawgivers of fashion among us, their illiberality will appear a hundred fold more ungracious. These exclusive laws are the more severely felt in Chihuahua, because in that city there are no *cafés*, nor reading rooms, nor in short any favorite public resorts, except of a gambling character, at which gentlemen can meet to lounge or amuse themselves.

Besides the cock-pit, the gaming-table, and the *Alameda*, which is the popular promenade for the wealthy and the indolent, one of the most favorite pastimes of the females generally is shopping; and the most fashionable time for this is by candle-light, after they have partaken of their chocolate and their *cigarritos*. The streets and shops are literally filled from dusk till nine or ten o'clock; and many a time have I seen the counter of a store actually lined till a late hour, with the fairest and most fashionable señoritas of the city. On such occasions it is not a little painful as well as troublesome to be compelled to keep a strict eye to the rights of property, not that the dealers are all dishonest, but because there never fail to be some present who are painfully afflicted with the self-appropriating mania,

even among the fairest-looking señoritas.
This, with other purposes no less culpable,
has no doubt tended to establish the custom
of night-shopping.

It may already be generally known perhaps, that the predominant party, in Mexico,
(and particularly in the North), is decidedly
anti-masonic. During my stay in Chihuahua
I had an opportunity to test their antipathy for
that mysterious brotherhood. This was evinced in the seizure of a dozen or two cotton
handkerchiefs, which, unknown to myself,
happened to bear the stamp of the 'masonic
carpet.' These obnoxious articles having attracted the attention of some lynx-eyed friar,
one day, much to my consternation, my store
was suddenly invaded by the alcalde and
some ecclesiastics. The handkerchiefs were
seized without ceremony, and by an *auto de fe*,
condemned to be publicly burned.

CHAPTER VII.

HAVING closed all my affairs in Chihuahua,
and completed my preparations for departing,
I took my leave of that city for the North, on
the 31st of October, 1839. I was accompanied by a caravan consisting of twenty-two
wagons (all of which save one belonged to
me), and forty odd men, armed to the teeth,
and prepared for any emergency we might be
destined to encounter: a precaution altogether
necessary, in view of the hordes of hostile savages which at all times infested the route before us.

We also set out provided with an ample
stock of bread and other necessaries; for, from
the suburbs of Chihuahua to the village of

Carrizal, a distance of nearly a hundred and fifty miles, there are no settlements on the route, from whence to procure supplies. To furnish the party with meat, I engaged twenty sheep, to be delivered a few miles on the way, which were to be driven along for our daily consumption. But the contractor having failed, we found ourselves entering the wilderness without a morsel of meat. The second day our men began to murmur—it was surely 'dry living' upon mere bread and coffee: in fact, by the time we entered the 'territory' of the Hacienda de Encinillas, spoken of in another chapter, they were clearly suffering from hunger. I was therefore under the necessity of sending three Mexican muleteers of our party to *lazo* a beef from a herd which was grazing at some distance from where we had pitched our camp; being one of those buffalo-like droves which run so nearly wild upon this extensive domain. It had been customary, from time immemorial, for travellers when they happened to be distressed for meat, to supply their wants out of the wild cattle which nominally belonged to this hacienda, reserving to themselves the privilege of paying a reasonable price afterwards to the proprietor for the damage committed. I must say, however, that, although I had travelled over the same road nine times, I had never before resorted to this summary mode of procuring food; nor should I, on the present occasion, have deviated from my regular practice, though thus partially authorized by a custom of the country, but for the strait in which we found ourselves, and the fact that I was confident I should meet either with a *mayordomo* or some of the *vaqueros*, to whom I could pay the value of the beef, before passing beyond the purlieus of the hacienda, upon the lands of which we had yet to travel for sixty or eighty miles.

The muleteers had just commenced giving chase to the cattle, when we perceived several horsemen emerge from behind a contiguous eminence, and pursue them at full speed. Believing the assailants to be Indians, and seeing them shoot at one of the men, chase another, and seize the third, bearing him off prisoner, several of us prepared to hasten to the rescue, when the other two men came running in and informed us that the aggressors were Mexican vaqueros. We followed them, notwithstanding, to the village of Torreon, five or six miles to the westward, where we found a crowd of people already collected around our poor friend, who was trembling from head to foot, as though he had really fallen into the hands of savages. I immediately inquired for the mayordomo, when I was informed that the proprietor himself, Don Angel Trias, was present. Accordingly I addressed myself to *su señoría*, setting forth the innocence of my servant, and declaring myself solely responsible for whatever crime had been committed. Trias, however, was immovable in his determination to send the boy back to Chihuahua to be tried for robbery, and all further expostulation only drew down the grossest and coarsest insults upon myself, as well as my country, of which he professed no inconsiderable knowledge.*

The altercation was at first conducted solely in Spanish; but the princely señor growing weary of hearing so many unpalatable truths told of himself in the vernacular of his own humble and astounded menials, he stepped out from among the crowd, and addressed me in English,—a language in which he had acquired some proficiency in the course of his travels. The change of language by no means altered his views, nor abated his pertinacity. At last, finding there was nothing to be gained by this war of words, I ordered the boy to mount his horse and rejoin the wagons. "Beware of the consequences!" vociferated the enraged Trias. "Well, let them come," I replied; "here we are." But we were suffered to depart in peace with the prisoner.

That the reader may be able to form some idea of the pusillanimity of this lordly *haciendero*, it is only necessary to add, that when the altercation took place we were inside of the fortifications, from which our egress might easily have been prevented by simply closing the outer gate. We were surrounded by the whole population of the village, besides a

* Trias, while yet a youth, was dispatched by his adopted father to take the tour of Europe and the United States. He was furnished for 'pocket money' (as I have been told) with nearly a hundred *barras de plata*, each worth a thousand dollars or upwards. This money he easily got rid of during his travels, but retained most of his innate bigotry and self-importance : and, with his knowledge of the superiority of the people among whom he journeyed, grew his hatred for foreigners.

small detachment of regular troops, whose commandant took a very active part in the controversy, and fought most valiantly with his tongue. But the valor of the illustrious Señor Don Angel knew a much safer course than to vent itself where there was even a remote chance of personal risk. His influence could not fail to enlist the public in his behalf, and he thought no doubt that his battles might just as well be fought by the officers of justice as by himself.

Yet ignorant of his designs, and supposing the matter would end at this, we continued our march the next day, and by the time night approached we were full twenty miles from the seat of our late troubles. While at breakfast on the following morning we were greatly surprised by the appearance of two American gentlemen direct from Chihuahua, who had ridden thus far purposely to apprise us of what was brewing in the city to our detriment. It appeared that Trias had sent an express to the governor accusing me of rescuing a culprit from the hands of justice by force of arms, and that great preparations were accordingly being made to overtake and carry me back. That the reader may be able to understand the full extent and enormity of my offence, he has only to be informed that the proprietor of an hacienda is at once governor, justice of the peace, and everything besides which he has a mind to fancy himself—a perfect despot within the limits of his little dominion. It was, therefore, through contempt for *his* 'excellency' that I had insulted the majesty of the laws!

Having expressed my sentiments of gratitude to my worthy countrymen for the pains they had taken on my account, we again pursued our journey, determined to abide the worst. This happened on the 3d of November: on the 5th we encamped near the Ojo Caliente, a hundred and thirty miles from Chihuahua. About eleven o'clock at night, a large body of men were seen approaching. They very soon passed us, and quietly encamped at a distance of several hundred yards. They were over a hundred in number.

Nothing further occurred till next morning, when, just as I had risen from my pallet, a soldier approached and inquired if I was up. In a few minutes he returned with a message from *El Señor Capitan* to know if he could see me. Having answered in the affirmative, a very courteous and agreeable personage soon made his appearance, who, after bowing and scraping until I began to be seriously afraid that his body would break in two, finally opened his mission by handing me a packet of letters, one of which contained an order from the Governor for my immediate presence in Chihuahua, together with the three muleteers whom I had sent after the cattle; warning me, at the same time, not to give cause, by my resistance, for any other measure, which might be unpleasant to my person. The next document was from Señor Trias himself, in which he expressed his regret at having carried the matter to such an extreme, and ended with the usual offer of his services to facilitate an adjustment. Those, however, which most influenced my course, were from Don José Artalejo (*Juez de Hacienda*, Judge of the Customs, of Chihuahua), who offered to become responsible for a favorable issue if I would peaceably return; and another from a Mr. Sutton, with whom I had formerly been connected in business. The manly and upright deportment of this gentleman had inspired me with the greatest confidence, and therefore caused me to respect his opinions. But, besides my obligation to submit to a mandate from the government, however arbitrary and oppressive, another strong motive which induced me to return, in obedience to the Governor's order, was a latent misgiving lest any hostile movement on my part, no matter with what justice or necessity, might jeopardize the interests if not the lives of many of my countrymen in Chihuahua.

With regard to ourselves and our immediate safety, we would have found but very little difficulty in fighting our way out of the country. We were all well-armed, and many appeared even anxious to have a brush with the besiegers. However, I informed the captain that I was willing to return to Chihuahua, with the three 'criminals,' provided we were permitted to go armed and free, as I was not aware of having committed any crime to justify an arrest. He rejoined that this was precisely in accordance with his orders, and politely tendered me an escort of five or six soldiers, who should be placed under my command, to strengthen us against the Indians, that were known to infest our route. Thanking him for his favor, I at once started for Chihuahua, leaving the wagons to continue slowly on the journey, and the amiable captain with his band of *valientes* to retrace their steps at leisure towards the capital.

Late on the evening of the third day, I reached the city, and put up at the American Fonda, where I was fortunate enough to meet with my friend Artalejo, who at once proposed that we should proceed forthwith to the Governor's house. When we found ourselves in the presence of his excellency, my valued friend began by remarking that I had returned according to orders, and that he would answer for me with his person and property; and then, without even waiting for a reply, he turned to me and expressed a hope that I would make his house my residence while I remained in the city. I could not, of course, decline so friendly an invitation, particularly as I thought it probable that, being virtually my bail, he might prefer to have me near his person. But, as soon as we reached the street, he very promptly removed that suspicion from my mind. "I invite you to my house," said he, "as a friend, and not as a prisoner. If you have any business to transact, do not hold yourself under the least restraint. To-morrow I will see the affair satisfactorily settled."

The *Junta Departamental,* or State Council, of which Señor Artalejo was an influential member, was convened the following day. Meanwhile, every American I met with expressed a great deal of surprise to see me at liberty, as, from the excitement which had existed in the city, they expected I would have been lodged in the safest calabozo. I was advised not to venture much into the streets, as the rabble were very much incensed against me; but, although I afterwards wandered about pretty freely, no one offered to molest me; in fact, I must do the 'sovereigns of the city' the justice to say, that I was never more politely treated than during this occasion. Others suggested that, as Trias was one of the most wealthy and influential citizens of Chihuahua, I had better try to pave my way out of the difficulty with *plata,* as I could stand no chance in law against him. To this, however, I strenuously objected. I felt convinced that I had been ordered back to Chihuahua mainly for purposes of extortion, and I was determined that the *oficiales* should be disappointed. I had unbounded confidence in the friendship and integrity of Don José Artalejo, who was quite an exception to the general character of his countrymen. He was liberal, enlightened and honorable, and I shall ever remember with gratitude the warm interest he took in my affair, when he could have had no other motive for befriending me except what might spring from the consciousness of having performed a generous action.

At first, when the subject of my liberation was discussed in the *Junta Departamental,* the symptoms were rather squally, as some bigoted and unruly members of the Council seemed determined to have me punished, right or wrong. After a long and tedious debate, however, my friend brought me the draft of a petition which he desired me to copy and sign, and upon the presentation of which to the Governor, it had been agreed I should be released. This step, I was informed, had been resolved upon, because, after mature deliberation, the Council came to the conclusion that the proceedings against me had been extremely arbitrary and illegal, and that, if I should hereafter prosecute the Department, I might recover heavy damages. The wholesome lesson which had so lately been taught the Mexicans by France was perhaps the cause of the fears of the Chihuahua authorities. A clause was therefore inserted in the petition, wherein I was made to renounce all intention on my part of ever troubling the Department on the subject, and became myself a suppliant to have the affair considered as concluded.

This petition I would never have consented to sign, had I not been aware of the arbitrary power which was exercised over me. Imprisonment, in itself, was of but little consequence; but the total destruction of my property, which might have been the result of further detention, was an evil which I deemed it necessary to ward off, even at a great sacrifice of feeling. Moreover, being in duress, no forced concession would, of course, be obligatory upon me after I resumed my liberty. Again, I felt no very great inclination to sue for redress where there was so little prospect of procuring anything. I might certainly have represented the matter to the Mexican government, and even have obtained perhaps the acknowledgment of my claims against Chihuahua for damages; but the payment would have been extremely doubtful. As to our own Government, I had too much experience to rely for a moment upon her interposition.

During the progress of these transactions, I strove to ascertain the character of the charges made against me; but in vain. All I knew was, that I had offended a *rico*, and had been summoned back to Chihuahua at his instance; yet whether for 'high treason,' for an attempt at robbery, or for contempt to his *señoria*, I knew not. It is not unusual, however, in that 'land of liberty,' for a person to be arrrested and even confined for weeks without knowing the cause. The writ of *Habeas Corpus* appears unknown in the judicial tribunals of Northern Mexico.

Upon the receipt of my petition, the Governor immediately issued the following decree, which I translate for the benefit of the reader, as being not a bad specimen of Mexican grand eloquence:

" In consideration of the memorial which you have this day directed to the Superior Government, His Excellency, the Governor, has been pleased to issue the following decree:

" ' That, as Don Angel Trias has withdrawn his prosecution, so far as relates to his personal interests, the Government, using the equity with which it ought to look upon faults committed without a deliberate intention to infringe the laws, which appears presumable in the present case, owing to the memorialist's ignorance of them, the grace which he solicits is granted to him; and, in consequence, he is at liberty to retire when he chooses: to which end, and that he may not be interrupted by the authorities, a copy of this decree will be transmitted to him.'

" In virtue of the above, I inclose the said decree to you, for the purposes intended.

" God and Liberty. Chihuahua, Nov. 9, 1839.

" AMADO DE LA VEGA, Sec.

" To DON JOSIAH GREGG."

Thus terminated this 'momentous' affair. The moral of it may be summed up in a few words. A citizen of the United States who, under the faith of treaties, is engaged in his business, may be seized and harassed by the arbitrary authorities of Chihuahua with perfect impunity, because experience has proved that the American Government winks at almost every individual outrage, as utterly unworthy of its serious consideration. At the same time, the Indians may enter, as they frequently do, the suburbs of the city,—rob, plunder, and destroy life, without a single soldier being raised, or an effort made to bring the savage malefactors within the pale of justice. But a few days before the occasion of my difficulty at Torreon, the Apaches had killed a ranchero or two in the immediate neighborhood of the same village; and after-

wards, at the very time such a bustle was being made in Chihuahua to raise troops for
my 'special benefit,' the Indians entered the
corn-fields in the suburbs of the city, and killed several *labradores* who were at work in
them.   In neither of these cases, however,
were there any troops at command to pursue
and chastise the depredators—though a whole
army was in readiness to persecute our party.
The truth is, they felt much less reluctance to
pursue a band of civil traders, who, they were
well aware, could not assume a hostile attitude, than to be caught in the wake of a
band of savages, who would as little respect
their lives as their laws and their property.

Early on the morning of the 10th, I once
more, and for the last time, and with anything
but regret, took my leave of Chihuahua, with
my companions in trouble.   Towards the afternoon we met my old friend the captain,
with his valiant followers, whom I found as
full of urbanity as ever—so much so, indeed,
that he never even asked to see my passport.

On the evening of the next day, now in the
heart of the savage haunts, we were not a little alarmed by the appearance of a large body
of horsemen in the distance.   They turned
out, however, to be *Paseños*, or citizens of the
Paso del Norte.   They were on their way to
Chihuahua with a number of pack-mules
laden with apples, pears, grapes, wine, and
aguardiente—proceeds of their productive orchards and vineyards.   It is from El Paso that
Chihuahua is chiefly supplied with fruits and

liquors, which are transported on mules or in carretas. The fruits, as well fresh as in a dried state, are thus carried to the distant markets. The grapes, carefully dried in the shade, make excellent *pasas* or raisins, of which large quantities are annually prepared for market by the people of that delightful town of vineyards and orchards, who, to take them altogether, are more sober and industrious than those of any other part of Mexico I have visited; and are happily less infested by the extremes of wealth and poverty.

On the 13th, I overtook my wagons a few miles south of El Paso, whence our journey was continued, without any additional casualty, and on the 6th of December we reached Santa Fé, in fine health and spirits.

CHAPTER VIII.

ABOUT the beginning of February, 1840, and just as I was making preparations to return to the United States, the small-pox broke out among my men in a manner, which at first occasioned at least as much astonishment as alarm. One of them, who had travelled in a neighboring district, where there were some cases of small-pox, complained of a little fever, which was followed by slight eruptions, but so unlike true variolous pustules, that I treated the matter very lightly; not even suspecting a varioloid. These slight symptoms having passed off, nothing more was thought of it until eight or ten days after, when every unvaccinated member of our company was attacked by that fell disease, which soon began to manifest very malignant features. There were no fatal cases, however; yet much apprehension was felt, lest the disease should break out again on the route; but, to our great joy, we escaped this second scourge.

A party that left Santa Fé for Missouri soon afterward, was much more unfortunate. On the way, several of their men were attacked by the small-pox, some of whom died; and others retaining the infection till they approached the Missouri frontier, they were compelled to undergo a 'quarantine' in the bordering prairie, before they were permitted to enter the settlements.

On the 25th of February we set out from Santa Fé; but owing to some delays, we did not leave San Miguel till the 1st of March. As the pasturage was yet insufficient for our animals, we here provided ourselves with over six hundred bushels of corn, to feed them on the way. This time our caravan consisted of twenty-eight wagons, two small cannons, and forty-seven men, including sixteen Mexicans and a Comanche Indian who acted in the capacity of guide.* Two gentlemen of Bal-

* Manuel *el Comanche* was a full Indian, born and bred upon the great prairies. Long after having arrived at the state of manhood, he accompanied some Mexican *Comancheros* to the frontier village of San Miguel, where he fell in love with a Mexican girl—married her—and has lived in that place, a sober, 'civilized' citizen for the last ten or twelve years—endowed with much more good-

timore, Messrs. S. Wethered and J. R. Ware, had joined our caravan with one wagon and three men, making up the aggregate above-mentioned. We had also a caballada of more than two hundred mules, with nearly three hundred sheep and goats. The sheep were brought along partially to supply us with meat in case of emergency : the surplusage, how-ever, could not fail to command a fair price in the United States.

Instead of following the trail of the year before, I determined to seek a nearer and bet-ter route down the south side of the Canadian river, under the guidance of the Comanche; by which movement, we had again to travel a distance of four hundred miles over an en-tirely new country. We had just passed the Laguna Colorada, where, the following year, a division of Texan volunteers, under General McLeod, surrendered to Col. Archuleta, when our fire was carelessly permitted to communi-cate with the prairie grass. As there was a head-wind blowing at the time, we very soon got out of reach of the conflagration : but the next day, the wind having changed, the fire was again perceived in our rear approaching us at a very brisk pace. The terror which these prairie conflagrations are calculated to inspire, when the grass is tall and dry, as was the case in the present instance, has often

ness of heart and integrity of purpose than a majority of his Mex-ican neighbors. He had learned to speak Spanish quite intelligibly, and was therefore an excellent Comanche interpreter : and being familiar with every part of the prairies, he was very serviceable as a guide.

been described, and though the perils of these disasters are not unfrequently exaggerated, they are sometimes sufficient to daunt the stoutest heart. Mr. Kendall relates a frightful incident of this kind which occurred to the Texan Santa Fé Expedition; and all those who have crossed the Prairies have had more or less experience as to the danger which occasionally threatens the caravans from these sweeping visitations. The worst evil to be apprehended with those bound for Santa Fé is from the explosion of gunpowder, as a keg or two of twenty-five pounds each, is usually to be found in every wagon. When we saw the fire gaining so rapidly upon us, we had to use the whip very unsparingly; and it was only when the lurid flames were actually rolling upon the heels of our teams, that we succeeded in reaching a spot of short-grass prairie, where there was no further danger to be apprehended.

The headway of the conflagration was soon after checked by a small stream which traversed our route; and we had only emerged fairly from its smoke, on the following day (the 9th), when our Comanche guide returned hastily from his accustomed post in advance, and informed us that he had espied three buffaloes, not far off. They were the first we had met with, and, being heartily anxious for a change from the dried beef with which we were provided, I directed the Comanche, who was by far our surest hunter, to prepare at once for the *chasse*. He said he preferred to hunt on

horseback and with his bow and arrow; and
believing my riding-horse the fleetest in company (which, by the by, was but a common
pony, and thin in flesh withal), I dismounted
and gave him the bridle, with many charges
to treat him kindly, as we still had a long
journey before us. "Don't attempt to kill
but one—that will serve us for the present!"
I exclaimed, as he galloped off. The Comanche was among the largest of his tribe—
bony and muscular—weighing about two
hundred pounds: but once at his favorite
sport, he very quickly forgot my injunction, as
well as the weakness of my little pony. He
soon brought down two of his game,—and
shyly remarked to those who followed in his
wake, that, had he not feared a scolding from
me, he would not have permitted the third to
escape.

On the evening of the 10th our camp was
pitched in the neighborhood of a ravine in the
prairie, and as the night was dark and dreary,
the watch tried to comfort themselves by
building a rousing fire, around which they
presently drew, and commenced 'spinning
long yarns' about Mexican fandangoes, and
black-eyed damsels. All of a sudden the still-
ness of the night was interrupted by a loud
report of fire-arms, and a shower of bullets
came whizzing by the ears of the heedless
sentinels. Fortunately, however, no one was
injured; which must be looked upon as a
very extraordinary circumstance, when we
consider what a fair mark our men, thus hud-

dled round a blazing fire, presented to the
rifles of the Indians.   The savage yells, which
resounded from every part of the ravine, bore
very satisfactory testimony that this was no
false alarm ; and the ' Pawnee whistle' which
was heard in every quarter, at once impressed
us with the idea of its being a band of that
famous prairie banditti.

Every man sprang from his pallet with
rifle in hand ; for, upon the Prairies, we always
sleep with our arms by our sides or under our
heads.   Our Comanche seemed at first very
much at a loss what to do.   At last, thinking
it might possibly be a band of his own nation,
he began a most boisterous harangue in his
vernacular tongue, which he continued for
several minutes ; when finding that the enemy took no notice of him, and having become
convinced also, from an occasional Pawnee
word which he was able to make out, that he
had been wasting breath with the mortal foes
of his race, he suddenly ceased all expostu-
lations, and blazed away with his rifle, with a
degree of earnestness which was truly edify-
ing, as if convinced that that was the best he
could do for us.

It was now evident that the Indians had
taken possession of the entire ravine, the
nearest points of which were not fifty yards
from our wagons : a warning to prairie travellers to encamp at a greater distance from
whatsoever might afford shelter for an enemy.
The banks of the gully were low, but still they
formed a very good breastwork, behind which

the enemy lay ensconced, discharging volleys of balls upon our wagons, among which we were scattered. At one time we thought of making an attempt to rout them from their fortified position; but being ignorant of their number, and unable to distinguish any object through the dismal darkness which hung all around, we had to remain content with firing at random from behind our wagons, aiming at the flash of their guns, or in the direction whence any noise appeared to emanate. Indeed their yelling was almost continuous, breaking out every now and then in the most hideous screams and vociferous chattering, which were calculated to appal such timorous persons as we may have had in our caravan. All their screeching and whooping, however, had no effect—they could not make our animals break from the enclosure of the wagons, in which they were fortunately shut up; which was no doubt their principal object for attacking us.

I cannot forbear recording a most daring feat performed by a Mexican muleteer, named Antonio Chavez, during the hottest of the first onset. Seeing the danger of my two favorite riding horses, which were tethered outside within a few paces of the savages, he rushed out and brought safely in the most valuable of the two, though fusil-balls were showering around him all the while. The other horse broke his halter and made his escape.

Although sundry scores of shots had been fired at our people, we had only two men wounded. One, a Mexican, was but slightly injured in the hand, but the wound of the other, who was an Italian, bore a more serious aspect, and deserves especial mention. He was a short, corpulent fellow, and had been nicknamed 'Dutch'—a loquacious, chicken-hearted *fainéant*, and withal in the daily habit of gorging himself to such an enormous extent, that every alternate night he was on the sick list. On this memorable occasion, Dutch had 'foundered' again, and the usual prescription of a double dose of Epsom salts had been his supper potion. The skirmish had continued for about an hour, and although a frightful groaning had been heard in Dutch's wagon for some time, no one paid any attention to it, as it was generally supposed to be from the effects of his dose. At length, however, some one cried out, 'Dutch is wounded!'' I immediately went to see him, and found him writhing and twisting himself as if in great pain, crying all the time that he was shot. "Shot!—where?" I inquired. "Ah! in the head, sir?" "Pshaw! Dutch, none of that; you've only bumped your head in trying to hide yourself." Upon lighting a match, however, I found that a ball had passed through the middle of his hat, and that, to my consternation, the top of his head was bathed in blood. It turned out, upon subsequent examination, that the ball had glanced upon the skull, inflicting a serious-looking wound, and so deep that an inch of sound skin separated the holes at which the bullet had entered and passed out. Notwithstanding I at first apprehended a fracture of the scull, it very soon healed, and Dutch was 'up and about' again in the course of a week.

Although teachers not unfrequently have cause to deplore the thickness of their pupils' skulls, Dutch had every reason to congratulate himself upon possessing such a treasure, as it had evidently preserved him from a more serious catastrophe. It appeared he had taken shelter in his wagon at the commencement of the attack, without reflecting that the boards and sheets were not ball-proof: and as Indians, especially in the night, are apt to shoot too high, he was in a much more dangerous situation than if upon the ground.

The enemy continued the attack for nearly three hours, when they finally retired, so as to make good their retreat before daylight. As it rained and snowed from that time till nine in the morning, their 'sign' was almost entirely obliterated, and we were unable to discover whether they had received any injury or not. It was evidently a foot party, which we looked upon as another proof of their being Pawnees; for these famous marauders are well known to go forth on their expeditions of plunder without horses, although they seldom fail to return well mounted.

Their shot had riddled our wagons considerably: in one we counted no less than eight bullet-holes. We had the gratification to believe, however, that they did not get a single one of our animals: the horse which broke away at the first onset, doubtless made his escape; and a mule which was too badly wounded to travel, was dispatched by the muleteers, lest it should fall into the hands of the savages, or into the mouths of the wolves; and they deemed it more humane to leave it to be eaten dead than alive. We also experienced considerable damage in our stock of sheep, a number of them having been devoured by wolves. They had been scattered at the beginning of the attack; and, in their anxiety to fly from the scene of action, had jumped, as it were, into the very jaws of their ravenous enemies.

On the 12th of March, we ascended upon the celebrated *Llano Estacado*, and continued along its borders for a few days. The second night upon this dreary plain, we experienced one of the strongest and bleakest 'northwesters' that ever swept across those prairies; during which, our flock of sheep and goats, being left unattended, fled over the plain, in search of some shelter, it was supposed, from the furious element. Their disappearance was not observed for some time, and the night being too dark to discern anything, we were obliged to defer going in pursuit of them till the following morning. After a fruitless and laborious search, during which the effects of the mirage proved a constant source of annoyance and disappointment, we were finally obliged to relinquish the pursuit, and return to the caravan without finding one of them.

These severe winds are very prevalent
upon the great western prairies, though they
are seldom quite so inclement. At some seasons, they are about as regular and unceasing
as the 'trade winds' of the ocean. It will
often blow a gale for days, and even weeks
together, without slacking for a moment,
except occasionally at night. It is for this
reason, as well as on account of the rains,
that percussion guns are preferable upon
the Prairies, particularly for those who understand their use. The winds are frequently
so severe as to sweep away both sparks and
priming from a flint lock, and thus render
it wholly ineffective.

The following day we continued our
march down the border of the Llano Estacado. Knowing that our Comanche guide was
about as familiar with all those great plains
as a landlord with his premises, I began to
question him, as we travelled along, concerning the different streams which pierced them
to the southward. Pointing in that direction,
he said there passed a water-course, at the
distance of a hard day's ride, which he designated as a *cañada* or valley, in which there
was always water to be found at occasional
places, but that none flowed in its channel
except during the rainy season. This cañada
he described as having its origin in the Llano
Estacado some fifty or sixty miles east of Rio
Pecos, and about the same distance south of
the route we came, and that its direction was
a little south of east, passing to the southward

of the northern portion of the Witchita mountains, known to Mexican Ciboleros and Comancheros as *Sierra Jumanes*. It was, therefore, evident that this was the principal northern branch of Red River. The False Washita, or *Rio Negro*, as the Mexicans call it, has its rise, as he assured me, between the Canadian and this cañada, at no great distance to the southeastward of where we were then travelling.

On the 15th, our Comanche guide, being fearful lest we should find no water upon the plain, advised us to pursue a more northwardly course, so that, after a hard day's ride, we again descended the *ceja* or brow of the Llano Estacado, into the undulating lands which border the Canadian; and, on the following day, we found ourselves upon the southern bank of that stream.

Although, but a few days' travel above where we now were, the Canadian runs pent up in a narrow channel, scarcely four rods across, we here found it spread out to the width of from three to six hundred yards, and so full of sand-bars (only interspersed with narrow rills) as to present the appearance of a mere sandy valley instead of the bed of a river. In fact, during the driest seasons, the water wholly disappears in many places. Captain Boone, of the U. S. Dragoons, being upon an exploring expedition in the summer of 1843, came to the Canadian about the region of our western boundary, where he found the channel perfectly dry. Notwithstanding

it presents the face of one of the greatest
rivers of the west during freshets, yet even
then it would not be navigable on account of
its rapidity and shallowness. It would appear almost incredible to those unacquainted
with the prairie streams, that a river of about
1500 miles in length, and whose head wears
a cap of perennial snow (having its source in
the Rocky Mountains), should scarcely be
navigable, for even the smallest craft, over
fifty miles above its mouth.

We pursued our course down the same side
of the river for several days, during which
time we crossed a multitude of little streams
which flowed into the Canadian from the adjoining plains, while others presented nothing
but dry beds of sand. One of these was so
remarkable, on account of its peculiarity and
size, that we named it 'Dry River.' The bed
was at least 200 yards wide, yet without a
vestige of water ; notwithstanding, our guide
assured us that it was a brisk-flowing stream
some leagues above : and from the drift-wood
along its borders, it was evident that, even
here, it must be a considerable river during
freshets.

While travelling down the course of the
Canadian, we sometimes found the buffalo
very abundant. On one occasion, two or
three hunters, who were a little in advance
of the caravan, perceiving a herd quietly
grazing in an open glade, they 'crawled upon'
them after the manner of the 'still hunters.'
Their first shot having brought down a fine

fat cow, they slipped up behind her, and, resting their guns over her body, shot two or three others, without occasioning any serious disturbance or surprise to their companions; for, extraordinary as it may appear, if the buffalo neither see nor smell the hunter, they will pay but little attention to the crack of guns, or to the mortality which is being dealt among them.

The slaughter of these animals is frequently carried to an excess, which shows the depravity of the human heart in very bold relief. Such is the excitement that generally prevails at the sight of these fat denizens of the prairies, that very few hunters appear able to refrain from shooting as long as the game remains within reach of their rifles; nor can they ever permit a fair shot to escape them. Whether the mere pleasure of taking life is

13*

the incentive of these brutal excesses, I will
not pretend to decide; but one thing is very
certain, that the buffalo killed yearly on these
prairies far exceeds the wants of the traveller, or what might be looked upon as the
exigencies of rational sport.*

But in making these observations, I regret
that I cannot give to my precepts the force of
my own example: I have not always been
able wholly to withstand the cruel temptation.
Not long after the incident above alluded to,
as I was pioneering alone, according to my
usual practice, at a distance of a mile or two
ahead of the wagons, in search of the best
route, I perceived in a glade, a few rods in
front of me, several protuberances, which at
first occasioned me no little fright, for I took
them, as they loomed dimly through the tall
grass, for the tops of Indian lodges.   But I
soon discovered they were the huge humps
of a herd of buffalo, which were quietly
grazing.

I immediately alighted, and approached unobserved to within forty or fifty yards of the
unsuspecting animals.   Being armed with one
of Cochran's nine-chambered rifles, I took
aim at one that stood broad-side, and 'blazed
away.'   The buffalo threw up their heads and
looked about, but seeing nothing (for I remained concealed in the grass), they again

* The same barbarous propensity is observable in regard to wild
horses.   Most persons appear unable to restrain this wanton inclination to take life, when a mustang approaches within rifle-shot.
Many a stately steed thus falls a victim to the cruelty of man.

went on grazing as though nothing had happened. The truth is, the one I had shot was perhaps but little hurt; for, as generally happens with the inexperienced hunter—and often with those who know better, the first excitement allowing no time for reflection—I no doubt aimed too high, so as to lodge the ball in the hump. A buffalo's heart lies exceedingly low, so that to strike it the shot should enter not over one-fourth of the depth of the body above the lower edge of the breast bone.

The brutes were no sooner quiet, than I took another and more deliberate aim at my former victim, which resulted as before. But believing him now mortally wounded, I next fired in quick succession at four others of the gang. It occurred to me, by this time, that I had better save my remaining three shots; for it was possible enough for my firing to attract the attention of strolling savages, who might take advantage of my empty gun to make a sortie upon me—yet there stood my buffalo, some of them still quietly feeding.

As I walked out from my concealment, a party of our own men came galloping up from the wagons, considerably alarmed. They had heard the six shots, and, not recollecting my repeating rifle, supposed I had been attacked by Indians, and therefore came to my relief. Upon their approach the buffalo all fled, except three which appeared badly wounded—one indeed soon fell and expired. The other two would doubtless have fol-

lowed the example of the first, had not a
hunter, anxious to dispatch them more speedi-
ly, approached too near; when, regaining
strength from the excitement, they fled before
him, and entirely escaped, though he pursued
them for a considerable distance.

A few days after this occurrence, Mr. Wethered returned to the camp one evening with
seven buffalo tongues (the hunter's usual trophy) swung to his saddle. He said that, in
the morning, one of the hunters had ungene-
rously objected to sharing a buffalo with him;
whereupon Mr. W. set out, vowing he would
kill buffalo for himself, and 'no thanks to
any one.' He had not been out long when he
spied a herd of only seven bulls, quietly feeding near a ravine; and slipping up behind the
banks, he shot down one and then another,
until they all lay before him; and their seven
tongues he brought in to bear testimony of
his skill.

Not long after crossing Dry River, we ascended the high grounds, and soon found ourselves upon the high ridge which divides the
waters of the Canadian and False Washita,
whose 'breaks' could be traced descending
from the Llano Estacado far to the southwest.

By an observation of an eclipse of one of
Jupiter's satellites, on the night of the 25th of
March, in latitude 35° 51' 30", I found that
we were very near the 100th degree of longitude west from Greenwich. On the following day, therefore, we celebrated our entrance
into the United States territory. Those who

have never been beyond the purlieus of the land of their nativity, can form but a poor conception of the joy which the wanderer in distant climes experiences on treading once more upon his own native soil! Although we were yet far from the abodes of civilization, and further still from home, nevertheless the heart within us thrilled with exhilarating sensations; for we were again in our own territory, breathed our own free atmosphere, and were fairly out of reach of the arbitrary power which we had left behind us.

As we continued our route upon this narrow dividing ridge, we could not help remarking how nearly these streams approach each other: in one place they seemed scarcely five miles apart. On this account our Comanche guide, as well as several Mexicans of our party, who had some acquaintance with these prairies, gave it as their opinion that the Washita or *Rio Negro* was in fact a branch of the Canadian; for its confluence with Red River was beyond the bounds of their peregrinations.

As the forest of Cross Timbers was now beginning to be seen in the distance, and fearing we might be troubled to find a passway through this brushy region, south of the Canadian, we forded this river on the 29th, without the slightest trouble, and very soon entered our former trail, a little west of Spring Valley. This gave a new and joyful impulse to our spirits; for we had been travelling over twenty days without even a trail, and through a region of which we knew absolutely nothing, except from what we could gather from our Comanche pilot. This trail, which our wagons had made the previous summer, was still visible, and henceforth there was an end to all misgivings.

If we take a retrospective view of the country over which we travelled, we shall find but little that can ever present attractions to the agriculturist. Most of the low valleys of the Canadian, for a distance of five hundred miles, are either too sandy or too marshy for cultivation; and the upland prairies are, in many places, but little else than sand-hills. In some parts, it is true, they are firm and fertile, but wholly destitute of timber, with the exception of a diminutive branch of the Cross Timbers, which occupies a portion of the ridge betwixt the Canadian and the North Fork. The Canadian river itself is still more bare of timber than the upper Arkansas. In its whole course through the plains, there is but little except cottonwood, and that very scantily scattered along its banks—in some places, for leagues together, not a stick is to be seen. Except it be near the Mountains, where the valleys are more fertile, it is only the little narrow valleys which skirt many of its tributary rivulets that indicate any amenity. Some of these are rich and beautiful in the extreme, timbered with walnut, mulberry, oak, elm, hackberry, and occasionally cedar about the bluffs.

We now continued our journey without encountering any further casualty, except in crossing the Arkansas river, where we lost several mules by drowning; and on the 22d of April we made our entrance into Van Buren. This trip was much more tedious and protracted than I had contemplated—owing, in the first part of the journey, to the inclemency of the season, and a want of pasturage for our animals; and, towards the conclusion, to the frequent rains, which kept the route in a miserable condition.

Concerning this expedition, I have only one or two more remarks to offer. As regards the two different routes to Santa Fé, although Missouri, for various reasons which it is needless to explain here, can doubtless retain the monopoly of the Santa Fé trade, the route from Arkansas possesses many advantages. Besides its being some days' travel shorter,* it is less intersected with large streams; there are fewer sandy stretches, and a greater variety of wood-skirted brooks, affording throughout the journey very agreeable camping-places. Also, as the grass springs up nearly a month earlier than in Upper Missouri, caravans could start much sooner, and the proprietors would have double the time to conduct their mercantile transactions. Moreover, the return companies would find better pasturage on their way back, and reach their homes before the season of frost had far advanced. Again, such as should desire to engage in the 'stock

* The latitude of Independence, Mo., is 39° 8′, while that of Van Buren is 35° 26′,—within a few miles of the parallel of Santa Fé: and being on about the same meridian as Independence, the distance, of course, is considerably shorter.

trade' would at once bring their mules and horses into a more congenial climate—one more in accordance with that of their nativity; for the rigorous winters of Missouri often prove fatal to the unacclimated Mexican animals.

This was my last trip across the Plains, though I made an excursion, during the following summer, among the Comanche Indians, and other wild tribes, living in the heart of the Prairies, but returned without crossing to Mexico. The observations made during this trip will be found incorporated in the notices, which are to follow, of the Prairies and their inhabitants.

Since that time I have striven in vain to reconcile myself to the even tenor of civilized life in the United States; and have sought in its amusements and its society a substitute for those high excitements which have attached me so strongly to Prairie life. Yet I am almost ashamed to confess that scarcely a day passes without my experiencing a pang of regret that I am not now roving at large upon those western plains. Nor do I find my taste peculiar; for I have hardly known a man, who has ever become familiar with the kind of life which I have led for so many years, that has not relinquished it with regret.

There is more than one way of explaining this apparent incongruity. In the first place —the wild, unsettled and independent life of the Prairie trader, makes perfect freedom from nearly every kind of social dependence an absolute necessity of his being. He is in daily, nay, hourly exposure of his life and property, and in the habit of relying upon his own arm and his own gun both for protection and support. Is he wronged? No court or jury is called to adjudicate upon his disputes or his abuses, save his own conscience; and no powers are invoked to redress them, save those with which the God of Nature has endowed him. He knows no government—no laws, save those of his own creation and adoption. He lives in no society which he must look up to or propitiate. The exchange of this untrammelled condition—this sovereign independence, for a life in civilization, where both his physical and moral freedom are invaded at every turn, by the complicated machinery of social institutions, is certainly likely to commend itself to but few, —not even to all those who have been educated to find their enjoyments in the arts and elegancies peculiar to civilized society;—as is evinced by the frequent instances of men of letters, of refinement and of wealth, voluntarily abandoning society for a life upon the Prairies, or in the still more savage mountain wilds.

A 'tour on the Prairies' is certainly a *dangerous* experiment for him who would live a quiet contented life at home among his friends and relatives: not so dangerous to life or health, as prejudicial to his domestic habits. Those who have lived pent up in our large cities, know but little of the broad, unembarrassed freedom of the Great Western Prairies. Viewing them from a snug fire-side, they seem crowded with dangers, with labors and with sufferings; but once upon them, and these appear to vanish—they are soon forgotten.

There is another consideration, which, with most men of the Prairies, operates seriously against their reconciliation to the habits of civilized life. Though they be endowed naturally with the organs of taste and refinement, and though once familiar with the ways and practices of civilized communities, yet a long absence from such society generally obliterates from their minds most of those common laws of social intercourse, which are so necessary to the man of the world. The awkwardness and the *gaucheries* which ignorance of their details so often involves, are very trying to all men of sensitive temperaments. Consequently, multitudes rush back to the Prairies, merely to escape those criticisms and that ridicule, which they know not how to disarm.

It will hardly be a matter of surprise then, when I add, that this passion for Prairie life, how paradoxical soever it may seem, will be very apt to lead me upon the Plains again, to spread my bed with the mustang and the buffalo, under the broad canopy of heaven,— there to seek to maintain undisturbed my confidence in men, by fraternizing with the little prairie dogs and wild colts, and the still wilder Indians—the *unconquered Sabœans* of the Great American Deserts.

CHAPTER IX.

CONCLUSION OF THE SANTA FÉ TRADE.

Decline of Prices—Statistical Table—Chihuahua Trade—Its Extent—Different Ports through which Goods are introduced to that Market—Expedition between Chihuahua and Arkansas—The more recent Incidents of the Santa Fé Caravans—Adventures of 1843—Robbery and Murder of Chavez—Expedition from Texas—Defeat of Gen. Armijo's Van-guard—His precipitate Retreat—Texan Grievances—Unfortunate Results of Indiscriminate Revenge—Want of Discipline among the Texans—Disarmed by Capt. Cook—Return of the Escort of U. S. Dragoons, and of the Texans—Demands of the Mexican Government—Closing of the Santa Fé Trade.

BEFORE proceeding to the graver matters to be presented in the succeeding chapters, a few words to those who are curious about the history of the Santa Fé trade intervening between the conclusion of my personal narrative and the closing of the trade by the Mexican government, in 1843, may not be amiss.

The Santa Fé trade, though more or less fluctuating from its origin, continued to present an average increase and growth down to the year 1831. During the same period, the prices of goods continued to go down in even a more rapid ratio. Since 1831, the rates of

sales have continued steadily to fall, to the
latest period of the trade, although there has
been no average increase in the number of
adventurers, or amount of merchandise.*

* Some general statistics of the Santa Fé Trade may prove not
wholly without interest to the mercantile reader. With this view, I
have prepared the following table of the probable amounts of merchandise invested in the Santa Fé Trade, from 1822 to 1843 inclusive, and about the portion of the same transferred to the Southern
markets (chiefly Chihuahua) during the same period ; together
with the approximate number of wagons, men and proprietors engaged each year :

Years	Amt. Mdse.	W'gs.	Men.	Pro's.	T'n to Ch'a.	Remarks.
1822	15,000		70	60		Pack-animals only used.
1823	12,000		50	30		do. do.
1824	35,000	26	100	80	3,000	do. and wagons.
1825	65,000	37	130	90	5,000	do. do.
1826	90,000	60	100	70	7,000	Wagons only henceforth.
1827	85,000	55	90	50	8,000	
1828	150,000	100	200	80	20,000	3 men killed, being the first.
1829	60,000	30	50	20	5,000	1st U. S. Es.—1 trader killed.
1830	120,000	70	140	60	20,000	First oxen used by traders.
1831	250,000	130	320	80	80,000	Two men killed.
1832	140,000	70	150	40	50,000	⎰ Party defeated on Canadian
1833	180,000	105	185	60	80,000	⎱ 2 men killed, 3 perished.
1834	150,000	80	160	50	70,000	2d U. S. Escort.
1835	140,000	75	140	40	70,000	
1836	130,000	70	135	35	60,000	
1837	150,000	80	160	35	80,000	
1838	90,000	50	100	20	40,000	
1839	250,000	130	250	40	100,000	Arkansas Expedition.
1840	50,000	30	60	5	10,000	Chihuahua Expedition.
1841	150,000	60	100	12	80,000	Texan Santa Fe Expedition.
1842	160,000	70	120	15	90,000	
1843	450,000	230	350	30	300,000	3d U.S. Es.—Ports closed.

The foregoing table is not given as perfectly accurate, yet it is believed to be about as nearly so as any that could be made out at the
present day.   The column marked " Pro's." (Proprietors), though
even less precise than the other statistics, presents, I think, about
the proportion of the whole number engaged each year who were
owners.   At first, as will be seen, almost every individual of
each caravan was a proprietor, while of late the capital has been

From 1831 to the present date, prices have scarcely averaged, for medium calicoes, thirty-seven cents, and for plain domestic cottons thirty-one cents per yard. Taking assortments round, 100 per cent. upon United States costs were generally considered excellent sales: many stocks have been sold at a still lower rate. The average prices of Chihuahua are equally low, yet a brisker demand has rendered this the most agreeable and profitable branch of the trade.

held by comparatively few hands. In 1843, the greater portion of the traders were New Mexicans, several of whom, during the three years previous, had embarked in this trade, of which they bid fair to secure a monopoly.

The amount of merchandise transported to Santa Fé each year, is set down at its probable cost in the Eastern cities of the United States. Besides freights and insurance to Independence, there has been an annual investment, averaging nearly twenty-five per cent. upon the cost of the stocks, in wagons, teams, provisions, hire of hands, &c., for transportation across the Prairies. A large portion of this remaining unconsumed, however, the ultimate loss on the outfit has not been more than half of the above amount. Instead of purchasing outfit, some traders prefer employing freighters, a number of whom are usually to be found on the frontier of Missouri, ready to transport goods to Santa Fé, at ten to twelve cents per pound. From thence to Chihuahua the price of freights is six to eight cents—upon mules, or in wagons.

The average gross returns of the traders has rarely exceeded fifty per cent. upon the cost of their merchandise, leaving a net profit of between twenty and forty per cent.; though their profits have not unfrequently been under ten per cent.: in fact, as has before been mentioned, their adventures have sometimes been losing speculations. (a)

(a) Those who are familiar with Mr. Mayer's very interesting work on Mexico, will observe that a portion of the preceding table corresponds substantially with one presented on page 318 of that work. In justice to myself, I feel compelled to state, that, in 1841, I published, in the Galveston "Daily Advertiser," a table of the Santa Fé trade from 1831 to 1840 inclusive, of which that of Mr. Mayer embraces an exact copy. I have since made additions, and corrected it to some extent, but still the correspondence is such as seemed to require of me this explanation.

14*

The first attempt to introduce American goods into the more southern markets of Mexico from Santa Fé, was made in the year 1824. The amounts were very small, however, till towards the year 1831. For a few of the first years, the traders were in the habit of conveying small lots to Sonora and California; but this branch of the trade has, I believe, latterly ceased altogether. Yet the amounts transferred to Chihuahua have generally increased; so that for the last few years, that trade has consumed very nearly half of the entire imports by the Missouri Caravans.

The entire consumption of foreign goods in the department of Chihuahua, has been estimated by intelligent Mexican merchants, at from two to three millions annually; the first cost of which might be set down at nearly one half. Of this amount the Santa Fé trade, as will be seen from the accompanying table, has not furnished a tenth part; the balance being introduced through other ports, viz.: *Matamoros*, whence Chihuahua has received nearly half its supplies—*Vera Cruz* via the city of Mexico, whence considerable amounts have been brought to this department—*Tampico* on the Gulf of Mexico, and *Mazatlan* on the Pacific, via Durango, whence the imports have been of some importance—while nearly all the west of the department, and especially the heavy consumption of the mining town of Jesus-Maria, receives most of its supplies from the port of *Guaymas* on the Gulf of

California; whence, indeed, several stocks of goods have been introduced as far as the city of Chihuahua itself. In 1840, a large amount of merchandise was transported directly from the Red River frontier of Arkansas to Chihuahua; but no other expedition has ever been made in that direction.*

* With a view to encourage adventurers, the government of Chihuahua agreed to reduce the impost duties to a very low rate, in favor of a pioneer enterprise; and to furnish an escort of dragoons for the protection of the traders.

The expedition was undertaken chiefly by Mexicans; but one American merchant, Dr. H. Connelly, having invested capital in it, I obtained from this intelligent gentleman a very interesting sketch of the adventures of this pioneer party, which I regret that my plan will not permit me to present in detail.

The adventurers set out from Chihuahua on the 3d of April, 1839, amidst the benisons of the citizens, and with the confident hope of transferring the valuable trade of the North to their city. The caravan (including fifty dragoons), consisted of over a hundred men, yet only about half a dozen of the number were proprietors. Though they had but seven wagons, they brought about seven hundred mules, and two or three hundred thousand dollars in specie and bullion, for the purposes of their adventure.

They took the Presidio del Norte in their route, and then proceeding northwestwardly, finally arrived at Fort Towson after a protracted journey of three months; but without meeting with any hostile savages, or encountering any serious casualty, except getting bewildered, after crossing Red River, which they mistook for the Brazos. This caused them to shape their course thence nearly north, in search of the former stream, until they reached the Canadian river, where they met with some Delaware Indians, of whom they obtained the first correct information of their whereabouts; and by whom they were piloted safely to Fort Towson.

It had been the intention of these adventurers to return to Chihuahua the ensuing fall; but from various accidents and delays, they were unable to get ready until the season had too far advanced; which, with an incessant series of rains that followed, prevented them from travelling till the ensuing spring. Learning that the Texans were friendly disposed towards them, they now turned their course through the midst of the northern settlements of that republic. Of the kind treatment they experienced during their transit, Dr. Connelly speaks in the following terms: " I have never been more hospitably treated, or had more efficient assistance, than

By far the greatest portion of the introductions through the sea-ports just alluded to, have been made by British merchants. It is chiefly the preference given to American manufactures, which has enabled the merchandise of the Santa Fé adventurers to compete in the Southern markets, with goods introduced through the sea-ports, which have had the

was given by the citizens of Red River. All seemed to vie with each other in rendering us every aid in their power; and our Mexican friends, notwithstanding the hostile attitude in which the two countries stood towards each other, were treated with a kindness which they still recollect with the warmest feelings of gratitude." This forms a very notable contrast with the treatment which the Texan traders, who afterwards visited Santa Fé, received at the hands of the Mexicans.

The caravan now consisted of sixty or seventy wagons laden with merchandise, and about two hundred and twenty-five men, including their escort of Mexican dragoons. They passed the Texan border early in April, and expected to intersect their former track beyond the Cross Timbers, but that trail having been partially obliterated, they crossed it unobserved, and were several days lost on the waters of the Brazos river. Having turned their course south for a few days, however, they fortunately discovered their old route at a branch of the Colorado.

After this they continued their journey without further casualty; for notwithstanding they met with a large body of Comanches, they passed them amicably, and soon reached the Rio Pecos. Though very narrow, this stream was too deep to be forded, and they were compelled to resort to an expedient characteristic of the Prairies. There being not a stick of timber anywhere to be found, of which to make even a raft, they buoyed up a wagon-body by binding several empty water-kegs to the bottom, which served them the purpose of a ferry-boat.

When they reached Presidio del Norte again, they learned that Gov. Irigóyen, with whom they had celebrated the contract for a diminution of their duties, had died during their absence. A new corps of officers being in power, they were now threatened with a charge of full tariff duties. After a delay of forty-five days at the Presidio, however, they made a compromise, and entered Chihuahua on the 27th of August, 1840.

The delays and accumulated expenses of this expedition caused it to result so disastrously to the interests of all who were engaged in it, that no other enterprise of the kind has since been undertaken.

benefit of the draw-back. In this last respect
our traders have labored under a very unjust
burden.

It is difficult to conceive any equitable reason why merchants conveying their goods
across the Prairies in wagons, should not be
as much entitled to the protection of the
Government, as those who transport them in
vessels across the ocean. This assistance
might have enabled our merchants to monopo-
lize the rich trade of Chihuahua; and they
would, no doubt, have obtained a share of
that of the still richer departments of Durango
and Zacatecas, as well as some portion of the
Sonora and California trade. Then rating
that of Chihuahua at two millions, half that
of Durango at the same, and a million from
Zacatecas, Sonora, etc., it would ascend to the
clever amount of some five millions of dollars
per annum.

In point of revenue, the Santa Fé trade has
been of but little importance to the government of Mexico. Though the amount of duties collected annually at this port has usually been fifty to eighty thousand dollars, yet
nearly one-half has been embezzled by the
officers of the customs, leaving an average
net revenue of perhaps less than forty thousand dollars per annum.

It is not an unimportant fact to be known,
that, since the year 1831, few or none of the
difficulties and dangers which once environed
the Santa Fé adventurer have been encountered. No traders have been killed by the

savages on the regular route, and but few animals stolen from the caravans. On the whole, the rates of insurance upon adventures in this trade should hardly be as high as upon marine adventures between New York and Liverpool. While I declare, however, the serious dangers and troubles to have been in general so slight, I ought not to suppress at least an outline of the difficulties that occurred on the Prairies in 1843, which were attended with very serious consequences.

It had been reported in Santa Fé as early as November, 1842, that a party of Texans were upon the Prairies, prepared to attack any Mexican traders who should cross the Plains the succeeding spring; and as some Americans were accused of being spies, and in collusion with the Texans, many were ordered to Santa Fé for examination, occasioning a deal of trouble to several innocent persons. Than this, however, but little further attention was paid to the report, many believing it but another of those rumors of Texan invasion which had so often spread useless consternation through the country.

So little apprehension appeared to exist, that, in February, 1843, Don Antonio José Chavez, of New Mexico, left Santa Fé for Independence, with but five servants, two wagons, and fifty-five mules. He had with him some ten or twelve thousand dollars in specie and gold bullion, besides a small lot of furs. As the month of March was extremely inclement, the little party suffered inconceivably from cold and privations. Most of them were frost-bitten, and all their animals, except five, perished from the extreme severity of the season; on which account Chavez was compelled to leave one of his wagons upon the Prairies. He had worried along, however, with his remaining wagon and valuables, till about the tenth of April, when he found himself near the Little Arkansas; at least a hundred miles within the territory of the United States. He was there met by fifteen men from the border of Missouri, professing to be Texan troops, under the command of one John M'Daniel. This party had been collected, for the most part, on the frontier, by their leader, who was recently from Texas, from which government he professed to hold a captain's commission. They started no doubt with the intention of joining one Col. Warfield (also said to hold a Texan commission), who had been upon the Plains near the Mountains, with a small party, for several months—with the avowed intention of attacking the Mexican traders.

Upon meeting Chavez, however, the party of M'Daniel at once determined to make sure of the prize he was possessed of, rather than take their chances of a similar booty beyond the U. S. boundary. The unfortunate Mexican was therefore taken a few miles south of the road, and his baggage rifled. Seven of the party then left for the settlements with their share of the booty, amounting to some four or five hundred dollars apiece; making the journey on foot, as their horses had taken

a *stampede* and escaped.   The remaining
eight, soon after the departure of their comrades, determined to put Chavez to death,—
for what cause it would seem difficult to con-
jecture, as he had been, for two days, their
unresisting prisoner.   Lots were accordingly
cast to determine which four of the party
should be the cruel executioners; and their
wretched victim was taken off a few rods and
shot down in cold blood.   After his murder a
considerable amount of gold was found about
his person, and in his trunk.   The body of
the unfortunate man, together with his wagon
and baggage, was thrown into a neighboring
ravine; and a few of the lost animals of the
marauders having been found, their booty was
packed upon them and borne away to the
frontier of Missouri.

Great exertions had been made to intercept
this lawless band at the outset; but they escaped the vigilance even of a detachment of
dragoons that had followed them over a hundred miles.   Yet the honest citizens of the
border were too much on the alert to permit
them to return to the interior with impunity.
However, five of the whole number (including three of the party that killed the man)
effected their escape, but the other ten were
arrested, committed, and sent to St. Louis for
trial before the United States Court.   It appears that those who were engaged in the
killing of Chavez have since been convicted
of murder; and the others, who were only
concerned in the robbery, were found guilty

of larceny, and sentenced to fine and imprisonment.

About the first of May of the same year, a
company of a hundred and seventy-five men,
under one Col. Snively, was organized in the
north of Texas, and set out from the settlements for the Santa Fé trace. It was at first
reported that they contemplated a descent upon Santa Fé; but their force was evidently
too weak to attempt an invasion at that crisis.
Their prime object, therefore, seems to have
been to attack and make reprisals upon the
Mexicans engaged in the Santa Fé trade, who
were expected to cross the Prairies during the
months of May and June.

After the arrival of the Texans upon the
Arkansas, they were joined by Col. Warfield
with a few followers. This officer, with about
twenty men, had some time previously attacked the village of Mora, on the Mexican
frontier, killing five men (as was reported)
and driving off a number of horses. They
were afterwards followed by a party of Mexicans, however, who *stampeded* and carried
away, not only their own horses, but those of
the Texans. Being left afoot, the latter burned
their saddles, and walked to Bent's Fort, where
they were disbanded; whence Warfield passed to Snively's camp, as before mentioned.

The Texans now advanced along the Santa
Fé road, beyond the sand hills south of the
Arkansas, when they discovered that a party
of Mexicans had passed towards the river.
They soon came upon them, and a skirmish

ensuing, eighteen . Mexicans were killed, and as many wounded, five of whom afterwards died. The Texans suffered no injury, though the Mexicans were a hundred in number. The rest were all taken prisoners except two, who escaped and bore the news to Gen. Armijo, encamped with a large force at the Cold Spring, 140 miles beyond. As soon as the General received notice of the defeat of his vanguard, he broke up his camp most precipitately, and retreated to Santa Fé. A gentleman of the caravan which passed shortly afterward, informed me that spurs, lareats and other scraps of equipage, were found scattered in every direction about Armijo's camp—left by his troops in the hurly-burly of their precipitate retreat.

Keeping beyond the territory of the United States, the right of the Texans to harass the commerce of Mexicans will hardly be denied, as they were at open war: yet another consideration, it would seem, should have restrained them from aggressions in that quarter. They could not have been ignorant that but a portion of the traders were Mexicans— that many American citizens were connected in the same caravans. The Texans assert, it is true, that the lives and property of Americans were to be respected, *provided* they abandoned the Mexicans. But did they reflect upon the baseness of the terms they were imposing? What American, worthy of the name, to save his own interests, or even his life, could deliver up his travelling companions to be sacrificed? Then, after having abandoned the Mexicans, or betrayed them to their enemy—for such an act would have been accounted treachery—where would they have gone? They could not then have continued on into Mexico; and to have returned to the United States with their merchandise, would have been the ruin of most of them.

The inhuman outrages suffered by those who were captured in New Mexico in 1841, among whom were many of the present party, have been pleaded in justification of this second Texan expedition. When we take their grievances into consideration, we must admit that they palliate, and indeed justify almost any species of revenge consistent with the laws of Nature and of nations: yet whether, under the existing circumstances, this invasion of the Prairies was proper or otherwise, I will leave for others to determine, as there seems to be a difference of opinion on the subject. The following considerations, however, will go to demonstrate the unpropitious consequences which are apt to result from a system of indiscriminate revenge.

The unfortunate Chavez (whose murder, I suppose, was perpetrated under pretext of the cruelties suffered by the Texans, in the name of whom the party of M'Daniel was organized) was of the most wealthy and influential family of New Mexico, and one that was anything but friendly to the ruling governor, Gen. Armijo. Don Mariano Chavez, a brother to the deceased, is a gentleman of very amiable character, such as is rarely to be met with in that unfortunate land. It is asserted that he furnished a considerable quantity of provisions, blankets, etc., to Col. Cooke's division of Texan prisoners. Señora Chavez (the wife of Don Mariano), as is told, crossed the river from the village of Padillas, the place of their residence, and administered comforts to the unfortunate band of Texans. Though the murder of young Chavez was evidently not sanctioned by the Texans generally, it will, notwithstanding, have greatly embittered this powerful family against them—a family whose liberal principles could not otherwise have been very unfavorable to Texas.*

The attack upon the village of Mora, though of less important results, was nevertheless an unpropitiatory movement. The inhabitants of that place are generally very simple and innocent rancheros and hunters, and, being separated by the snowy mountains from the principal settlements of New Mexico, their hearts seem ever to have been inclined to the Texans. In fact, the village having been founded by some American denizens, the Mexican inhabitants appear in some degree to have imitated their character.

The defeat of Armijo's vanguard was attended by still more disastrous consequences, both to the American and Texan interest. That division was composed of the militia of

* This family is very distinct from one Manuel Chavez (who, though Gov. Armijo's nephew, is a very low character), a principal agent in the treacheries practised upon the Texan Santa Fé Expedition.

the North—from about Taos—many of them Taos Pueblos. These people had not only remained embittered against Gov. Armijo since the revolution of 1837, but had always been notably in favor of Texas. So loth were they to fight the Texans, that, as I have been assured, the governor found it necessary to bind a number of them upon their horses, to prevent their escape, till he got them fairly upon the Prairies. And yet the poor fellows were compelled to suffer the vengeance which was due to their guilty general!

When the news of their defeat reached Taos, the friends and relatives of the slain— the whole population indeed, were incensed beyond measure; and two or three naturalized foreigners who were supposed to favor the cause of Texas, and who were in good standing before, were now compelled to flee for their lives; leaving their houses and property a prey to the incensed rabble. Such appears to have been the reaction of public sentiment resulting from the catastrophe upon the Prairies!

Had the Texans proceeded differently— had they induced the Mexicans to surrender without battle, which they might no doubt easily have accomplished, they could have secured their services, without question, as guides to Gen. Armijo's camp, and that unmitigated tyrant might himself have fallen into their hands. The difficulty of maintaining order among the Texans was perhaps the cause of many of their unfortunate proceed-

15*

ings. And no information of the caravan
having been obtained, a detachment of seventy
or eighty men left, to return to Texas.

The traders arrived soon after, escorted by
about two hundred U. S. Dragoons under the
command of Capt. Cook. Col. Snively with
a hundred men being then encamped on the
south side of the Arkansas river, some ten to
fifteen miles below the point called the ' Caches,' he crossed the river and met Capt.
Cook, who soon made known his intention
of disarming him and his companions,—an
intention which he at once proceeded to
put into execution. A portion of the Texans, however, deceived the American captain in this wise. Having concealed their
own rifles, which were mostly Colt's repeat-
ers, they delivered to Capt. Cook the worthless fusils they had taken from the Mexicans;
so that, when they were afterwards released,
they still had their own valuable arms; of
which, however, so far as the caravan in question was concerned, they appear to have had
no opportunity of availing themselves.

These facts are mentioned merely as they
are said to have occurred. Capt. Cook has
been much abused by the Texans, and accused
of having violated a friendly flag—of having
taken Col. Snively prisoner while on a friendly visit. This is denied by Capt. Cook, and
by other persons who were in company at the
time. But apart from the means employed
by the American commander (the propriety
or impropriety of which I shall not attempt

to discuss), the act was evidently the salvation of the Santa Fé caravan, of which a considerable portion were Americans. Had he left the Texans with their arms, he would doubtless have been accused by the traders of escorting them to the threshold of danger, and then delivering them over to certain destruction, when he had it in his power to secure their safety.

Capt. Cook with his command soon after returned to the United States,* and with him some forty of the disarmed Texans, many of whom have been represented as gentlemen worthy of a better destiny. A large portion of the Texans steered directly home from the Arkansas river; while from sixty to seventy men, who elected Warfield their commander, were organized for the pursuit and capture of the caravan, which had already passed on some days in advance towards Santa Fé. They pursued in the wake of the traders, it is said, as far as the Point of Rocks (twenty miles east of the crossing of the Colorado or Canadian), but made no atttempt upon them —whence they returned direct to Texas. Thus terminated the ' Second Texan Santa Fé Expedition,' as it has been styled; and

* As U. S. troops cannot go beyond our boundary, which, on this route is the Arkansas river, these escorts afford but little protection to the caravans. Such an extensive, uninhabitable waste as the great prairies are, ought certainly to be under maritime regulations. Some international arrangements should be made between the United States and Texas or Mexico (accordingly as the proprietorship of the region beyond our boundary may be settled), whereby the armies of either might indiscriminately range upon this desert, as ships of war upon the ocean.

though not so disastrous as the first, it turned out about as unprofitable.

Although this expedition was composed wholly of Texans, or persons not claiming to be citizens of the United States, and organized entirely in Texas—and, notwithstanding the active measures adopted by the United States government to defend the caravans, as well of Mexicans as of Americans, against their enemy—Señor Bocanegra, Mexican Minister of Foreign Relations, made a formal demand upon the United States (as will be remembered), for damages resulting from this invasion. In a rejoinder to Gen. Thompson (alluding to Snively's company), he says, that " Independence, in Missouri, was the starting point of these men." The preceding narrative will show the error under which the honorable secretary labored.

A portion of the party who killed Chavez was from the frontier of Missouri; but witness the active exertions on the border to bring these depredators to justice—and then let the contrast be noted betwixt this affair and the impunity with which robberies are every day committed throughout Mexico, where well-known highwaymen often run at large, unmolested either by the citizens or by the authorities. What would Señor Bocanegra say if every other government were to demand indemnity for all the robberies committed upon their citizens in Mexico ?

But the most unfortunate circumstance attending this invasion of the Prairies—unfortunate at least to the United States and to New Mexico—was the closing of the Northern ports to foreign commerce, which was doubt-less, to a great degree, a consequence of the before-mentioned expedition, and which of course terminated the Santa Fé Trade, at least for the present.*

I am of the impression, however, that little apprehension need be entertained, that this decree of Gen. Santa Anna will be permitted much longer to continue, unless our peaceful relations with Mexico should be disturbed; an event, under any circumstances, seriously to be deprecated. With the continuation of peace between us, the Mexicans will certainly be compelled to open their northern frontier ports, to avoid a revolution in New Mexico, with which they are continually threatened while this embargo continues. Should the obnoxious decree be repealed, the Santa Fé Trade will doubtless be prosecuted again with renewed vigor and enterprise.

* The following is the substance of Santa Anna's decree, dated at his Palace of Tacubaya, August 7, 1843 :

" Article 1st. The frontier custom-houses of Taos, in the depart-ment of New Mexico, Paso del Norte and Presidio del Norte in that of Chihuahua, are entirely closed to all commerce.

"Art. 2d. This decree shall take effect within forty-five days after its publication in the capital of the Republic."

It should be understood that the only port in New Mexico for the introduction of foreign goods was nominally Taos, though the cutsom-house was at Santa Fé, where all the entrances were made.

CHAPTER X.

GEOGRAPHY OF THE PRAIRIES.

WHILE I have endeavored in the preceding pages to give the reader some general idea of life upon the Prairies, I feel that I have wholly failed thus far to convey any adequate notions of their natural history. I propose in the following pages to repair this deficiency as far as I am able, and to present a rapid sketch of the vastness of those mighty territories; of their physical geography; and of the life, as well vegetable as animal, which they sustain. It is to be regretted that this ample field for observation should have received so little of the consideration of scientific men; for there is scarcely a province in the whole wide range of Nature's unexplored domains, which is so worthy of study, and yet has been so little studied by the natural philosopher.

If we look at the Great Western Prairies, independently of the political powers to which portions of them respectively belong, we shall find them occupying the whole of that extensive territory lying between the spurs of the Rocky Mountains on the north, and the rivers of Texas on the south—a distance of some seven or eight hundred miles in one direction.; and from the frontiers of Missouri and Arkansas on the east to the eastern branches of the southern Rocky Mountains on the west— about six hundred miles in the transverse direction: the whole comprising an area of about 400,000 square miles, some 30,000 of which are within the original limits of Texas, and 70,000 in those of New Mexico (if we extend them east to the United States boundary), leaving about 300,000 in the territory of the United States.

This vast territory is not interrupted by any important mountainous elevations, except along the borders of the great western sierras, and by some low, craggy ridges about the Arkansas frontier—skirts of the Ozark mountains. There is, it is true, high on the dividing ridge between Red River and the False Washita, a range of hills, the southwestern portion of which extends about to the 100th degree of longitude west from Greenwich; that is, to the United States boundary line. These are generally called the Witchita mountains, but sometimes *Towyash* by hunters, perhaps from *tóyavist*, the Comanche word for mountain. I inquired once of a Comanche Indian how his nation designated this range of mountains, which was then in sight of us. He answered, " *Tóyavist.*" " But this simply means a mountain," I replied. " How do you distinguish this from any other mountain ?" " There are no other mountains in the Comanche territory," he rejoined—" none till we go east to your country, or south to Texas, or west to the land of the Mexican."

With these exceptions, there are scarcely any elevations throughout these immense plains which should be dignified by the title of mountains. Those seen by the Texan Santa Fé Expedition about the sources of Red River, were without doubt the *cejas* or brows of the elevated table plains with which the Prairies abound, and which, when viewed from the plain below, often assume the appearance of formidable mountains; but once upon their summit, the spectator sees another vast plain before him.

These *table lands*, or *mesas*, as the Mexicans term them, of which there are many thousands of square miles lying between the frontier of the United States and the Rocky Mountains, are level plains, elevated a considerable distance above the surrounding country, and may be likened to the famous steppes of Asia. They are cut up with numerous streams, the largest of which are generally bordered for several miles back by hilly uplands, which are for the most part sandy, dry and barren.

The most notable of the great *plateaux* of the Prairies is that known to Mexicans as *El Llano Estacado*, which is bounded on the north by the Canadian river—extends east about to the United States boundary, including the heads of the False Washita and other branches of Red River—and spreads southward to the sources of Trinity, Brazos and Colorado rivers, and westward to Rio Pecos. It is quite an elevated and generally a level plain, without important hills or ridges, unless we distinguish as such the craggy breaks of the streams which border and pierce it. It embraces an area of about 30,000 square miles, most of which is without water during three-fourths of the year; while a large proportion of its few perennial streams are too brackish to drink of.

I have been assured by Mexican hunters and Indians, that, from Santa Fé southeastward, there is but one route upon which this plain can be safely traversed during the dry season; and even some of the watering-places on this are at intervals of fifty to eighty miles, and hard to find. Hence the Mexican traders and hunters, that they might not lose their way and perish from thirst, once staked out this route across the plain, it is said; whence it has received the name of *El Llano Estacado*, or the Staked Plain.

In some places the brows of these *mesas* approach the very borders of the streams. When this occurs on both sides, it leaves deep chasms or ravines between, called by the Mexicans *cañones*, and which abound in the vicinity of the mountains. The Canadian river flows through one of the most remarkable of these cañones for a distance of more than fifty miles—extending from the road of the Missouri caravans downward—throughout the whole extent of which the gorge is utterly impassable for wagons, and almost so for animals.

Intersecting the direct route from Missouri, this cañon was a source of great annoyance to some of the pioneers in the Santa Fé trade. In 1825, a caravan with a number of wagons reached it about five miles below the present ford. The party was carelessly moving along, without suspecting even a ravine at hand, as the bordering plains were exceedingly level, and the opposite margins of equal height, when suddenly they found themselves upon the very brink of an immense precipice, several hundred yards deep, and almost perpendicular on both sides of the river. At the bottom of those cliffs, there was, as is usually the case, a very narrow but fertile valley, through which the river wound its way, sometimes touching the one bluff and sometimes the other.

Ignorant of a ford so near above, the caravan turned down towards the crossing of the former traders. " We travelled fifty miles," says Mr. Stanley, who was of the caravan, "the whole of which distance the river is bound in by cliffs several hundred feet high, in many places nearly perpendicular. We at length came to the termination of the table land; but what a scene presented itself! The valley below could only be reached by descending a frightful cliff of from 1200 to 1500 feet, and more or less precipitous. After a search of several hours, a practicable way was found; and, with the greatest fatigue and exertion, by locking wheels, holding on with ropes, and literally lifting the wagons down in places, we finally succeeded in reaching the bottom. . . . . How did the Canadian and other streams in New Mexico sink themselves to such immense depths in the solid rock? It seems impossible that the water should have worn away the rock while as hard as in its present state. What a field of speculation for the geologist, in the propositions—Were the chasms made for the streams, or did the streams make the chasms? Are they not of volcanic origin?"

Nor are the flat prairies always free from this kind of annoyance to travellers. They are not unfrequently intersected by diminutive chasms or water-cuts, which, though sometimes hardly a rod in width, are often from fifty to a hundred feet deep. These little cañones are washed out by the rains, in their descent to the bordering streams, which is soon effected after an opening is once made through the surface; for though the clayey foundation is exceedingly firm and hard while dry, it seems the most soluble of earths, and melts almost as rapidly as snow under the action of water. The tenacious turf of the 'buffalo grass,' however, retains the marginal surface, so that the sides are usually perpendicular—indeed, often shelving inward at the base, and therefore utterly impassable. I have come unsuspectingly upon the verge of such a chasm; and though, to a stranger, the appearance would indicate the very head of the ravine, I would sometimes be compelled to follow its meandering course for miles without being able to double its 'breaks.' These I have more especially observed high on the borders of the Canadian.

The geological constitution of the Prairies is exceedingly diversified. Along the eastern border, especially towards the north, there is an abundance of limestone, interspersed with sandstone, slate, and many extensive beds of bituminous coal. The coal is particularly abundant in some of the regions bordering the Neosho river; where there are also said to be a few singular bituminous or 'tar springs,' as they are sometimes called by the hunters. There are also many other mineral, and particularly sulphur springs, to be met with.

Further westward, the sandstone prevails; but some of the table plains are based upon strata of a sort of friable calcareous rock, which has been denominated 'rotten limestone:' yet along the borders of the mountains the base of the plains seems generally to be of trap and greenstone. From the waters of Red River to the southwest corner of Missouri, throughout the range of the Ozark mountains, granite, limestone, flint and sandstone prevail. But much of the middle portion of the Prairies is without any apparent rocky foundation—we sometimes travel for days in succession without seeing even as much as a pebble.

On passing towards Santa Fé in 1839, and returning in 1840, I observed an immense range of plaster of Paris, both north and south of the Canadian river, and between thirty and fifty miles east of the United States western boundary. The whole country seemed based upon this fossil, and cliffs and huge masses of it were seen in every direction. It ranges from the coarsest compact sulphate of lime or ordinary plaster, to the most transparent gypsum or selenite, of which last there is a great abundance. By authentic accounts from other travellers, this range of gypsum extends, in a direction nearly north, almost to the Arkansas river.

Of metallic minerals, iron, lead, and perhaps copper, are found on the borders of the Prairies; and it is asserted that several specimens of silver ores have been met with on our frontier, as well as about the Witchita and the Rocky Mountains. Gold has also been found, no doubt, in different places; yet it is questionable whether it has anywhere been discovered in sufficient abundance to render it worth the seeking. Some trappers have report-

16*

ed an extensive gold region about the sources
of the Platte river; yet, although recent search
has been made, it has not been discovered.

The most valuable perhaps, and the most
abundant mineral production of the Prairies
is *Salt*. In the Choctaw country, on the waters of Red River, there are two salt-works in
operation; and in the Cherokee nation salt
springs are numerous, three or four of which
are now worked on a small scale; yet a sufficient quantity of salt might easily be produced to supply even the adjoining States.
The *Grand Saline*, about forty miles above
Fort Gibson, near the Neosho river, was considered a curiosity of its kind, before its natural beauties were effaced by 'improvements.'
In the border of a little valley, a number of
small salt springs break out, around the orifice of each of which was formed, in the shape
of a pot, a kind of calcareous saline concre-
tion. None of the springs are very bold, but
the water is strong, and sufficiently abundant
for extensive works.

There have been several *Salines*, or mines
(if we may so term them) of pure salt, discovered in different parts of the Prairies. The
most northern I have heard of, is fifty or sixty
miles west of the Missouri river, and thirty
or forty south of the Platte, near a tributary
called the Saline; where the Otoes and other
Indians procure salt. It is described as resembling the *salinas* of New Mexico, and the
quantity of salt as inexhaustible. South of the
Arkansas river and a degree or two further

westward, there are several of these salines, which are perhaps still more extensive.

I have been favored with some extracts from the journal of Capt. Nathan Boone* of the United States' Dragoons, who made an exploring tour through those desolate regions during the summer of 1843. In his journey, between the Canadian and Upper Arkansas, he found efflorescent salt in many places, as well as a superabundance of strongly impregnated salt-water; but, besides these, he visited two considerable salines.

Of the first, which he calls the ' Salt Plain,' he remarks, that "the approach was very gratifying, and from the appearance one might expect to find salt in a solid mass, for the whole extent of the plain, of several feet in thickness." This is situated in the forks of the Salt Fork of the Arkansas. The plain is described as being level as a floor, and evidently sometimes overflowed by the streams which border it. Yet the extent of salt, it would seem, did not realize Capt. Boone's anticipations, as he remarks that it was covered "with the slightest possible film of crystallized salt on the surface, enough to make it white." But he explored only a small portion of the plain, which was very extensive.

However, the most wonderful saline is the great *Salt Rock*, which he found further to the

* Capt. Boone is a son of the late Col. Daniel Boone, the celebrated pioneer of the West. Being of practical habits, and of extensive experience upon those deserts, much weight is due to his observations.

southwestward, on the main Red Fork. " The whole cove on the right of the two forks of the river," says Capt. Boone, "appears to be one immense salt spring of water so much concentrated, that, as soon as it reaches the point of breaking forth, it begins depositing its salt. In this way a large crust, or rock is formed all over the bottom for perhaps 160 acres. Digging through the sand for a few inches anywhere in this space, we could find the solid salt, so hard that there was no means in our power of getting up a block of it. We broke our mattock in the attempt. In many places, through this rock-salt crust the water boiled up as clear as crystal . . . . . . but so salt that our hands, after being immersed in it and suffered to dry, became as white as snow. Thrusting the arm down into these holes, they appeared to be walled with salt as far down as one could reach. The cliffs which overhang this place are composed of red clay and gypsum, and capped with a stratum of the latter. . . . . . We found this salt a little bitter from the impurities it contained, probably Epsom salts principally." As it is overhung with sulphate of lime, and perhaps also based upon the same, might not this 'salt-rock' be heavily impregnated with this mineral, occasioning its excessive hardness ? Capt. Boone also speaks of gypsum in various other places, both north and south of this, during his travel.

Mr. Sibley (then of Fort Osage), who was quite familiar with the western prairies, visited a saline, over thirty years ago, which would seem to be the 'Salt Plain' first mentioned by Capt. Boone. The former, it is true, found the salt much more abundant than as described by the latter; but this may be owing to Capt. Boone's not having penetrated as far as the point alluded to by Mr. Sibley,—whose description is in the following language :*

"The Grand Saline is situated about 280 miles southwest of Fort Osage, between two forks of a small branch of the Arkansas, one of which washes its southern extremity, and the other, the principal one, runs nearly parallel, within a mile of its opposite side. It is a hard level plain of reddish colored sand, and of an irregular or mixed figure. Its greatest length is from northwest to southeast, and its circumference about thirty miles. From the appearance of the driftwood that is scattered over, it would seem the whole plain is at times inundated by the overflowing of the streams that pass near it. This plain is entirely covered in dry hot weather, from two to six inches deep, with a crust of beautiful clean white salt, of a quality rather superior to the imported blown salt. It bears a striking resemblance to a field of brilliant snow after a rain, with a light crust on its top."

This is, in extent and appearance, nearly as described by several hunters and Indian traders with whom I have conversed. Col. Logan, a worthy former agent of the Creek Indi-

* Brackenbridge's Voyage up the Missouri River, p. 205.

ans, visited no doubt the same, not far from the same period; and he describes it in a similar manner—only representing the depth of the salt as greater. Everywhere that he dug through the stratum of earth about the margin, at the depth of a few inches he came to a *rock of solid salt*, which induced him to believe that the whole country thereabouts was based upon a stratum of 'rock salt.' This was of a reddish cast, partaking of the color of the surface of the surrounding country. Mr. Sibley remarks that "the distance to a navigable branch of Arkansas is about eighty miles"— referring perhaps to the Red Fork; though the saline is no doubt at a still less distance from the main stream.

With such inexhaustible mines of salt within two or three days' journey of the Arkansas river, and again within the same distance of the Missouri, which would cost no further labor than the digging it up and the transporting of it to boats for freighting it down those streams, it seems strange that they should lie idle, while we are receiving much of our supplies of this indispensable commodity from abroad.

Besides the *salines* already mentioned, there is one high on the Canadian river, some two hundred miles east of Santa Fé. Also, it is said, there are some to be found on the waters of Red River; and numerous others are no doubt scattered throughout the same regions, which have never been discovered.

Many of the low valleys of all the western

streams (Red River as well as Arkansas and its branches), are impregnated with salinous qualities, and, during wet weather, ooze saltish exudations, which effloresce in a thin scum. This is sometimes pure salt, but more frequently compounded of different salts—not only of the muriate, but of the sulphate of soda, and perhaps magnesia; often strongly tinctured with nitre. Some of the waters of these sections (particularly when stagnant) are so saturated with this compound during dry weather, that they are insupportable even for brutes—much to the consternation of a forlorn traveller. In these saline flats nothing grows but hard wiry grass, which a famished beast will scarcely eat.

It is from these exudations, as well as from the salines or salt plains before mentioned, that our western waters, especially from Arkansas to Red River, acquire their brackishness during the low seasons; and not from the mountains, as some have presumed. Such as issue from thence are there as pure, fresh and crystalline as snow-fed rills and icy fountains can make them.

It will now readily be inferred that the Great Prairies from Red River to the western sources of the Missouri, are, as has before been intimated, chiefly uninhabitable—not so much for want of wood (though the plains are altogether naked), as of soil and of water; for though some of the plains appear of sufficiently fertile soil, they are mostly of a sterile character, and all too dry to be cultivated.

These great steppes seem only fitted for the haunts of the mustang, the buffalo, the antelope, and their migratory lord, the prairie Indian. Unless with the progressive influence of time, some favorable mutation should be wrought in nature's operations, to revive the plains and upland prairies, the occasional fertile valleys are too isolated and remote to become the abodes of civilized man.

Like the table plains of Northern Mexico, these high prairies could at present only be made available for grazing purposes, and that in the vicinity of the water-courses. The grass with which they are mostly clothed, is of a superior quality. The celebrated 'buffalo grass' is of two kinds, both of which are species of the *grama* of New Mexico, and equally nutritious at all seasons. It is the same, I believe, that is called 'mezquite grass' in Texas, from the mezquite tree which grows there in the same dry regions with it. Of this unequalled pasturage the great western prairies afford a sufficiency to graze cattle for the supply of all the United States. It is particularly adapted to sheep-raising, as is shown by example of the same species in New Mexico.

But from the general sterility and unhabitableness of the Prairies is excepted, as will be understood, that portion, already alluded to, which borders our western frontier. The uplands from the Arkansas boundary to the Cross Timbers, are everywhere beautifully interspersed with isolated prairies and glades, many of which are fertile, though some are too flat, and consequently inclined to be marshy. The valleys of the streams are principally of a rich loam, rather subject to inundations, but mostly tillable. The timbered uplands are mostly of fair quality, except on the broken ridges and mountainous sections before referred to. Some of the uplands, however, known usually as 'post-oak flats,' like the marshy prairies, seem to be based upon quick-sand. The soil is of a dead unproductive character, and covered with small lumps or mounds of various sizes, and of irregular shapes.

The country lying west of Missouri, which includes the sources of the Neosho, the Verdigris, the Marais-des-Cygnes and other branches of the Osage, and the lower sections of the Kansas river, vies with any portion of the Far West in the amenity of its upland prairies—in the richness of its alluvial bottoms—in the beauty and freshness of its purling rills and rivulets—and in the salubrity of its atmosphere.

We have here then, along the whole border, a strip of country, averaging at least two hundred miles wide by five hundred long—and even more if we extend it up the Missouri river—affording territory for two States, respectable in size, and though more scant in timber, yet more fertile, in general, than the two conterminous States of Missouri and Arkansas. But most of this delightful region has been ceded to the different tribes of the Frontier Indians.

Concerning that portion of the Prairies which lies south of Red River, in Northern Texas, I learn from some interesting memoranda, politely furnished me by Dr. Henry Connelly, one of the principals of the pioneer expedition from Chihuahua to Arkansas, of which I have already spoken, that, besides some beautiful lands among the Cross Timbers, there is a great deal of delightful country still further west, of a part of which that gentleman holds the following language:—
"Between the Brazos and Red River, there is surely the most beautiful and picturesque region I have ever beheld. I saw some of the finest timber, generally oak—not that scrubby oak which characterizes so much of the Texan territory—but large black and bur-oak; such as would answer all the purposes for which the largest timber is useful. Between those two rivers, no doubt there is destined to be one of the most dense and prosperous settlements. The fertility of the soil is not exceeded by any I have seen; and, from the high and undulating character of the country, there can be no doubt of its being very healthy."
To the westward of Rio Brazos, and south of some sandy and saline regions which border the upper portions of this stream, the same enterprising traveller represents many of the valleys as rich and beautiful, and the uplands as being in many places sparsely timbered with mezquite trees. This is particularly the case on the sources of the Colorado, where the country is delightfully watered. But im-

mediately north of this sets in that immense desert region of the Llano Estacado.

The chief natural disadvantage to which the Great Western Prairies are exposed, consists in the absence of navigable streams. Throughout the whole vast territory which I have been attempting to describe, there is not a single river, except the Missouri, which is navigable during the whole season. The remaining streams, in their course through the plains, are and must continue to be, for all purposes of commerce, comparatively useless.

The chief of these rivers are the Missouri, the Arkansas, and Red River, with their numerous tributaries. The principal western branches of the Missouri are the Yellow Stone, the Platte and the Kansas. Small 'flats' and 'buffalo boats' have passed down the two former for a considerable distance, during high water; but they are never navigable to any extent by steamboats.

The *Arkansas* river penetrates far into the Rocky Mountains, its ramifications, interlocking with some of the waters of the Missouri, Columbia, San Buenaventura, Colorado of the West, and Rio del Norte. The channel of this stream, in its course through the Prairies, is very wide and shallow, with banks in many places hardly five feet above low water. It will probably measure nearly 2000 miles in length, from its source to the frontier of Arkansas. It is called *Rio Napeste* by the Mexicans; but among the early French voyagers it acquired the name of *Arkansas,* or rather

*Akansa,** from a tribe of the Dahcotah or Osage stock, who lived near its mouth. This river has numerous tributaries, some of which are of great length, yet there is not one that is at all navigable, except the Neosho from the north, which has been descended by small boats for at least a hundred miles.

Red River is much shorter and narrower from the frontier westward than the Arkansas, bearing but little over half the volume of water. Even in its serpentine course it can hardly exceed 1200 miles from the Arkansas boundary to its source. This river rises in the table plains of the Llano Estacado, and has not, as I have been assured by traders and hunters, any mountainous elevations about its source of any consequence; although we are continually hearing the inhabitants of its lower borders speak of the "*June freshets* produced by the melting of the snow in the mountains."

The upper portions of this river, and emphatically from the mouth of the False Washita (or Faux Ouachittâ) upward, present little or no facilities for navigation; being frequently spread out over sand-bars to the width of several hundred yards. A very credible Indian trader, who had been on Red River

---

* A stranger would be led to suppose we were without a system of orthography, from the fact of our so generally adopting the French spelling of Indian names, whereby all sight is soon lost of the original. The French first corrupt them, and we, by adapting our pronunciation to their orthography, at once transform them into new names. Thus 'polite usage' has converted into *Arkan'sas* the plural of the primitive *Arkansa* or *Arkonsah;* though an approximate, *Ar'kansaw,* is still the current 'vulgar' pronunciation. *Osage* and a great many others have suffered similar metamorphoses.

some two hundred miles above the False Washita, informed me, that, while in some places he found it not over fifty yards wide, in others it was at least five hundred. This and most other prairie streams have commonly very low banks with remarkably shallow channels, which, during droughts, sometimes go dry in their transit through the sandy plains.*

It would be neither interesting nor profitable to present to my readers a detailed account of all the tributaries of the three principal rivers already mentioned. They may be

* Of all the rivers of this character, the Cimarron, being on the route from Missouri to Santa Fé, has become the most famous. Its water disappears in the sand and reappears again, in so many places, that some travellers have contended that it ' ebbs and flows' periodically. This is doubtless owing to the fact, that the little current which may flow above the sand in the night, or in cloudy weather, is kept dried up, in an unshaded channel, during the hot sunny days. But in some places the sand is so porous that the water never flows above it, except during freshets.

I was once greatly surprised upon encountering one of these sandy sections of the river after a tremendous rain-storm. Our caravan was encamped at the ' Lower Cimarron Spring:' and, a little after night-fall, a dismal, murky cloud was seen gathering in the western horizon, which very soon came lowering upon us, driven by a hurricane, and bringing with it one of those tremendous bursts of thunder and lightning, and rain, which render the storms of the Prairies, like those of the tropics, so terrible. Hail-stones, as large as turkeys' eggs, and torrents of rain soon drenched the whole country; and so rapidly were the banks of the river overflowed, that the most active exertions were requisite to prevent the mules that were ' staked' in the valley from drowning. Next morning, after crossing the neck of a bend, we were, at the distance of about three miles, upon the river-bank again; when, to our astonishment, the wetted sand, and an occasional pool, fast being absorbed, were the only vestiges of the recent flood—no water was flowing there!

In these sandy stretches of the Cimarron, and other similar ' dry streams,' travellers procure water by excavating basins in the channel, a few feet deep, into which the water is filtrated from the saturated sand.

found for the most part laid down, with their bearings and relative magnitudes, upon the map which accompanies this work. It is only necessary to say in addition, that none of them can ever be availed of to any considerable extent for purposes of navigation.

With regard to the productions of the soil of these regions, the reader will probably have formed, in the main, a tolerably correct idea already; nevertheless a few further specifications may not be altogether unacceptable.

The timber of that portion of the United States territory which is included between the Arkansas frontier and the Cross Timbers, throughout the highlands, is mostly oak of various kinds, of which black-jack and post-oak predominate, as these, and especially the former, seem only capable of withstanding the conflagrations to which they are exposed, and therefore abound along the prairie borders. The black-jack presents a blackened, scrubby appearance, with harsh rugged branches—partly on account of being so often scorched and crisped by the prairie fires. About the streams we find an intermixture of elm, hackberry, paccan (or pecan), ash, walnut, mulberry, cherry, persimmon, cottonwood, sycamore, birch, etc., with varieties of hickory, gum, dogwood, and the like. All of the foregoing, except paccan, gum and dogwood, are also found west of Missouri, where, although the uplands are almost wholly prairie, the richest growths predominate in the valleys.

In many of the rich bottoms from the Canadian to Red River, for a distance of one or two hundred miles west of the frontier, is found the celebrated *bois-d'arc* (literally, *bow-wood*), usually corrupted in pronunciation to *bowdark*. It was so named by the French on account of its peculiar fitness for *bows*. This tree is sometimes found with a trunk two or three feet in diameter, but, being much branched, it is rarely over forty or fifty feet high. The leaves are large, and it bears a fruit a little resembling the orange in general appearance, though rougher and larger, being four or five inches in diameter; but it is not used for food. The wood is of a beautiful light orange color, and, though coarse, is susceptible of polish. It is one of the hardest, firmest and most durable of timbers, and is much used by wagon-makers and millwrights, as well as by the wild Indians, who make bows of the younger growths.

On the Arkansas and especially its southern tributaries as far west as the Verdigris, and up those of Red River nearly to the False Washita, the bottoms are mostly covered with cane. And scattered over all the south to about the same distance westward, the sassafras abounds, which grows here in every kind of soil and locality.

The celebrated *Cross Timbers*, of which frequent mention has been made, extend from the Brazos, or perhaps from the Colorado of Texas, across the sources of Trinity, traversing Red River above the False Washita, and thence west of north, to the Red Fork of Arkansas, if not further. It is a rough hilly range of country, and, though not mountainous, may perhaps be considered a prolongation of that chain of low mountains which pass to the northward of Bexar and Austin city in Texas.

The Cross Timbers vary in width from five to thirty miles, and entirely cut off the communication betwixt the interior prairies and those of the great plains. They may be considered as the 'fringe' of the great prairies, being a continuous brushy strip, composed of various kinds of undergrowth; such as black-jacks, post-oaks, and in some places hickory, elm, etc., intermixed with a very diminutive dwarf oak, called by the hunters 'shin-oak.' Most of the timber appears to be kept small by the continual inroads of the 'burning prairies;' for, being killed almost annually, it is constantly replaced by scions of undergrowth; so that it becomes more and more dense every reproduction. In some places, however, the oaks are of considerable size, and able to withstand the conflagrations. The underwood is so matted in many places with grape-vines, green-briars, etc., as to form almost impenetrable 'roughs,' which serve as hiding-places for wild beasts, as well as wild Indians; and would, in savage warfare, prove almost as formidable as the hammocks of Florida.

South of the Canadian, a branch of these Cross Timbers projects off westward, and afterwards crosses the stream; and, having continued up for a hundred miles, it inclines north-west beyond the North Fork, and ultimately ceases, no doubt, in the great sandy plains in that direction.

The region of the Cross Timbers is gene-rally well-watered; and is interspersed with romantic and fertile tracts. The bottoms of the tributaries of Red River, even for some distance west of the Cross Timbers (perhaps almost to the U. S. boundary), are mostly very fertile, and timbered with narrow stripes of elm, hackberry, walnut, hickory, mulberry, bur-oak and other rich growths.

But further north, and west of the Cross Timbers, even the streams are nearly naked. The Cimarron river for more than a hun-dred miles is absolutely without timber; and the Arkansas, for so large a stream, is remarka-bly scant. The southern border, being pro-tected from the prairie fires by a chain of sand-hills, which extends for two hundred miles along it, is not so bare as the northern bank; though even here it is only skirted with occasional sparsely set groves of cotton-wood in the nooks and bends. It is upon the abundance of islands which intersperse its channel, that the greatest quantity of timber (though purely cottonwood) is to be found; yet withal, there are stretches of miles with-out a tree in view. The banks of the Ca-nadian are equally naked; and, having fewer islands, the river appears still more barren. In fact, there is scarce anything else but cot-tonwood, and that very sparsely scattered along the streams, throughout most of the far-western prairies.

It is unquestionably the prairie conflagrations that keep down the woody growth upon most of the western uplands. The occasional skirts and fringes which have escaped their rage, have been protected by the streams they border. Yet may not the time come when these vast plains will be covered with timber? It would seem that the prairie region, long after the discovery of America, extended to the very banks of the Mississippi. Father Marquette, in a voyage down this river, in 1673, after passing below the mouth of the Ohio, remarks :—" The banks of the river began to be covered with high trees, which hindered us from observing the country as we had done all along ; but we judged from the bellowing of the oxen [buffalo] that the meadows are very near."—Indeed, there are parts of the southwest now thickly set with trees of good size, that, within the remembrance of the oldest inhabitants, were as naked as the prairie plains ; and the appearance of the timber in many other sections indicates that it has grown up within less than a century. In fact, we are now witnessing the encroachment of the timber upon the prairies, wherever the devastating conflagrations have ceased their ravages.

The high plains seem too dry and lifeless to produce timber; yet might not the vicissitudes of nature operate a change likewise upon the seasons? Why may we not sup-

pose that the genial influences of civilization—that extensive cultivation of the earth—
might contribute to the multiplication of
showers, as it certainly does of fountains? Or
that the shady groves, as they advance upon
the prairies, may have some effect upon the
seasons? At least, many old settlers maintain that the droughts are becoming less oppressive in the West. The people of New
Mexico also assure us that the rains have
much increased of latter years, a phenomenon
which the vulgar superstitiously attribute to
the arrival of the Missouri traders. Then may
we not hope that these sterile regions might
yet be thus revived and fertilized, and their
surface covered one day by flourishing settlements to the Rocky Mountains?

With regard to fruits, the Prairies are of
course not very plentifully supplied. West
of the border, however, for nearly two hundred
miles, they are covered, in many places, with
the wild strawberry; and the groves lining the
streams frequently abound in grapes, plums,
persimmons, mulberries, paccans, hackberries,
and other 'sylvan luxuries.' The high prairies beyond, however, are very bare of fruits.
The prickly pear may be found over most of
the dry plains; but this is neither very palata-
ble nor wholesome, though often eaten by
travellers for want of other fruits. Upon the
branches of the Canadian, North Fork, and
Cimarron, there are, in places, considerable
quantities of excellent plums, grapes, choke-
cherries, gooseberries, and currants—of the

latter there are three kinds, black, red, and white. About the ravines and marshy grounds (particularly towards the east) there are different kinds of small onions, with which the traveller may season his fresh meats. On the plains, also, I have met with a species resembling garlic in flavor.

But the flowers are among the most interesting products of the frontier prairies. These gay meadows wear their most fanciful piebald robes from the earliest spring till divested of them by the hoary frosts of autumn. When again winter has fled, but before the grassy green appears, or other vegetation has ventured to peep above the earth, they are bespeckled in many places with a species of *erythronium*, a pretty lilaceous little flower, which springs from the ground already developed, between a pair of lanceolate leaves, and is soon after in full bloom. But the floriferous region only extends about two hundred miles beyond the border: the high plains are nearly as destitute of flowers as they are of fruits.

The *climate* of most parts of the Prairies is no doubt healthy in the extreme; for a purer atmosphere is hardly to be found. But the cold rains of the 'wet season,' and the colder snows of winter, with the annoying winds that prevail at nearly all times, often render it very unpleasant. It can hardly be said, it is true, that the Prairies have their regular 'dry and rainy seasons;' yet the summers are often so droughty, that, unless some change should be effected in nature's functions, cultivators would generally find it necessary, no doubt, to resort to irrigation. That portion, however, which is conterminous with our western border, and to the distance of nearly two hundred miles westward, in every respect resembles the adjacent States of Missouri and Arkansas in climate. The south is a little disposed to chills and fevers; but the northern portion is as healthy as the most salubrious uplands of Missouri.

CHAPTER XI.

ANIMALS OF THE PRAIRIES.

The Mustang or Wild Horse—Capturing him by 'Creasing,' and with the Lazo — Horse-flesh — The Buffalo — Its Appearance — Excellence of its Meat — General Utility to the Indian and Traveller — Prospect of its Extinction — Hunting the Buffalo with Bow and Arrows, the Lance, etc.—'Still-hunting'—The Buffalo ferocious only when wounded—Butchering, etc.—The Gray Wolf—Its Modes of killing Buffalo —Their great Numbers—A 'Wolf-scrape'—The Prairie Wolf, or 'Jackal of the Prairies'—Elk, Deer and Bear—The Antelope—The Bighorn—The Prairie Dog—Owls and Rattlesnakes—The Horned Frog—Fowls—Bees, etc.

THE zoology of the Prairies has probably attracted more attention than any other feature of their natural history. This has not arisen altogether from the peculiar interest the animals of the Prairies possess; but they constitute so considerable a portion of the society of the traveller who journeys among them, that they get to hold somewhat the same place in his estimation that his fellow-creatures would occupy if he were in civilization. Indeed, the animals are *par éminence* the communities of the Prairies.

By far the most noble of these, and therefore the best entitled to precedence in the brief notice I am able to present of the animals of those regions, is the *mustang** or wild horse of the Prairies. As he is descended from the stock introduced into America by the first Spanish colonists, he has no doubt a partial mixture of Arabian blood. Being of domestic origin, he is found of various colors, and sometimes of a beautiful piebald.

It is a singular fact in the economy of nature, that all *wild* animals of the same species should have one uniform color (with only occasional but uniform differences between males and females); while that of the *domestic* animals, whether quadruped or fowl, is more or less diversified.

The beauty of the mustang is proverbial. One in particular has been celebrated by hunters, of which marvellous stories are told. He has been represented as a medium-sized stallion of perfect symmetry, milk-white, save a pair of black ears—a natural 'pacer,' and so fleet, it has been said, as to leave far behind every horse that had been tried in pursuit of him, without breaking his 'pace.' But I infer that this story is somewhat mythical, from the difficulty which one finds in fixing the abiding place of its equine hero. He is familiarly known, by common report, all over the great Prairies. The trapper celebrates him in the vicinity of the northern Rocky

Mustang would most naturally seem a corruption of the Spanish adjective *mostrenco* (without owner), but the Mexicans call wild horses *mesteñas,* a synonyme in one of its senses with *mostrenco.*

Mountains; the hunter, on the Arkansas, or in the midst of the Plains; while others have him pacing at the rate of half a mile a minute on the borders of Texas. It is hardly a matter of surprise, then, that a creature of such an ubiquitary existence should never have been caught.

The wild horses are generally well formed, with trim and clean limbs; still their elegance has been much exaggerated by travellers, because they have seen them at large, abandoned to their wild and natural gaiety. Then, it is true, they appear superb indeed; but when caught and tamed, they generally dwindle down to ordinary ponies. Large droves are very frequently seen upon the Prairies, sometimes of hundreds together, gambolling and curvetting within a short distance of the caravans. It is sometimes difficult to keep them from dashing among the loose stock of the traveller, which would be exceedingly dangerous; for, once together, they are hard to separate again, particularly if the number of mustangs is much the greatest. It is a singular fact, that the gentlest wagon-horse (even though quite fagged with travel), once among a drove of mustangs, will often acquire in a few hours all the intractable wildness of his untamed companions.

The mustang is sometimes taken by the cruel expedient of 'creasing,' which consists in shooting him through the upper *crease* of the neck, above the cervical vertebræ; when, the ball cutting a principal nerve, he falls as sud-

denly as if shot in the brain, and remains
senseless for a few minutes, during which he
is secured with a rope.   He soon recovers
from the shock, however, and springs to his
feet, but finds himself deprived of his liberty.
He is easily tamed after this, and the wound
heals without leaving any physical injury.
But 'creasing' is so nice an operation that
many are killed in the attempt.   If the ball
pass a little too low, it fractures a vertebra
and kills the poor brute instantly.

But the most usual mode, among the Mexicans and Indians, of taking the *mesteña* (as
the former call these animals), is with the
lazo.   They pursue them on fleet horses, and
great numbers are thus noosed and tamed.
The mustang has been taken in Texas in
considerable numbers by preparing a strong
pen at some passway or crossing of a river,
into which they are frightened and caught.

Upon the plains, I once succeeded in separating a gay-looking stallion from his herd of
mesteñas, upon which he immediately joined
our *caballada*, and was directly lazoed by a
Mexican.   As he curvetted at the end of the
rope, or would stop and gaze majestically at
his subjecters, his symmetrical proportions
attracted the attention of all; and our best
jockeys at once valued him at five hundred
dollars.   But it appeared that he had before
been tamed, for he soon submitted to the
saddle, and in a few days dwindled down to
scarce a twenty-dollar hackney.

Prairie travellers have often been reduced
18*

to the necessity of eating the flesh of the mustang; and, when young and tender, it has been accounted savory enough; but, when of full age, it is said to be exceedingly rancid, particularly when fat. They are sometimes hunted by Mexicans for their oil, which is used by the curriers.

The *buffalo*, though making no pretensions to the elegance and symmetry of the mustang, is by far the most important animal of the Prairies to the traveller. It is sufficiently well known that these animals bear but little resemblance to the buffalo of India; but that they are a species of bison, or *bos Americanus*, according to naturalists. They are called *Cíbolos* by the Mexicans; and it would certainly have prevented ambiguity, had they been distinguished by some other name than buffalo with us.

Their dusky black color becomes much paler during the season of long hair.* The phenomenon of a white buffalo has frequently been remarked upon the Prairies; but as the white skin is said to have been used in the mystic ceremonies of many of the northern tribes of Indians, this probably created such a demand for them, that they have become nearly extinct. Their unusual color has commonly been considered a *lusus naturæ*, yet it is probable that they stand in about the same relation to the black or brown buffalo that black sheep do to white ones. The horns of

---

* The bulls usually shed in the spring, from the shoulders back, but not in front, which imparts to them quite a lion-like appearance.

the buffalo are short and black, and almost concealed under the frightfully shaggy frontlets of long woolly hair that crown the foreheads of the bulls; which, with the goat-like beard, and ill-shapen hump, form the chief distinction between them and the domestic cattle: in fact, they are so nearly of the same species that they will breed together; though the offspring, like the mule, is said to be unfruitful. Between the males and females there is still a greater disproportion in size than among the domestic cattle. A buffalo cow is about as heavy as a common ox, while a large fat bull will weigh perhaps double as much.

These are very gregarious animals. At some seasons, however, the cows rather incline to keep to themselves; at other times they are mostly seen in the centre of the gang, while the bulls are scattered around, frequently to a considerable distance, evidently guarding the cows and calves. And on the outskirts of the buffalo range, we are apt to meet with small gangs of bulls alone, a day or two's travel distant, as though performing the office of 'piquet guards' for the main herds.

The flesh of the buffalo is, I think, as fine as any meat I ever tasted: the old hunter will not admit that there is anything equal to it. Much of its apparent savoriness, however, results perhaps from our sharpened 'prairie appetites,' and our being usually upon salt provisions awhile before obtaining it. The flesh is of coarser texture than beef, more juicy, and the fat and lean better distributed. This meat is also very easy of digestion,* possessing even aperient qualities. The circumstance that bulls of all ages, if fat, make good beef, is a further proof of the superiority of buffalo meat. These are generally selected for consumption in the winter and early spring, when the cows, unless barren, are apt to be poor; but during most of the year, the latter are the fattest and tenderest meat. Of these, the udder is held as hardly second to the tongue in delicacy. But what the tail of the beaver is to the trapper, the tongue of the buffalo is to the hunter. Next to this are the 'marrow-bones,' the tender-loins, and the hump-ribs. Instead of a gristly substance, as sometimes stated, the hump is produced by a convex tier of vertical ribs, which project from the spine, forming a gradual curve over the shoulders: those of the middle being sometimes nearly two feet in length. The 'veal' is rarely good, being generally poor, owing to the scanty supply of milk which their dams afford, and to their running so much from hunters and wolves.

This animal furnishes almost the exclusive food of the prairie Indians, as well as covering for their wigwams and most of their clothing; also their bedding, ropes, bags for their meat, &c.; sinews for bow-strings, for sewing moccasins, leggins, and the like; be-

---

* It has often been remarked by travellers, that however much buffalo meat one may eat, no inconvenience is ever suffered from it.

sides sustenance for the numerous travellers
and trappers who range upon their grazing
regions. Were they only killed for food, however, their natural increase would perhaps re-
plenish the loss: yet the continual and wanton slaughter of them by travellers and hunters, and the still greater havoc made among
them by the Indians, not only for meat, but
often for the skins and tongues alone (for
which they find a ready market among their
traders), are fast reducing their numbers, and
must ultimately effect their total annihilation
from the continent. It is believed that the
annual 'export' of *buffalo rugs** from the Prairies and bordering ' buffalo range,' is about a
hundred thousand: and the number killed
wantonly, or exclusively for meat, is no doubt
still greater, as the skins are fit to dress scarcely
half the year. The vast extent of the prairies
upon which they now pasture is no argument
against the prospect of their total extinction,
when we take into consideration the extent of
country from which they have already disappeared; for it is well known, that, within the
recollection of our oldest pioneers, they were
nearly as abundant east of the Mississippi as
they now are upon the western prairies; and
from history we learn, that they once ranged
to the Atlantic coast. Even within thirty
years, they were abundant over much of the
present States of Missouri and Arkansas; yet
they are now rarely seen within two hundred
miles of the frontier. Indeed, upon the high

* Often, but it would seem improperly, called ' buffalo *robes*.'

plains they have very sensibly decreased within the last ten years. Nevertheless, the number of buffalo upon the Prairies is still immense. But, as they incline to migrate *en masse* from place to place, it sometimes happens, that, for several days' travel together, not a single one is to be met with; but, in other places, many thousands are often seen at one view.

The Indians, as well as Mexicans, hunt the buffalo mostly with the bow and arrows. For this purpose they train their fleetest horses to run close beside him; and, when near enough, with almost unerring aim, they pierce him with their arrows, usually behind the short ribs, ranging forward, which soon disables and brings him to the ground. When an arrow has been ill-directed, or does not enter deep enough, and even sometimes when it has penetrated a vital part, but is needed to use again, the hunter sometimes rides up and draws it out while the animal is yet running. An athletic Indian will not unfrequently discharge his darts with such force, that I have seen them (30 inches long) wholly buried in the body of a buffalo: and I have been assured by hunters that the arrows, missing the bones, have been known to pass entirely through the huge carcass and fall upon the ground.

The dexterity acquired by these wild hunters in shooting the buffalo, is very surprising. On one occasion, upon the prairies, a party of Witchita Indians were encamped near us; and a drove of buffalo passing in the vicinity, I requested a chief to take my horse and kill one 'upon the shares.' He delighted in the sport: so, gathering his arrows, he mounted the pony, which was slow, and withal very lean, and giving chase, in a few minutes he had two buffaloes lying upon the plain, and two others went off so badly wounded, that, with a little exertion, they might have been secured.

But the dexterity of the Comanches in the buffalo chase is perhaps superior to that of any other tribe. The Mexican *Ciboleros*, however, are scarcely if at all inferior to the Indians in this sport. I once went on a hunting expedition with a Cibolero, who carried no arms except his bow and arrows and a butcher's knife. Espying a herd of buffalo, he put spurs to his horse, and, though I followed as fast as a mule I rode could trudge, when I came up with him, after a chase of two or three miles, he had the buffalo partly skinned! This was rather unusual dispatch, to be sure, for the animal oftener lingers awhile after receiving the fatal dart.

In the chase, the experienced hunter singles out the fattest buffalo as his victim, and having given him a mortal wound, he in like manner selects another, and so on, till the plain is sometimes literally strewed with carcasses.

It seems that Capt. Bonneville marvelled greatly that some Indians, during his peregrinations in the Rocky Mountains, should have killed buffalo "without guns or arrows, and with only an old spear;" and he was no doubt mistaken in supposing "that they had chased the herds of buffalo at full speed, until they tired them down, when they easily dispatched them with the spear:" for both Indians and Mexicans often chase with a long-handled spear or lance, which, if the horse be well trained, is still a more expeditious mode of killing them than with the bow and arrow. An expert lancer will enter a drove, and drawing up alongside, will pierce buffalo after buffalo until several are brought down.

In default of bow or lance, they chase with the fusil, but seldom so successfully as with the former weapons. The Americans generally prefer 'running' with the horseman's pistol; yet the Indian is apt to kill double as many with his arrows or lance.

In all these modes of hunting, the buffalo is sometimes dangerous; for, becoming enraged from his wounds, he will often make desperate lunges at his pursuer; and, if the horse be not well trained, he may be himself disembowelled, leaving his rider at the mercy of the buffalo, as has happened on some occasions. But if the steed understand his business, he will dodge the animal with the expertness of a fencer.

Buffalo calves (but not full-grown buffalo) are often taken with the lazo by Mexicans and Indians; yet, being separated from their dams and the droves during chases, these simple little creatures not unfrequently take up with the riding animals of the hunters, and follow them to the camp as tamely as though they were their dams. If provided with domestic cows, they may be raised without much difficulty.

Some of the northern Indians, particularly the Assinaboins, are said to practise still a distinct mode of taking the buffalo. A staunch pound is erected at some convenient point, and, after a course of mystic rites by their medicine-men, they start upon the enterprise. A gang of buffalo is frightened towards the pen, while an Indian, covered with one of their woolly skins, runs at a distance ahead. Being seen by the animals, they mistake him for one of their kind, and follow him into the pen. Once secured in the enclosure, they leisurely dispatch them with their arrows, as they are said to believe it would offend the Great Spirit and render future hunts unpropitious to use fire arms in killing their imprisoned game.

However, of all other modes, our backwoodsmen prefer 'still-hunting' — that is, stealing upon their game afoot with the rifle. Buffalo are much more easily approached than deer. When the hunter perceives a herd at rest, or quietly feeding, he crawls upon them behind a bank, a shrub, or a tuft of grass, with the greatest facility, provided he 'has the wind of them,' as hunters say—that is, if the wind blows from the buffalo; but if the reverse, he will find it impossible to approach them, however securely he may have concealed himself from their sight. In fact, their scent being acute, they seem to depend more upon it than their sight; for if a gang of buffalo be frightened, from any quarter whatever, they are apt to shape their course against the wind, that they may scent an enemy in their way.

If the hunter succeed in 'bringing down' his first shot, he may frequently kill several out of the same herd; for, should the game neither see nor smell him, they may hear the rifle cracks, and witness their companions fall one after another, without heeding, except to raise their heads, and perhaps start a little at each report. They would seem to fancy that the fallen are only lying down to rest, and they are loth to leave them. On one occasion, upon the Cimarron river, I saw some ten or a dozen buffaloes lying upon a few acres of ground, all of which had been shot from the same herd by a couple of our hunters. Had not the gang been frightened by the approaching caravan, perhaps a dozen more of them might have fallen.

A dextrous hunter will sometimes 'crawl upon' a gang of buffalo, on a perfectly level plain. As their sight is at best not acute, and is always more or less obscured by the shaggy hair of their foreheads, they will hardly observe an approaching enemy when they are feeding, unless the wind bears them the scent. The hunter is, therefore, careful to 'have the wind' of them, and crawls slowly and closely upon the ground, until within gun-shot. If he bring down the first, the others will perhaps retire a little, when he may sometimes approach behind the fallen buffalo, and shoot several others.

The tenacity of these animals for life is often very extraordinary. When one receives even a mortal shot, he frequently appears not hurt —he seems to disdain to flinch—but will curl his tail and step about as though he neither felt nor feared anything! If left undisturbed, however, he begins to stagger, and in a few moments expires: but if provoked, he might run for miles before he would fall. I have seen a party of hunters around a wounded and enraged bull, fire, at a few paces distance, a dozen or two shots, aimed at his very heart, without their seeming to have any effect till his anger cooled, when in an instant he would lie lifeless upon the ground. In such cases, the inexperienced hunter often aims to shoot them in the brain, but without success. Owing not only to the thickness of the scull, but to the matted wool upon it, I have never witnessed an instance of a rifle-ball's penetrating to the brain of a buffalo bull.

The 'still-hunter' must needs be upon his guard; for the wounded buffalo is prone to make battle, upon the too near approach of his enemy. With a little presence of mind, however, his attacks are easily shunned. If he make a lunge, the pedestrian hunter has only to wheel abruptly to one side; for the animal is apt to pass on in a direct line. I have never heard of a serious accident of the kind; yet some frightful though amusing incidents have occurred in such cases.

The buffalo never attacks, however, except when wounded. Even the largest droves (the opinion of some travellers to the contrary notwithstanding), though in the wildest career, are easily turned from their course by a single man who may intercept their way. I have crouched in the tall grass in the direct route of a frighted gang, when, firing at them on their near approach, they would spread in consternation to either side. Still their advance is somewhat frightful—their thundering rumble over the dry plain—their lion-like fronts and dangling beards—their open mouths and hanging tongues—as they come on, puffing like a locomotive engine at every bound, does at first make the blood settle a little heavy about the heart.

The gait of these animals is a clumsy gallop, and any common pony can overtake them in the chase; though, as the hunter would express it, they 'lumber' over the ground rather deceivingly. The cows are usually much faster than the bulls. It has been the remark of travellers that the buffalo jumps up from the ground differently from any other animal. The horse rises upon his fore feet first, and the cow upon her hind feet, but the buffalo seems to spring up on them all at once.

American hunters, as well as Indians, to butcher the buffalo, generally turn it upon the belly, and commence on the back. The hump-ribs, tender-loins, and a few other choice bits being appropriated, the remainder is commonly left for the wolves. The skin is chiefly used for buffalo rugs, but for which it is only preserved by the Indians during fall and winter (and then rarely but from the cows and bullocks), when the hair is long and woolly. I have never seen the buffalo hide tanned, but it seems too porous and spongy to make substantial leather. Were it valuable, thousands of hides might be saved that are annually left to the wolves upon the Prairies.

Although the buffalo is the largest, he has by no means the control among the prairie animals: the sceptre of authority has been lodged with the large *gray wolf*. Though but little larger than the wolf of the United States, he is much more ferocious. The same species abound throughout the north of Mexico, where they often kill horses, mules and cattle of all sizes; and on the Prairies they make considerable havoc among the buffalo.

Many curious tales are told of the wiles and expedients practised by these animals to secure their prey. Some assert that they collect in companies, and chase a buffalo by turns, till he is fatigued, when they join and soon dispatch him: others, that, as the buffalo runs with the tongue hanging out, they snap at it in the chase till it is torn off, which preventing him from eating, he is reduced by starvation, and soon overpowered: others, that, while running, they gnaw and lacerate

19*

the legs and ham-strings till they disable him,
and then he is killed by the gang.   Be this
as it may, certain it is that they overcome
many of the largest buffaloes, employing perhaps different means of subduing them, and
among these is doubtless the last mentioned,
for I have myself seen them with the muscles
of the thighs cruelly mangled—a consequence
no doubt of some of these attacks.   Calves
are constantly falling victims to the rapacity
of these wolves; yet, when herds of buffalo
are together, they defend their offspring with
great bravery.

Though the color of this wolf is generally a
dirty gray, they are sometimes met with nearly
white.   I am of opinion, however, that the
diversity of color originates chiefly from the
different ages of the hair, and partially from
the age of the animal itself.   The few white
wolves I have seen, have been lean, long-
haired, and apparently very old.   There are
immense numbers of them upon the Prairies.
Droves are frequently to be seen following in
the wake of caravans, hunting companies,
and itinerant Indian bands, for weeks together
—not, like the jackal, so much to disinter the
dead (though this they sometimes do), as to
feast upon the abandoned carcasses of the
buffalo which are so often wantonly killed
and wasted.   Unless in these cases, they are
rarely seen, except in the neighborhood of
buffalo ; therefore, when the hungry traveller
meets with wolves, he feels some assurance
that supplies of his favorite game are at hand.

I have never known these animals, rapacious as they are, extend their attacks to man, though they probably would, if very hungry and a favorable opportunity presented itself. I shall not soon forget an adventure with one of them, many years ago, on the frontier of Missouri. Riding near the prairie border, I perceived one of the largest and fiercest of the gray species, which had just descended from the west, and seemed famished to desperation. I at once prepared for a chase; and, being without arms, I caught up a cudgel, when I betook me valiantly to the charge, much stronger, as I soon discovered, in my cause than in my equipment. The wolf was in no humor to flee, however, but boldly met me full half-way. I was soon disarmed, for my club broke upon the animal's head. He then 'laid to' my horse's legs, which, not relishing the conflict, gave a plunge and sent me whirling over his head, and made his escape, leaving me and the wolf at close quarters. I was no sooner upon my feet than my antagonist renewed the charge; but, being without weapon, or any means of awakening an emotion of terror, save through his imagination, I took off my large black hat, and using it for a shield, began to thrust it towards his gaping jaws. My *ruse* had the desired effect; for, after springing at me a few times, he wheeled about and trotted off several paces, and stopped to gaze at me. Being apprehensive that he might change his mind and return to the attack, and conscious that, under the compromise, I had the best of the bargain, I very resolutely——took to my heels, glad of the opportunity of making a drawn game, though I had myself given the challenge.

There is a small species called the *prairie wolf* on the frontier, and *coyote** by the Mexicans, which is also found in immense numbers on the Plains. It is rather smaller than an ordinary dog, nearly the color of the common gray wolf, and though as rapacious as the larger kind, it seems too cowardly to attack stout game. It therefore lives upon the remains of buffalo killed by hunters and by the large wolves, added to such small game as hares, prairie dogs, etc., and even reptiles and insects. It will lie for hours beside a 'dog-hole,' watching for the appearance of the little animal, which no sooner peeps out than the enemy pounces upon it.

The coyote has been denominated the 'jackal of the Prairies;' indeed, some have reckoned it really a species of that animal, yet it would seem improperly, as this creature

---

* *Canis latrans*, a distinction to which its noisiness emphatically entitles it. Clavigero says of this animal: " El *coyotl*, ó *coyote*, como dicen los Españoles, es una fiera semejante al lobo en la voracidad, á la zorra en la astucia, al perro en la forma, y en otras propiedades al *adive*, ó *chacal*; por lo que algunos escritores Megicanos lo han numerado entre varias de aquellas especias; pero es indudable que se diferencia de todas ellas," etc.—*Hist. Ant. de Még. Tom. I. p.* 40.

A similar propensity is observable among us to refer nearly all American animals to European species, whereas but very few that are legitimately indigenous to this continent, agree in every particular with those of the Old World. It would surely have contributed to the copiousness and euphony of the language, as well as to perspicuity in the distinction of species, had we, like the Mexicans, retained the Indian names of our indigenous animals.

partakes much less of the nature of the jackal
than of the common wolf. Still, however
noisy the former may be, he cannot exceed
the prairie wolf. Like ventriloquists, a pair
of these will represent a dozen distinct voices
in such quick succession—will bark, chatter,
yelp, whine, and howl in such variety of note,
that one would fancy a score of them at hand.
This, added to the long and doleful bugle-note
of the large wolf, which often accompanies it,
sometimes makes a night upon the Prairies
perfectly hideous. Some hunters assert that
the coyote and the dog will breed together. Be this as it may, certain it is that the
Indian dogs have a wonderfully wolfish appearance.

The *elk* as well as the *deer* is found somewhat abundant upon the Arkansas river, as
high as the Santa Fé road, but from thence
westward they are both very scarce ; for these
animals do not resort to the high prairie plains.
Further south, however, in the prairies bordering the brushy tributaries of the Canadian
and Red River, deer are exceedingly plenty—
herds of hundreds are sometimes seen together; but in these southern regions there are
but few elks.

About the thickety streams above-mentioned, as well as among the Cross Timbers, the
black bear is common, living chiefly upon
acorns and other fruits. The grape vines and
the branches of the scrubby oaks, and plum-
bushes, are in some places so torn and broken
by the bear in pursuit of fruits, that a stranger

would conclude a violent hurricane had passed among them.

That species of gazelle known as the *antelope* is very numerous upon the high plains. This beautiful animal, though reckoned a link between the deer and goat, is certainly much nearest the latter. It is about the size and somewhat of the figure of a large goat. Its horns also resemble those of the latter, being likewise persistent; but they are more erect, and have a short prong projecting in front. The ground of this animal's color a little resembles that of the common deer, but it is variegated with a whitish section or two on each side.

The antelope is most remarkable for its fleetness: not bounding like the deer, but skimming over the ground as though upon skates. The fastest horse will rarely overtake them. I once witnessed an effort to catch one that had a hind-leg broken, but it far outstripped our fleetest 'buffalo-horse.' It is, therefore, too swift to be hunted in the chase. I have seen dogs run after this animal, but they would soon stop and turn about, apparently much ashamed of being left so far behind.

The flesh of the antelope is, like that of the goat, rather coarse, and but little esteemed: consequently, no great efforts are made to take them. Being as wild as fleet, the hunting of them is very difficult, except they be entrapped by their curiosity. Meeting a stranger, they seem loth to leave him until they have fully found him out. They will often take a circuit around the object of their curiosity, usually approaching nearer and nearer, until within rifle-shot—frequently stopping to gaze. Also, they are often decoyed with a scarlet coat, or a red handkerchief attached to the tip of a ramrod, which will sometimes allure them within reach of the hunter's aim. But this interesting animal, like the buffalo, is now very rarely seen within less than 200 miles of the frontier: though early voyagers tell us that it once frequented regions east of the Mississippi.

The *bighorn* (*carnero cimarron*, as called by Mexicans, and sometimes known to trappers as the mountain sheep), so abundant in most of the Rocky Mountain chain, is found in the spurs and table-plain cliffs about the sources of the Cimarron river (whence this stream acquired its name), as well as in the highland gorges, and other parts of those mountain borders. Its flesh is said to be excellent, and is preferred by many hunters to venison. It is larger than a common sheep, and covered with brownish hair instead of wool—darker than the deer, but whitish on the belly. It is most remarkable for its huge spiral horns, resembling in shape and curvature those of the sheep, but sometimes over three feet long, and four to six inches in diameter at the base.*

---

* Mr. Irving furnishes the following dimensions of a male of this species: " From the nose to the base of the tail, five feet; length of the tail, four inches; girth of the body, four feet; height, three feet eight inches," &c.—*Rocky Mts., Vol. I., p.* 48.

The bighorn is quite celebrated for its agility, and its habit of secluding itself among the most inaccessible mountain crags. It seems to delight in perching and capering upon the very verge of the most frightful precipices and overhanging cliffs, and in skipping from rock to rock, regardless of the yawning chasms, hundreds of feet in depth, which intervene. In fact, when pursued, it does not hesitate, as I have been assured, to leap from a cliff into a valley a hundred or more feet below, where, lighting upon its huge horns, it springs to its feet uninjured; for the neck is so thick and strong as to support the greatest shock the animal's weight can bring upon it. Being exceedingly timorous, it rarely descends to the valleys, but feeds and sleeps about such craggy fastnesses as are inaccessible to the wolves and other animals of prey. This animal seems greatly to resemble the *moufflon* of Buffon, in color, figure and horns, but the *chamois* in habits.

But of all the prairie animals, by far the most curious, and by no means the least celebrated, is the little *prairie dog*. This singular quadruped is but little larger than a common squirrel, its body being nearly a foot long, with a tail of three or four inches. The color ranges from brown to a dirty yellow. The flesh, though often eaten by travellers, is not esteemed savory. It was denominated the 'barking squirrel,' the 'prairie ground-squirrel,' etc., by early explorers, with much more apparent propriety than the present establish-

ed name. Its yelp, which resembles that
of the little toy-dog, seems its only canine
attribute. It rather appears to occupy a middle ground betwixt the rabbit and squirrel—
like the former in feeding and burrowing—
like the latter in frisking, flirting, sitting erect,
and somewhat so in its barking.

The prairie dog has been reckoned by some
naturalists a species of the marmot (*arctomys
ludoviciana*); yet it seems to possess scarce any
other quality in common with this animal except that of burrowing. Some have supposed,
it is true, that like the marmot, they lie torpid
during the cold season; and it is observed in
'Long's Expedition,' that, "as they pass the
winter in a lethargic state, they lay up no provisions," &c.: but this is no doubt erroneous;
for I have the concurrent testimony of several
persons, who have been upon the Prairies in
winter, that, like rabbits and squirrels, they issue from their holes every soft day; and therefore lay up no doubt a hoard of 'hay' (as there
is rarely anything else to be found in the
vicinity of their towns), for winter's use.

A collection of their burrows has been
termed by travellers a 'dog town,' which comprises from a dozen or so, to some thousands
in the same vicinity; often covering an area of
several square miles. They generally locate
upon firm dry plains, coated with fine short
grass, upon which they feed; for they are no
doubt exclusively herbivorous. But even
when tall coarse grass surrounds, they seem
commonly to destroy this within their 'streets,'

which are nearly always found 'paved' with a fine species suited to their palates. They must need but little water, if any at all, as their 'towns' are often, indeed generally, found in the midst of the most arid plains—unless we suppose they dig down to subterranean fountains. At least they evidently burrow remarkably deep. Attempts either to dig or drown them out of their holes have generally proved unsuccessful.

Approaching a 'village,' the little dogs may be observed frisking about the 'streets'—passing from dwelling to dwelling apparently on visits—sometimes a few clustered together as though in council—here feeding upon the tender herbage—there cleansing their 'houses,' or brushing the little hillock about the door—yet all quiet. Upon seeing a stranger, however, each streaks it to its home, but is apt to stop at the entrance, and spread the general alarm by a succession of shrill yelps, usually sitting erect. Yet at the report of a gun or the too near approach of the visitor, they dart down and are seen no more till the cause of alarm seems to have disappeared.

Two other animals are said to live in communion with the prairie dogs—the *rattle-snake* and a small *owl;* * but both are no doubt intruders, resorting to these burrows for shelter, and to feed, it is presumed, upon the 'pups' of the inmates.

* This has been called the *Coquimbo owl.* Its note, whether natural or imitative, much resembles that of the prairie dog.

'DOG TOWN,' OR SETTLEMENT OF PRAIRIE DOGS.

V. de also p. 36.

Rattle-snakes are exceedingly abundant upon these plains : scores of them are sometimes killed in the course of a day's travel; yet they seem remarkably harmless, for I have never witnessed an instance of a man's being bitten, though they have been known to crawl even into the beds of travellers.* Mules are sometimes bitten by them, yet very rarely, though they must daily walk over considerable numbers.

The *horned frog*, as modern travellers have christened it, or horned lizard,† as those of earlier times more rationally called it, is the most famed and curious reptile of the plains. Like the prairie dog, it is only found in the dry regions, often many miles from water. It no doubt lives nearly, if not wholly, without drink. Its food probably consists chiefly of ants and other insects; though many Mexicans will have it, that the *camaleon* (as they call it) *vive del aire*—lives upon the air. It has been kept several months without partaking of a particle of aliment. I once took a pair of them upon the far-western plains, which I shut up in a box and carried to one of the eastern cities, where they were kept for several months before they died,—without having taken food or water, though repeatedly offered them.

* Though I never saw it tried, it has been said that snakes will not crawl over a hair-rope stretched upon the ground, and that consequently these form good barriers to keep these reptiles out of a bed.

† Orbicular lizard, as it has been technically denominated. It would seem a species of chamēleon, having apparently some, though very little, variability of color.

The whole length of the horned frog is from two to five inches—body flatted horizontally, oval-shaped, and between one and two inches wide in the middle. The back is beautifully variegated, with white and brown, and sometimes a yellowish purple. The belly is whitish and covered with brown specks. It acquired its name from a pair of short horns projecting from the top of the head—with other smaller horny protuberances upon the head and body. It has a short tail, which gives it a lizard-like appearance. It is a very inoffensive creature, and may be handled with perfect impunity, notwithstanding its uncouth appearance, and sometimes vicious demonstrations.

As birds mostly incline to the timbered regions, there is but a scant variety to be met with upon the plains. About the Cross Timbers and indeed on all the brushy creeks, especially to the southward, are quantities of wild *turkeys*, which are frequently seen ranging in large flocks in the bordering prairies. That species of American grouse, known west as the *prairie-hen*, is very abundant on the frontier, and is quite destructive, in autumn, to the prairie corn-fields. This fowl is rarely seen over two hundred miles beyond the border. Of *partridges*, the same is true; but their number is quite limited anywhere beyond the precincts of the settlements. About the streams there are different species of geese and ducks, as well as both sand-hill and white cranes: also flocks of a species of plover and curlew. Add to these numbers of hawks and ravens, and we have most of the fowls of the Prairies. Flocks of the latter follow in the wake of caravans with even greater constancy than wolves.

The *bee*, among Western pioneers, is the proverbial precursor of the Anglo-American population: in fact, the aborigines of the frontier have generally corroborated the notion; for they used to say, they knew the whites were not far behind, when bees appeared among them. This partial coincidence, I suppose, is the result of their emigration westward being at nearly an even pace with that of the settlers. As yet no honey-bees seem to have been discovered as far westward as any part of the Rocky Mountains. They are scattered, however, to the distance of two or three hundred miles west of the Missouri and Arkansas frontier, where there is timber affording them suitable habitations. On the Santa Fé route but few have been found beyond the Council Grove.

20*

CHAPTER XII.

ABORIGINES OF AMERICA.

IT will hardly be expected from a work making so little pretension as this to scientific accuracy and completeness, that the remarks which my plan necessarily leads me to make, concerning the aborigines of western America, should be either critical or comprehensive. Neither can I feel that it is a topic which I am at liberty wholly to disregard. The opportunities which I have enjoyed for obtaining a knowledge of the character and habits of the western Indians have been such, that I trust that a brief account of them may prove in some measure new, and not altogether uninteresting to a portion of my readers. Impressed with this belief, I propose, in the few following pages, to record such facts as shall seem to be most novel, and to corroborate, in my humble measure, occasional others which have before been related. With this view, I shall proceed to notice, in the present chapter, such leading characteristics of the aborigines generally, as shall seem most noteworthy; and then, in those that follow, ask the reader's attention to many peculiarities which make the most conspicuous differences between them.

No aboriginal nation or people has ever yet been discovered, to my knowledge, which has not professed to have a mysterious ancestry of a mythical character. It is interesting to mark the analogies and the differences between their various systems. Although among some tribes who have lived much in communication with the whites, their cosmogony has been confounded very much with the Mosaic or Scripture account, so that it is now often difficult to distinguish clearly the aboriginal from the imported, yet all the Americo-Indian tribes have more or less preserved their traditions on this subject. The old full-blood Choctaws, for instance, relate that the first of their tribe issued from a cave in Nunnewaya or Bending Mountain, in the 'Old Nation,' east of the Mississippi; yet this tradition has but little currency among the young men and mixed-bloods of the tribe. The minute account of this supposed origin cannot now be readily procured; yet some idea may be formed of it from a kindred tradition among the Mandans which has been preserved to us by Lewis and Clark, and is thus related:

"The whole nation resided in one large village under ground near a subterraneous lake: a grape vine extended its roots down to their habitation and gave them a view of the light: some of the most adventurous climbed up the vine, and were delighted with the sight of the earth, which they found covered with buffalo, and rich with every kind of fruits: returning with the grapes they had gathered, their countrymen were so pleased with the taste of them that their whole nation resolved to leave their dull residence for the charms of the upper regions; men, women and children ascended by means of the vine; but when about half the nation had reached the surface of the earth, a corpulent woman who was clambering up the vine broke it with her weight, and closed upon herself and the rest of the nation, the light of the sun."

Besides the Mandans it seems that other neighboring tribes had somewhat analogous notions of their origin. An early explorer relates that the Osages believed that their forefathers grew from a snail, which, having become a man, married the daughter of a beaver, whence sprang the present race.

The resemblance of the American Indians to each other, however, is not more conspicuous in anything than in their religious opinions. They seem to have no well-defined creeds: yet there are very few but profess a faith in some sort of First Cause—a Great

Spirit, a Master of Life, who rules the destinies of the world.   Though the different nations have not always typified their deity by
the same objects, yet by far the greater number seem to have, fixed upon the sun as the
fit object of their adoration.   "Next to *Vira-
chocha*, or their supreme God," says Father
Acosta, speaking of the Indians of Peru,
"that which most commonly they have and
do adore amongst the Infidells is the Sunne."
Many of the Mexican tribes* professed the
same faith, and particularly those of New
Mexico, as has already been mentioned.
This seems also the most current among the
Comanches and other wild tribes of the Prairies : and the Choctaws and several other
nations of the frontier appear at least to have
held the sun in great veneration.

But of all the Indian tribes, none appear to
have ascribed to the 'fountain of light' more
of the proper attributes of deity than the
Shawnees.   They argue, with some plausibility, that the sun animates everything—
therefore, he is clearly the Master of Life, or
the Great Spirit; and that everything is produced originally from the bosom of the earth
—therefore, she is the mother of creation.
The following anecdote† (as told to me by a
gentleman of integrity), which transpired upon

* Clavigero asserts of the Indians of Mexico, that their first heaven (that of the warriors, &c.) they called " *la casa del sol*" (the
house of the sun), which luminary they worshipped every morning at sunrise.

† I have since met with the same, in substance, related by Mr.
Schoolcraft.

the occasion of an interview of Tecumseh with Gen. Harrison, is as illustrative of the religious opinions of the Shawnees, as it is characteristic of the hauteur and independent spirit of that celebrated Shawnee chief. The General, having called Tecumseh for a 'talk,' desired him to take a seat, saying, " Come here, Tecumseh, and sit by your father." " You my father?" replied the chief, with a stern air—" No! yonder sun is my father (pointing towards it), and the earth is my mother; so I will rest on her bosom"—and immediately seated himself upon the ground, according to Indian custom.

But though the Shawnees consider the sun the type, if not the essence, of the Great Spirit, many also believe in an evil genius, who makes all sorts of bad things, to counterbalance those made by the Good Spirit. For instance, when the latter made a sheep, a rose, wholesome herbs, etc., the bad spirit matched them with a wolf, a thorn, poisonous plants, and the like. They also appear to think there is a kind of purgatory in which the spirits of the wicked may be cleansed before entering into their elysium.

The worship of all the aborigines seems to consist chiefly in feasting and dancing. A worthy missionary among the Shawnees related to me the following legendary tradition, as explanatory of their ideas of another world, and the institution of their worship, which may serve as a fair sample of the traditions of many other tribes.

In days of yore (say the Shawnees) there lived a pious brother and an affectionate sister, who were inordinately attached to each other. It came to pass that the sister sickened and died, and was carried to the world of spirits. The good brother was inconsolable, and for a while refused to eat or drink, or to partake of any kind of nourishment: he wished to follow his beloved sister. At length he resolved to set out in search of her; so he commenced his pilgrimage toward the setting sun. Steadily pursuing the same course for days and moons together, he at last came to where the sky and earth meet; and finding an opening, he ascended into the upper regions. He now turned his course towards the rising sun, which he continued, above the sky, till he came to the abode of his grandfather—which seems but another name for one of the good spirits. This sage, knowing his errand, gave him 'medicine' to transform him into a spirit, that he might pass through the celestial courts. He also gave him instructions how to proceed, and where he would find his sister. He said she would be at a dance; and when she rose to join in the amusement, he must seize and ensconce her in the hollow of a reed with which he was furnished, and cover the orifice with the end of his finger.

After an arduous peregrination through the land of spirits, the brother found and secured his sister as directed. He returned with his charge to the habitation of his grandfather, who gave another 'medicine' to transform them both into material beings again, that they might revisit their brothers on earth. The sage also explained to them the mysteries of heaven and the sacred rites of worship, that they might instruct their tribe therein. When about to start back, the venerable spirit told them that the route by which the brother had come was very circuitous—there was a much nearer way; and opening a trap-door through the sky, they beheld their native town just below them. So the good brother and sister descended; and returning home, a great feast was celebrated, accompanied by a solemn dance—in accordance with the grandfather's instructions. Thus originated, as they say, the sacred dances and other religious ceremonies now in practice.

As they believe the Indian heaven separate, and essentially different and distinct from that of the whites, and as they do not wish their people divided, this has often occasioned a serious opposition to the labors of the missionaries.* For the purpose of thwarting the

* The Shawnees have four missionary establishments among them, viz. a Methodist, Baptist, Moravian, and Quaker. There are also missionaries of different sects among most of the tribes of the border, the labors of whom have been attended with some degree of success. There is, I believe, but one Catholic Mission upon the frontier, which is among the Potawatomies, about a thousand of whom have embraced this faith. The Catholics, however, appear to have succeeded better than most other denominations, in their missionary efforts. It is so in Mexico, so in Canada, and appears so everywhere else that they have undertaken the Christianization of the heathen. I would not be understood to attribute this to any intrinsic superiority of their religion, but to the peculiarities of its forms and ceremonies. The pageantry of their worship, the palpable representation of the divine mysteries by the introduction

measures of these, a noted anti-christian sage 'played off,' a few years ago, the following 'vision.' Being very ill (as they relate), this sage, to all appearance, died, and became stiff and cold, except a spot upon his breast, which still retained the heat of life. In this state he remained a day or more, when he again breathed and returned among the living : and calling his friends about him, he related the scenes he had witnessed. He had ascended to the Indian's heaven, he said, which he described as usual: a fine country, abounding in all sorts of game, and everything an Indian could desire. There he met with his grandfather, who said to him, " It is meet, my son, that thou return to the earth, and warn thy brothers against the dangers that await them. Tell them to beware of the religion of the white man: that every Indian who embraces it is obliged to take the road to the white man's heaven ; and yet no red man is permitted to enter there, but will have to wander about for ever without a resting-place."

The identity of the notions which the different tribes have conceived of a future existence, and the character of the 'world of spirits,' seems still more general. They fancy

of images, better accords with their pristine idolatry, than a more spiritual faith. Catholics, indeed, have had the sagacity to permit the Indians (at least in some countries) to interweave many of their own heathen ceremonies with the sacred Christian rites, forming a singular *mêlée* of Romish and pagan worship, which is especially the case in Mexico. Also, the less rigid Catholic creed and customs do not debar them from their wonted favorite amusements, not to say vices. It is therefore that whole tribes sometimes simultaneously embrace this imposing creed.

heaven but another material world, superior, it is true, yet resembling this—a kind of elysian vale, or paradise—a 'happy hunting-ground,' abounding in game and all their comforts of life, which may be procured without labor. This elysium they generally seem to locate 'upon the sky,' which they fancy a material solid vault. It appears impossible for them, in their pristine barbarism, to conceive of a spiritual existence, or of a world differing materially from that which they see around them.

Father Hennepin (writing about 1680) relates, that the northern Indians inquired about the manner of living in heaven, and remarks: "When I made answer that they live there without eating or drinking, 'We will not go thither,' said they, 'because we must not eat;' and when I have added that there would be no occasion for food there, they clapt their hands to their mouths, as a sign of admiration, and said, '*Thou art a great liar!—is there anything can live without eating?*'"

Similar opinions, among many different tribes, I have heard declared in direct terms; yet, did we want further testimony, some of their burial customs and funeral rites would seem to indicate their ideas of the future state. The Cherokees, Choctaws, Creeks, Kansas, and kindred tribes, besides many others, or perhaps most others of the frontier, have been accustomed to inter the most valuable property of the deceased and many necessaries with them. "Their whole property was bu-

ried with them,"* says an intelligent Cherokee, in some manuscript notes concerning his
ancestors, I have in my possession : and I
have been assured by credible natives, that,
within their recollection, they have seen, at
these burials, provisions, salt, and other necessaries, interred with the dead for their
long journey.

There are very few of the prairie Indians
but practise something of this kind : many
kill the favorite hunting-horses, and deposite
the arms, etc., of the deceased, for his use in
the chase, when he arrives at the 'happy hunting ground.' We are also informed by Capt.
Bonneville, and other travellers, that this is
practised by some, if not all, of the natives
beyond the Rocky Mountains. The same
is told of the Navajoes, Apaches, and
other uncatholicized tribes of the north of
Mexico.

Peter Martyr, a learned and celebrated pro-
testant divine, who wrote his "Decades of
the Newe Worlde" towards the middle of the
sixteenth century, observes that, "in many
places of the firme lande, when any of the
kynges dye, all his housholde servauntes, as
well women as men which have continually
served hym, kyl themselves, beleavynge, as
they are taught by the devyl *Tuyra*, that they
which kyll themselves when the kynge dyeth,
go with hym to heaven and serve hym in the
same place and office as they dyd before on

* Adair, who resided forty years with the southern Indians, previous to 1775, speaks of the same among them all.

the earth whyle he lyved.* And that all that
refuse so to doo, when after they dye by theyr
naturall death or otherwyse, theyr soules to
dye with theyr bodyes, and to bee dissolved
into ayer and become nothynge as do the
soules of hogges, byrdes or fysshes, or other
brute beastes."† In corroboration of a similar custom among the natives along the Mississippi, in 1542, Herrera relates, that, after the
death of Fernando de Soto, and his party had
set out westward, they were joined by a
youth, who stated that he had fled to escape
being buried with his lord who had died;
which was the practice in that country. Travellers from the upper lakes to the Mississippi
speak of similar customs, at an early day,
among the tribes of that quarter.

It would appear that they believe everything, both animate and inanimate—beasts,
arms, ornaments, etc.—to possess immortal
attributes, subject to resurrection in the world
of spirits. However, did not their motives
seem so well defined by the direct allusions
to their notions of futurity, we might suppose,
as is frequently urged, that the burying of
property, slaves, etc., with the deceased, was
only intended as a mark of respect; which,
indeed, is hardly more irrational than the cus-

---

* Also Clavigero speaks of similar beliefs and practices among
the Mexican Indians, particularly in the obsequies of the kings;
and adds—" El número de víctimas correspondía á la grandeza del
funeral, y, segun algunos autores, llegaban á veces á doscientas."
† Edition of 1555, translated from the Latin, fol. 181.—In another place, the same author also says they buried corn, etc., with
the dead, for their use in the world to come.

tom of interring costly garniture and appendages with the dead among us.

Some of the modes of burial adopted by
the American aborigines are different, I believe, from those of any other people. Though,
as among civilized nations, even the wildest
tribes sometimes inter in ordinary graves, yet
they frequently deposit their dead, in a sitting
and even in a standing posture, in pits, caves,
and hollow trees; and occasionally, they lay
the corpse out upon scaffolds suspended from
the branches of trees, or resting upon them
where they will admit of it, so as to be out of
reach of the wolves and other beasts.

I was once, with a little caravan, travelling
up the course of the Arkansas river, when, a
thunder-storm coming up suddenly, and night
drawing near, we turned the wagons, as soon
as we could, to the river-bank, to encamp.
The bustle of ungearing and securing the
teams before they should be frightened by
the tempest, was hardly over, when we discovered a platform suspended above our
heads, upon the branches of a cottonwood,
which, upon examination, was found to contain an Indian corpse, from whose bones the
putrid flesh had not yet separated!

This mode of disposing of the dead would
seem once to have been quite extensive; for,
as well as upon the western prairies, it formerly prevailed among the Potawatomies of
the north, and the Choctaws of the south, at
least while on their expeditions. In this case,
if practicable, they would leave a band of

aged men, known as 'bone-pickers,' to clean the bones, when the flesh decayed, and carry them to their village for interment.

Barbarians are generally superstitious to an extreme, believing in hobgoblins, witchcraft, legerdemain and all sorts of mummeries.* Like many grandmothers in backwoods life, they delight in recounting the extraordinary apparitions, transmigrations, sorceries, etc., which they pretend to have witnessed. Nothing seems too absurd for their belief. Among many other cases of similar cast, an intelligent Potawatomie once assured me that he had witnessed the death of one of his nation, who had received a stab in his side with a knife (probably in some illicit adventure); and it being unknown to his friends how the wound had been inflicted, it was currently reported and believed, that from their

* The Indians often so imposed upon the credulous ancients as to make them believe they had direct communication with Satan. The learned divine, Peter Martyr, has a whole chapter "Of the familiaritie which certeyne of the Indians have with the devyll, and howe they receave answere of hym of thynges to coome:" and very seriously and philosophically concludes, that, "the devyll beynge so auncient an Astronomer, knowethe the tymes of thynges, and seeth howe they are naturally directed:" to which he appends numerous instances of the evil spirit's revelations of the "tymes of thynges to coome" to his ministers, the magi. And even as late as 1721, Father Charlevoix gravely says, an instance he relates, and many others that he "knows, which are equally certain, prove that the Devil is sometimes concerned in the magic of the Savages." The Choctaws, and perhaps some others, used to punish witchcraft with all the rigor of our own ancestors, putting poor creatures to death upon the slightest proof of their tampering with the black art: but this barbarity is now prohibited by their more civilized laws. Yet the more barbarous tribes still have their conjurers and medicine-men, who deal in auguries and mystic ceremonies; which, with their dances, constitute the greater part of their worship.

present home on the frontier of Missouri, he had visited the 'Old Nation' in Michigan, poisoned an enemy there, received the fatal stab, and returned and died, all in one day.

If you tell an Indian that such things are absurd and impossible, he is apt to answer, "It may be so with the white man, but how do you know it to be impossible with the Indian? You tell us many strange things which happened to your fathers—we don't contradict them, though we believe such things never could have happened to the red man." Or, they will reply, perhaps, as they did to Father Hennepin in a similar case: "Fie, thou knowest not what thou sayest; thou may'st know what has passed in thy own Country, for thy Ancestors have told thee of them; but thou canst not know what has passed in ours before the Spirits (that is to say the Europeans) came hither."

In their matrimonial customs there is also a similarity among most of the American savages. Polygamy seems once to have been universal; and I believe still is so among the uncivilized tribes. Every man takes as many wives as he can obtain, or is able to support. The squaws, however, the more willingly consent to this multiplicity, as it affords additional helpmates in their labors. Polygamy among these savages would appear, indeed, not altogether an unwise provision. At least it seems palliated with such a belligerent people, who lose so many males in their continual wars, leaving a great surplus of females; and where the duties of the latter are so numerous and so severe.

The custom of buying wives, or at least making large presents to their parents, has always been very general; and still exists, not only among the more savage, but even with many of the partially civilized nations. Yet, notwithstanding their depravity in other respects, there is one thing truly remarkable in their marriages. All modern observers seem to agree with the ancient authors, that they universally abhor incestuous connections. Among the Creeks, even the marrying of cousins was punished by cutting off the ears. The Cherokees (according to some manuscript notes which I have of an intelligent member of the tribe) were prohibited from marrying in their own clans (i. e. kindred) under penalty of death; and their clans themselves were their executioners. But, although the Indians thus so strictly prohibit marriage within the degrees of consanguinity, it is not so with those of affinity among many tribes. The Otoes, Kansas, and others of the same stock, will not only marry several sisters, but their deceased brothers' wives; in fact, this last seems considered a duty, so that the orphan children of the brother may not be without a protector.*

While the aborigines of the New World

---

* Clavigero remarks of the Indians of Mexico, "Estaba severamente prohibido . . . . . . todo enlace matrimonial, entre parientes en primer grado de consanguinidad, ó de afinidad, excepto entre cuñados."

have been noted above almost every other uncivilized nation in history, for their vindictiveness and cruelty towards their enemies, there are, in these attributes, wide differences apparent among them. The Indians along the Pacific coast, as well as in most of Mexico, were always more mild and peaceable than those of the United States. Hence it is, in fact, that the Spaniards did not meet with that formidable resistance to their conquests which they encountered among the fiery tribes of Florida, or that relentless and desperate hostility which the Anglo-Americans experienced in the first settlement of most parts of the United States.

But in the common trait of hospitality to strangers all the western tribes are alike distinguished. The traveller who is thrown upon their charity, is almost universally received and treated with the greatest kindness; and, though they might pilfer him to the skin, and even place his person in jeopardy, if he show want of confidence in them, and endeavor to conceal his effects, yet his property is generally secure when under their charge: they appear to consider a breach of confidence one of the greatest crimes.

Among the wild tribes, as well as among most of the unadulterated border Indians, to set something to eat before a friend, and even a stranger, immediately upon his arrival at a lodge or a cabin, is deemed not only an act of hospitality but of necessary etiquette; and a refusal to partake is looked upon as an unfriendly token—an insult, in fact, to the family. Travellers are often severely taxed to preserve the good feeling of their hosts in this particular, especially among the prairie Indians. One at all fastidious in matters of diet, would find it hard to relish food from a greasy horn-spoon which every urchin had been using; and then to ladle it out of a pot which had been common for all the papooses and pups of the premises: or to partake from a slice rolled up in a musty skin, or a dirtier blanket. And yet an apology even of having already dined half-a-dozen times would scarcely palliate the insult of a refusal. Though one visit fifty lodges in the course of a day, he must taste the food of every one.

The Indian system of chiefs, which still prevails, and is nearly the same everywhere, except with the Cherokees, Choctaws, Chickasaws, and the Creeks to a degree, seems to bear a strong resemblance to that of the patriarchs of old; which, with their clans so analogous to those of our forefathers, perhaps affords as strong a proof as any other of their Asiatic origin.*   To this might be added their

* The origin of the American Indians has been discussed by too many able writers for me to enter into it here: nor will I attempt to show the general traits of similarity that are to be observed in their various languages: yet it may interest an occasional reader, to be informed of the relations of consanguinity which subsist between many of the different Indian tribes. They may be arranged principally under the following heads: 1. The Dahcotah stock, which is by far the most extensive of those indigenous west of the Mississippi. It embraces the Arkansas (of which the Quapaws are now the only remnant), the Osages, Kansas or Kaws, Iowas, Winnebagoes, Otoes, Missouries, Omahas, Poncas, and the various bands of the Sioux: all of whom speak a language still traceable

mode of naming; for the Indians universally
apply names significant of acts, qualities,
beasts, birds, etc., to their offspring,—a practice which seems to have prevailed generally
among the ancient Asiatics.* Surnames
have only been adopted by educated families

to the same origin, though some of them have been separated for
several centuries. I call these indigenous to the West, because
most of them have been so from the period of the earliest explorers on the Mississippi; yet the tradition among them is that they
came from about the northern lakes; which appears corroborated
by the fact, that the language of the Naudowessies, Assiniboins,
and perhaps others in that quarter, shows them to be of the same
family.—2. The different bands of the Comanches and Shoshonies
or Snakes, constitute another extensive stock, speaking one language.—3. The Blackfeet, Gros Ventres or Minnatarees, Crows
and Arrapahoes, speak dialects of another.—4. The Pawnees and
Rickaras of the north, and the Wacoes, Witchitas, Towockanoes,
Towyash and Keechyes, of Red River, are of the same origin.
The Chayennes, originally from near Lake Winnipeg, and the Kiawas (or Caiguas, according to Mexican orthography), appear unal-
lied to any of the foregoing nations.—5. Of those from the north
and east, the Algonquin stock appears most extensive,—embracing
the Potawatomies, Ottawas, Chippewas, Knisteneaux, Crees, Sacs
and Foxes; with whom the Delawares have also been classed,
though their language would now appear very distinct.—6. The
Wyandots, Senecas, and others of the Six Nations, are of the Hu-
ron or Iroquois.—7. The Shawnees and Kickapoos are of one
stock.—8. The Kaskaskias, Piorias, Piankeshaws and Weaws, are
descendants of the Miamies.—9. The Choctaws and Chickasaws are
nearly the same people.—10. The Creeks and Seminoles—though
old authors speak of the Creeks as being akin to the Choctaws,
yet there is now but little relationship to be traced in their language; while that of the Cherokees appears entirely *sui generis*.

* The *tribes* often take the names of the seceding chiefs who
originate them, or are called from some circumstance attending their
separation; but frequently they assume a name from an important
word in their languages: thus *Choctaw* and *Chickasaw* are said to
have been the names of chiefs; *Seminole* (or *Seminóleh*) and *Pioria*
imply runaways or seceders; while *Illinois*, in the language of
that ancient tribe, and *Lunnapáe*, by which the Delawares distinguished themselves, signify *man*. This last is perhaps most common; for, as each nation holds itself superior to all others, its
members call themselves *men*, in contradistinction to *boys* or *squaws*,
as they are wont to denominate their enemies.

and mixed-bloods of the border nations, and are generally taken from their missionaries or some favorite friends; except they inherit surnames from parents of white extraction.

That the Indians of America are decreasing in numbers is very well known, but many are dwindling away, perhaps, at a more rapid pace than is generally suspected. The number of the Osages, it is confidently believed, has diminished fifty per cent. within the last ten years: the once powerful tribe of Missouries is now reduced to a mere remnant; while the Mandans, as a nation, have become entirely extinct: and others have shared or bid fair soon to share the same fate. This has resulted partially from the ravages of the small-pox and other diseases, yet as much no doubt from the baneful effects of intoxicating liquors. On this account, their diminution has generally been less in proportion as they are more remote from the whites. But the 'red man' has suffered from his intercourse with the whites not in this respect alone. The incentives to luxury and avarice continually presented by them, have had a very pernicious influence. Formerly the savages were contented with the indispensables of life—generally sober, just and charitable; but now they will sacrifice their comfort—risk their lives, and commit the most atrocious outrages, to gratify their vanity and lusts—to bedeck themselves with gewgaws and finery.

CHAPTER XIII.

THE FRONTIER INDIANS.

Causes of Removal West—Annuities, etc.—Dissatisfaction of
the Indians—Their Melioration by the Change—Superiority
of their present Location—Lands granted to them—Improvements, Agriculture, etc.—Their Slaves—Manufactures—Style
of Living, Dress, etc.—Literary Opportunities and Improvements—Choctaw Academy—Harpies and Frauds—Games—
Systems of Government—Polygamy—Ancient Laws and Customs—Intemperance—Preventive Measures—A Choctaw
Enactment—Marriage and Funeral Customs of the Choctaws
—The Creeks—Their Summary Executions—Mourning—
Indian Titles—The Northern Tribes—Census of the Frontier
Nations.

For the purpose of a somewhat more dis-
criminating notice of the Indian tribes beyond
our western border—for it is to those I intend
my remarks, in these pages, to be strictly confined—I will distinguish them, according to
the prevailing classification of the West, as
'Frontier' or 'Border Indians,' which title includes those occupying that district lying west
of and immediately adjoining Arkansas and
Missouri, and known as the *Indian Territory;*
and the 'Wild Tribes' or 'Prairie Indians,'
by which are meant those who are found west
of the others, and who range those immense

plains from the borders of the Indian Territory to the Rocky Mountains. Of these I will speak in their order.

The most important of the frontier tribes, as is well known, are the Cherokees, Choctaws and Chickasaws, Creeks and Seminoles, Shawnees, Delawares, etc. It is equally well known that most of these tribes were removed from within the States, not less because of the vicious propensities which they contracted and the imposition to which they were continually exposed, than on account of the difficulty of maintaining peaceful relations between them and our own citizens, while they remained in their midst. Their situation within the States certainly presented quite an anomaly in government—independent powers within the limits of others claiming sovereign jurisdiction.

A mistaken philanthropy — mistaken for 'want of a full knowledge of all the bearings of the subject—among some people, has occasioned much censure upon this branch of the policy of our government. But were we to take into consideration the treatment of other nations towards the aborigines of America, that of the United States, when placed in contrast, would certainly present a very benevolent aspect. They have always been removed by their own consent, obtained through their chiefs and councils; and have not only been given equal amounts of land, west of the border, but have generally been removed and furnished a year's subsistence at the expense of the government, and received valuable equivalents beside, in utensils and other necessaries, and in regular annuities. These are sums, generally in money, annually paid, for a series of years, to the several tribes, proportioned usually to the size of the tribe and the amount of territory acquired from it. This institution of annuities, however, though intended as the most charitable, has doubtless been the most injurious branch of the policy of the United States towards the Indians. Being thus afforded the means of living without much labor, they have neglected manufactures, and even agriculture, to a considerable degree, and many of them have acquired confirmed habits of indolence and dissipation; and now that their annuities are growing short, they are being left destitute, without the energy, the industry, or the 'means wherewith to procure a livelihood.

But, notwithstanding the constant efforts of the general government to make them comfortable, and the immense sums of money which have been paid them, and their being located in regions far better suited to their wants and their habits of life than those they abandoned, many of them appear greatly dissatisfied with the change and with the government; which seems painfully demonstrative of that perverse, restless disposition, which appears ever to have characterized the conduct of half-civilized nations.

One ostensible reason for their unwillingness to remove, has been a reluctance to abandon their native homes and the 'graves of their fathers.' Many fabulous legends are told of the attachment of the Indian to his native soil, yet but few who are acquainted with their habitudes, will place much stress on this. Their own traditions, as well as experience, have shown, that, when left to themselves, they incline to migrate; of which the Azteques of Mexico, and the Osages, with others of our border, afford striking examples: in fact, there is scarcely a tribe on the frontier which has not its traditions of migrations at some period. The Shawnees say their forefathers emigrated from the south to the regions north of the Ohio—the Creeks, as well as many of the Choctaws, that they were originally from west of the Mississippi—besides many other cases.

But, with regard to this passage of our country's history, I will merely say, in addition, that, so far as I am able to judge, the condition of the 'red man' has been very materially bettered by the change. The lands they at present occupy are, for the most part, of a more fertile character than those which they have left. The climate is equally, or perhaps more healthy, in general; notwithstanding the dreadful mortality which afflicted many of them shortly after their removal—a calamity which was attributable, primarily, to the change of climate, as well as to the change of habits which their new dwelling-places involved; and secondarily, to the too abundant use of spirituous liquors, with which they were frequently provided by both native and white peddlers and traders, before any measures, efficient enough to check the evil, were taken either by themselves or by the general government. But, although the latter cause still prevails to some degree, I have little doubt that the average mortality among the frontier tribes, at present, is less than it was before their removal.

To each tribe has generally been granted a greater number of acres, with definite metes and boundaries, than had been ceded by them east of the Mississippi. It is deemed unnecessary, however, to swell this brief notice with a statement of the several amounts of land given to each tribe, and their localities, as these may be seen with sufficient accuracy and definiteness by consulting the map which accompanies this work.

The lands of each tribe are the property of the Indian commonwealth; and, therefore, even among the most civilized of them, the settler has a title only in his improvement, which he holds by occupancy, and can sell at pleasure. To prevent collisions in improvements, the first occupant is entitled to a certain distance in every direction. Among the Cherokees, no one can build within a quarter of a mile of the house or field of another: so, to extend their possessions, the more wealthy sometimes make several isolated improvements, scattered in different directions, within half a mile of each other.

The game in the interspersed forests having now become scarce, and that of the western prairies being too remote, the frontier Indians have generally turned their attention to agriculture, and to the raising of stock ; and most of them have large numbers of horses, cattle, and hogs.

Some of these Indians, particularly of the southern nations, have very extensive farms : but the mass of their population extend their culture no further than they seem compelled by necessity. The traveller, passing through the Cherokee Nation, is struck with the contrast between an occasional stately dwelling, with an extensive farm attached, and the miserable hovels of the indigent, sometimes not ten feet square, with a little patch of corn, scarce large enough for a family garden. In fact, among all the tribes who have no slaves, what little there is of cultivation, is mostly the work of the women. Scattered through the country, one continually encounters dilapidated huts with trifling improvements, which have been abandoned by the owners for some fancy they may have taken to some other location at a distance, better adapted, as they think, to the promotion of their comfort, and upon which they may live with less labor.

Most of the labor among the wealthier classes of Cherokees, Choctaws, Chickasaws, Creeks and Seminoles, is done by negro slaves ; for they have all adopted substantially the Southern system of slavery. Some individuals of these nations own over fifty slaves each :

but they are the only slaveholders of the frontier tribes, except very few among the Shawnees.

With some tribes, and particularly among the lower classes of the Creeks, they are inclined to settle in 'towns,' as they call them, —making large fields, which are cultivated in common, and the produce proportionally distributed. But these 'towns' are rather settlements than villages, being but sparse clusters of huts without any regularity. Indeed, there is not, I believe, a regularly laid out town in all the Indian country, nor a place that could even merit the name of a village; except Doaksville near Fort Towson, and perhaps Park Hill in the Cherokee Nation.

Besides agriculture, most of the frontier tribes attend a little to manufactures, though with no greater energy. The women have generally learned to spin, weave and sew, at which they occupy themselves, occasionally, during recess from the labors of the field. But very few of the men acquire mechanical arts or follow trades of any kind: their carpenter, wheelwright and smith work is done by a few mechanics provided the several tribes in accordance with treaty stipulations. To each tribe is furnished in particular one or more blacksmiths from the United States.

These frontier Indians for the most part live in cabins of logs, like those of our backwoods settlers; and many of them are undistinguishable, except in color, language, and to some degree in costume, from the poorer classes of their white neighbors. Even in dress and language the more civilized are fast conforming to the latter. In many families, especially of the Cherokees, the English tongue only is spoken; and great numbers of these, as well as of the Choctaws and Chickasaws, dress according to the American fashions: but the ruder portions of even these, the most enlightened nations, as is also the case with nearly all of the northern tribes, wear the hunting-shirt, sometimes of buckskin, but now more commonly of calico, cotton plaid or linsey. Instead of using hats, they wreathe about their heads a fancy-colored shawl or handkerchief. Neither do the women of these classes wear bonnets, but leave their heads exposed, or protected only with a shawl, somewhat after the manner of the Mexican females; to the lower classes of whom, indeed, the mixed-bloods of these Indians bear a strong resemblance. Their most usual dress is a short petticoat of cotton goods, or as frequently with the tribes of the north, of coarse red or blue broad-cloth.

The literary opportunities afforded to the border tribes are so important in their consequences as to deserve some notice. To each tribe has been granted, by the United States, a school fund, generally somewhat proportioned to the extent of the tribe. The Cherokees and Choctaws seem to have availed themselves of this provision to the greatest advantage. These funds are for the most part invested in American stocks, and the proceeds appropriated to educational uses, establishing schools, etc.* The tuition is, I believe, in every case, free to the Indians; and yet it is painful to know that comparatively few of the common classes will send their children.

The most extensive literary institution which has ever been in operation, for the benefit of the 'red man,' was the 'Choctaw Academy,' established in Kentucky, and supported by a common fund of several different tribes. It was not as successful, however, as was anticipated by its projectors; and is now being transferred and merged into an academy near Fort Towson, in the Choctaw country, wholly supported out of the Choctaw fund. This Academy proved very unsatisfactory to many of the tribes concerned. They said, with apparent justice, that their boys, educated there, forgot all their customs, their language, their relatives, their national attachments; and, in exchange, often acquired indolent and effeminate, if not vicious habits; and were ren-

---

* Their schools are mostly conducted in English, yet among some tribes they are often taught in their native languages. As in other respects, the Cherokees have made the greatest advancement in a literary point. Their singular system of characters representing syllables, invented by an illiterate native, is no doubt known to most of my readers. In these characters, a considerable number of books have been printed in their vernacular tongue. Many Cherokees, however, as well as Choctaws, have received good English educations. In the language of the latter also a great number of books have been published, but in which the common letter is used. A few books have also been printed in the languages of the Creeks, Wyandots, Potawatomies and Ottawas, Shawnees, Delawares, and some in the different dialects of Osage, Kansas, Otoes, etc. There is now a printing-office in operation at Park Hill, in the Cherokee Nation, and another among the Shawnees at the Baptist Mission.

dered unfit to live among their people, or to earn a maintenance by labor. There seems but little doubt that the funds of each tribe might be employed to a much better advantage in their own country. The influence of the institutions would there be more likely to extend to all classes; and by gradual, the only practicable means, a change might be wrought upon the nation.

It is one of the calamities incident to the state of ignorance in which most of these poor Indians remain, and their close, indeed political connection with the more civilized people of the United States, that they are continually preyed upon by the unprincipled harpies who are ever prowling through their country, ready to seize every opportunity of deceiving and defrauding them out of their money or effects.*

* By no means the least considerable of the frauds practised upon the frontier Indians, have been by contractors and government agents. The character of these impositions may be inferred from the following instance, as it is told, and very generally believed, upon the southwestern frontier.

It had been pretty well known, that some of those who had been in the habit of contracting to furnish with subsistence several of the southern tribes, in the year 1838 *et seq.*, had been imposing most grossly upon the Indians as well as the Government, in the way of ' short rations ' and other delinquencies, which resulted in the gain of a very large sum to the parties concerned. About the close of their operations, one of the *employés,* who was rather more cunning than the principals, took it into his head, on account of some ill-treatment he had suffered, to make an *exposé* of their transactions. He happened to hold a letter of instructions (which were of course of a confidential character), wherein were set forth the processes by which these frauds were to be practised. And to turn the affair to his particular profit, he threatened the parties with a complete exposure, unless a satisfactory *gratification* should interpose. A compromise being indispensable to the welfare of ' all whom it concerned,' a negotiation was soon set on foot: but the ' noisy customer ' was not silenced, until he was paid $13,000 in

The most depraving agencies employed to this end are the ministration of intoxicating drinks, and gaming, of both which the Indians are passionately fond, and by which they are frequently robbed of their money as soon almost as received.

Apart from the usual games at cards, dice, etc., the Indians of the border have some peculiar games of their own, as well at cards as otherwise. Among these the most celebrated is the 'Ball Play', which resembles, in some respects, the old-fashioned game of *bandy*. The wagers are usually laid upon beating the majority of a given number, a dozen or more of these games; and large amounts in horses, blankets, and other goods, and even money, are frequently staked upon the result.

Besides the ball play, *dancing* is a most favorite amusement of these tribes, indeed of all the frontier as well as prairie Indians. They formerly had many kinds of dances,— the green-corn dance, the medicine, the eagle, the scalp and the war dances. But these are now only practised by the ruder portions of the border nations and the less improved tribes; among whom may still be witnessed frequently their genuine aboriginal frolics.

The green-corn dance generally lasts seve-

cash; whereupon he delivered up the obnoxious 'papers,' and agreed to abscond. Some notice of the facts of this case are said to have been brought to the knowledge of the Government; and how it has escaped an investigation—and, more especially, how it escaped the attention of the Superintendent of that immediate district, have been matters of great surprise to those who had a knowledge of the particulars.

ral days, commencing when the new crop begins to ripen. A large arbor of green branches is usually prepared, and numerous parties of both sexes dance in a body to their native songs and rude instrumental music, accompanied by their monotonous "heh! heh! heh!" with a chorus of yells at intervals; and their movements are attended with the most comical gesticulations. Having passed through a course of 'purification' by drinking a decoction of certain stimulant herbs, prepared by their medicine-men, and put out all the fires, they strike fire anew by rubbing sticks together; and a quantity of corn, pulse and other fruits of the season, being cooked with the 'new fire,' the dance is closed with a general feast. Each family, as it is said, then takes a supply from the 'new breed' of fire. A more interesting and salutary influence of this custom, which is said to prevail among some tribes at this festival, is the cancelling or composing of all old difficulties and disputes.

The most advanced of these border nations, the *Cherokees* and the united tribes of the *Choctaws* and *Chickasaws*, have adopted systems of government, which are based upon the constitutions of our States. The Cherokee being the most complete, some account of it may not be out of place in this connection.

A council or convention of the wise men of the nation was convened on the first of July, 1839, who framed a constitution, somewhat resembling one previously established in the 'Old Nation,' of which the following are the general features. The three powers, legislative, executive and judicial, are distinguished and established. The legislative consists of a National Committee and Council. The former is composed of two and the latter of three members from each of the eight or ten districts into which the nation was to be divided—elected for two years by the people. They convene annually on the first Monday in October, and each house elects a presiding officer out of its own body. Bills are introduced, discussed and passed according to parliamentary usage.

The executive, called Principal Chief, and an assistant chief, are elected for four years by the people. The executive has the usual veto and pardoning power. He is assisted by an ' Executive Council' of five, and the common cabinet of secretaries. The judiciary consists of a Supreme and Circuit Court, and the ordinary justices of the peace. Trial by jury is secured ; and the common law of England appears to have been generally adopted. Religious toleration is guarantied, but no person can hold a civil office who denies the existence of a God, and a future state of rewards and punishments.

According to laws subsequently enacted by the same council, the punishment for murder is death ; and for an attempt to kill, a fine correspondent to the damage, for the benefit of the injured party : for rape, a hundred lashes—but for infanticide, only twenty-five to fifty ! Whipping seems the punishment for all inferior crimes; which is the same with the Choctaws and Creeks, among whom the executioners are called the 'light-horse,' a kind of police-guard, also formerly in use by the Cherokees, but now their place is supplied by a common sheriff and *posse*.

As is to be inferred from their institutions, the Cherokees stand first among the 'red men' in civilization, though in industry, morality, and sobriety, they are no doubt excelled by the Choctaws and Chickasaws, who are reckoned the most quiet and Christian-like Indians of the border.

No laws have yet been passed to enforce the payment of debts, except by the Cherokees; and these found it necessary to suspend their operation for two years. Even the most improved have not prohibited polygamy by any law; though, from the example of the whites and of the more civilized among them, as well as the exertions of the missionaries, it is growing out of repute with most of the border nations. It is still occasionally practised, however; and the ruder classes among them all, I believe, sometimes still take any number of wives, and divorce them at pleasure. But the more enlightened are married by preachers, or authorized civil officers.

With the united nation of Choctaws and Chickasaws, the executive power is vested in four chiefs, called in Choctaw *mingoes*, who are selected one from each of the districts into which the country is divided, and of which the Chickasaw tribe constitutes one. These chiefs are vested with the usual veto and pardoning powers, and are elected for four years. Most of their other constitutional provisions resemble those of the Cherokees. The Choctaws, as well as the Creeks, punish the crime of murder with death by shooting, which is generally executed immediately after trial, by the 'light-horse.'

It has become evident, however, that written laws and courts of justice, judges and juries, are still rather in advance of the state of civilization of the ruder classes, even among these most enlightened tribes. It has been found very difficult to bring them under their subordination. They have had, notwithstanding, a salutary effect in many cases, and especially with regard to murder. Among most of these nations (as well as the wild tribes), it was formerly the custom to leave the punishment of homicide to the relatives of the murdered. With the Choctaws and Cherokees, in particular, the entire clan or family of the murderer were held responsible for the crime; and though the real offender might escape, the bereaved family had a right to kill any one of his nearest relatives that could be found, up to the most remote kindred. There seemed no exceptions for accidental homicide, or killing in self-defence: the Mosaic precept of 'life for life' must be fulfilled, unless satisfactorily commuted. This savage custom had at least one salutary effect, however: the relatives themselves, instead of as-

sisting the escape, as so often occurs in civilized life, were generally the first to apprehend
and bring the fugitive criminal to justice.

But among the Choctaws, at least, any one
might take the place of the murderer, and in
the death of the substitute the law was satisfied, and the true criminal remained exempt.
An intelligent and creditable Choctaw related
to me an affecting incident, for the truth of
which he vouched. An Indian had remained
responsible for the appearance, on a certain
day, of his brother, who had killed a man.
When the day arrived, the murderer exhibited
some reluctance to fulfil the pledge, when
the other said to him : " My brother, you are
no brave—you are afraid to die—stay here
and take care of my family—I will die in
your place:" whereupon he immediately attended the appointed spot, and was executed
accordingly.

The highest honor known among them, in
fact, being that of a 'great brave,' it reflected
the greatest credit to meet death boldly. Instead of being visited by his tribe with infamy
for the crime he had committed, it rather
tended to make his name illustrious, if he
met the consequences without fear or flinch-
ing : whereas, any effort to avoid death was
attributed to cowardice. It would have been
esteemed quite as ignominious for the murderer to flee the established forfeit of his life,
as for a 'gentleman' under the 'civilized code
of honor,' to back out from a duel.

But among most of the frontier, as also the

wild tribes, a commutation, though not honorable to the perpetrator, was and still is permitted, except by the Cherokees and Choctaws. Any recompense which would satisfy the bereft family, released the murderer from further penalty.

There is scarcely any temptation which the Indian tribes have to encounter so frequently, and so seriously fatal to their social improvement, as intemperance. Of this they are conscious themselves, and most of them have adopted measures for prohibiting the introduction of ardent spirits among them, and for checking the propensity to use them, with various degrees of success. Among the Choctaws, a law was passed upon this subject, which, though not entirely, was measurably successful; and the spirit which effected its passage was worthy of the most exalted state of civilization.

It seems that the tribe had generally become sensible of the pernicious influences of strong drinks upon their prosperity and happiness, and had attempted various plans for its suppression, without success. At last, it was determined by the chiefs, captains, and head men, to strike a blow which should reach the very root of the evil at once. A council was called, and many and long were the speeches which were made, and much enthusiasm was created against the monster 'Whiskey,' and all his brood of compound enormities. Still every one seemed loth to move his arrest and execution. Finally, a

23*

captain of more than ordinary temerity arose, and offered a resolution that each and every individual who should thenceforward dare to introduce any of the liquid curses into their country, should be punished with a hundred lashes on his bare back, and the liquor be poured out. This was passed, after some slight changes, by acclamation: but, with a due sense of the injustice of *ex-post-facto* restrictions, all those who had liquors on hand were permitted to sell them. The council adjourned; but the members soon began to canvass among each other the pernicious consequences which might result from the protracted use of the whiskey already in the shops, and therefore concluded the quicker it was drank up, the more promptly would the evil be over: so, falling to, in less than two hours Bacchus never mustered a drunker troop than were these same temperance legislators. The consequences of their determination were of lasting importance to them. The law, with some slight improvements, has ever since been rigorously enforced.

Among most of the Indian tribes the daughter has very little to do with the selection of her husband. The parents usually require to be satisfied first, and their permission being secured the daughter never presumes to offer any important resistance. There is a post-nuptial custom peculiar to the full-blood Indians of the Choctaws, which deserves particular notice. For years, and perhaps for life, after the marriage of her daughter, the mother is forbidden to look upon her son-in-law. Though they converse together, he must be hidden from her by a wall, a tent, a curtain, or, when nothing else offers, by covering the eyes. During their emigration, it is said these poor superstitious matrons were put to infinite trouble so as not to infract this custom. While travelling, or in camp often without tents, the mother-in-law was afraid to raise her head or open her eyes, lest they should meet the interdicted object.

It is another peculiarity, which they have in common with some of the more northern tribes, that the Choctaw wife, of the 'old school,' can never call her husband by name. But if they have offspring—she calls him "my son's father;" or, more commonly using the child's name, when, if Ok-le-no-wa, for instance, she calls the husband "Ok-le-no-wa's father." And yet another oddity regarding names: the ignorant Choctaw seems to have a superstitious aversion to telling his own name: indeed it appears impossible to get it from him, unless he have an acquaintance present, whom he will request to tell it for him.

In burials, the civilized Choctaws follow the customs of the whites, but the ruder classes still preserve their aboriginal usages. According to these, a painted pole with a flag is stuck up at the grave, which usually remains three months. During this period they have regular mourning exercises every morning and evening; and are always prompt to avail themselves, at any other hour of the day, of the assistance of any friend who may visit them to help them to weep. At the end of the prescribed term, the friends of the bereft family attend a feast at their house, and, after dancing all night, the next morning visit the grave and pull down the pole; which is called 'the pole-pulling.' After this all mourning ceases, and the family is permitted to join in the usual amusements and festivities of the tribe, which was not allowable before.

Though the *Creeks** are generally a very industrious people, raising an abundance of corn and vegetables, yet they are quite behind their neighbors, of whom I have been speaking, as well politically as in a social and lite-rary view. Their executive consists of two principal chiefs, and their legislature or coun-cil of about forty minor chiefs or captains, who are also, *ex officio*, justices of the peace. They have no trial by jury, and their judicial proceedings are exceedingly summary—fre-quently without witnesses; for the warriors are generally too proud to deny a charge, lest it be construed into cowardice. Executions sometimes take place within an hour after the commencement of trial. Murder, rape and a third conviction of stealing are punished with death, usually by shooting; but, in case of homicide, if claimed by the relatives of the

* These Indians call themselves *Muscogee* or *Muscóhgeh.* They acquired the name of *Creeks*, by the whites, from the great number of small streams that intersect the country which they formerly in-habited—being first called, " Indians of the country of *creeks.*"

deceased, the criminal is executed with the same kind of weapon, or, if possible, the very same, with which he committed the murder.

Most inferior crimes, as has been mentioned, are punished by whipping: for the first offence of stealing, fifty lashes; for the second, a hundred and ears cropped. Adultery is punished by cutting off both the nose and ears of the adulteress; but the husband has a right to say if the law shall be executed: in fact, he is generally the executioner, and that often without trial. Notwithstanding the severity of these laws, they are for the most part rigorously enforced; though a commutation satisfactory to the aggrieved is still permitted to release the offender. Their laws, in cases of accidental homicide, are still more barbarously rigid than those of the other nations.

The obsequies of the Creeks are peculiar in this,—that at the moment an Indian expires, a gun is discharged. Their graves are generally under the floors of their dwellings, and a husband's is apt to be under the bed of his widow. The fate of the unfortunate relict is miserable enough in any country, but among the Creeks her doom is barbarously rigorous. She remains in strict mourning for four years,* with dishevelled hair and with-

---

* This custom seems to have descended from antiquity. Adair, prior to 1775, writes, that " The Muscohge widows are obliged to live a chaste single life for the space of four years; and the Chikkasah women, for the term of three, at the risk of the law of adultery being executed against the recusants." But I have not heard this custom spoken of among the Chickasaws at the present day.

out combing,—unless the relatives of the deceased interfere; whereby it is sometimes put an end to in a few months, provided the sincerity of her grief be evident and her conduct meritorious. In their mourning, however, they do not weep and cry with such clamorous vehemence as the Choctaws and others. But the Shawnees and Delawares are still more celebrated for quiet mourning. As warlike nations, they appear to disdain to mourn and wail aloud, as is the practice among the greater portion of the savage tribes.

Though these people have no family names, they generally take a kind of honorary title or *sobriquet*, as is also the case with the wild tribes, upon the occurrence of any important incident, or the performance of a meritorious feat. A singular mode of inheritance prevails among the Cherokees, the Creeks, and perhaps others. Though the women in other respects are mostly held as very inferior beings, the clans are all reckoned by them: the children pertain to the mother, and the estates descend through the female branch of the family. They say it is easy enough to verify the mothers of families, but it is difficult to identify the fathers.

The remaining tribes, inhabiting the more northern frontier, as well as the Seminoles who are located among the Creeks, possess so few distinct or striking characteristics, and, indeed, are mostly so few in number, that a particular notice of them seems hardly to be required. Suffice it to say, that all of them, as I believe, still retain their ancient systems of arbitrary chiefs and councils of sages and braves, nearly in their primitive state; and that the greater portion of them live in log huts, and cultivate the soil to a considerable extent. Though the Shawnees, Delawares, and Kickapoos, are among the most agricultural of the northern Indians, yet a few of these spend the greater portion of their time on the Prairies in hunting and in trading with the wild tribes.*

* No complete census has been taken of the frontier Indians since their removal; but the aggregate population of those settled west of the border, exclusive of the Osages, Kansas, and others of the north (who are more appropriately ranked among the Prairie Indians), is 81,541, according to the Report of the Commissioner of Indian Affairs, for the year 1843. Of these, there are reckoned of Cherokees, 25,911; Choctaws, 15,177; Chickasaws, 4,930; Creeks, 24,594; Seminoles, or Florida Indians, 3,824; Senecas from Sandusky, 251; Senecas and Shawnees, 211; Quapaws, 476; Wyandots, 664; Potawatomies, Chippewas and Ottawas, located on the waters of the Osage, 2,350; Kaskaskias and Piorias, 150; Piankeshaws, 98; Weaws, 176; Shawnees, 887: Delawares, 1,059; Stockbridges, Munsees, &c., 278; Kickapoos, 505. In addition to these, there still remain east of the Mississippi, of Cherokees, 1,000; Choctaws, 3,323; Chickasaws, 80; Creeks, 744; Potawatomies, &c., 500; Weaws, 30; besides some entire remnant tribes.

Many of the foregoing amounts, however, have been standing numbers in the tables of the reports of the Indian Department, ever since the removal of these tribes, and as it is known that most of them have been on the decline, the above aggregate is no doubt excessive. For instance, instead of 25,911, as given in the report for the Cherokees, their very intelligent agent, Governor Butler, reckoned them, in 1842, at only about 18,000: the Creeks in place of 24,594, have, in like manner, been set down at about 20,000; and in the 'Choctaw Almanac' for 1843, I find the population of that nation rated at 12,690, instead of 15,177, as stated in the Commissioner's report.

CHAPTER XIV.

INDIANS OF THE PRAIRIES.

System of Chiefs — Mode of Warfare — War-Council—The
Scalp-dance—The Calumet or Pipe of Peace—Treaties—
Public News-criers—Arms of the Indians—Bow and Arrows,
etc.—Hunting—Dancing—Language of Signs—Telegraphs—
Wigwams or Lodges—Pack-dogs—Costumes—Painting, Tat-
tooing, etc.—Indian Dandies—Manufactures, and Dressing the
Buffalo Rug—Indian Diet, Fasting, etc.—Primitive Thomso-
nians—Their domestic Animals, the Dog and the Horse—
Wampum—Their Chronology.

THOSE savage hordes which may be considered as the Prairie Indians proper, have made
little or no perceptible progress in civilization.
They mostly live by plunder and the chase:
a few eke out a subsistence by agriculture.
They consist of various distinct tribes, but
among whom there is a greater diversity of
language than of habitudes. I would not
have it understood, however, that all the customs of every band are entirely similar: it is
this assumption, together with the practice
of setting down as standing customs what
they have observed on some particular occasions, that has frequently created such a dis-
crepancy between the accounts of transient
travellers.

There is scarcely a prairie tribe, however limited in numbers, but is subdivided into petty bands, each under the immediate control of its own chief. Their systems of government are frequently compounded of the patriarchal and military. The most influential heads of families exercise a petty rule, which often extends beyond their own household to a circle of adherents. Several of these clans, bound by the ties of consanguinity or friendship, are apt to come under the control, by common consent, of some more influential chief, who may have gained celebrity in their wars; but a regular hereditary descent seems rarely established. These petty bands seldom unite under one general leader, except for the common defence, when threatened with danger. Occasionally there springs up a master spirit—a great brave and a great sage, who is able to unite his whole tribe, in which he is generally aided by a sufficient knack at sorcerous tricks to give him the character of a great 'medicine-man.'

War seems to be the element of the prairie Indians, notwithstanding but few possess much intrinsic bravery. They are, in fact, the most cowardly savages east of the Rocky Mountains, bearing but little similitude in this respect to the aborigines of the interior of the United States. They rarely attack an enemy except with a decided advantage; for the prospect of losing even a single warrior will often deter them from undertaking the most flattering adventure. It is true that, in addition to their timidity, they are restrained by the fact that the loss of a man often casts a gloom upon the most brilliant victory, and throws a whole clan into mourning. On this account they generally attack by surprise, and in the night, when all are presumed to be asleep; having care, if against a formidable enemy, that it be long enough before the morning dawn to allow them to retire beyond reach of pursuit before daylight. When the moon rises at a late hour, just before she appears, is a favorite time; for then they will have a gleam of light by which to collect and drive off the prize of stock which they may be able to frighten away. These prowling parties around a camp sometimes employ a species of signals in imitation of wolves, owls and other nocturnal animals, by which they communicate with each other—mimicking so to the life as not to give alarm to unsuspecting travellers.

War is seldom concluded upon, or even a campaign undertaken, without a general council, in which all the chiefs and most distinguished braves and sages assemble. After all are seated in a circle, the pipe is passed around until their brains are sufficiently soothed to enable them to consult the Great Spirit, and take freely into advisement the important matters under consideration. Therefore the tobacco smoke is usually blown upwards, as a propitiatory incense to the invoked spirits or genii who dwell 'upon the sky.' In this operation the smoke is generally inhaled into

the lungs, and discharged in murky streams
from the olfactories. If a council be preparatory to a campaign, the warriors sometimes
catch the tobacco smoke in the hand, anoint-
ing their bodies with it; which they fancy
renders them, if not invulnerable, at least far
more secure from the darts of their enemies.

Although in their warfare they employ every
wile and stratagem, and faithless subterfuge,
to deceive their enemies, and in battle are relentless and cruel in the extreme, yet they
seldom resort to those horrid punishments
and tortures upon their prisoners which were
wont to be inflicted by the savages of the interior of the United States, during their early
wars with the whites. The practice of burning their captives alive, said to have prevailed
many years ago among some prairie tribes,
seems now to have grown quite out of use.

Upon returning from a campaign after a
defeat, the village resounds for many days with
the lamentations, the shrieks and wailings of
the women and children; in which, not only
the bereft families, but all the relatives and
most of the friends of the deceased join. If,
on the contrary, the warriors have been successful, and bring home scalps of their enemies, all join in their most famous festival, the
scalp-dance. In this fête the savage trophies
are usually elevated upon a pole in the centre
of the dance; or perhaps the brave captors
retain them in their hands, tossing and swing-
ing them about their heads; at the same time
vehemently apostrophizing these ghastly re-

presentatives of their enemies, with the most taunting and insulting bravadoes; branding the nation with cowardice and effeminacy; daring them to come forward and revenge the blood of their slain; then concluding with scoffs and exulting yells at the dastardly silence of their enemies, whom they represent as afraid to whisper a note of vengeance against their superiors and masters, the triumphing conquerors. After the warriors have become fatigued, the squaws and children generally continue the barbarous festivity; in the midst of which some vainglorious brave will rise perhaps, and repeat the apostrophic fanfaronades, representing that the very squaws and papooses hold them in cowering submission, and that henceforth these only will be sent to subdue them; their warriors being reserved for more noble enemies. These brutal rites and rodomontades being concluded, the scalps are handed to their owners, who cure and paint them for future war-dances and other kindred ceremonies.

When a tribe wishes to celebrate a treaty of peace with an enemy, a number of their warriors, as ambassadors, or perhaps a whole band, move to the neighborhood, and send the calumet or pipe of peace, which supplies the place of the flag of truce among civilized nations:* though, when the embassy

* This seems to have been of ancient and general use among the savages of North America. " I must speak here of the *Calumet*," remarks Father Marquette, " the most mysterious thing in the world. The sceptres of our kings are not so much respected; for the savages have such a deference for this pipe, that one may call

is to the whites, a flag usually accompanies, as they have learned that this is our token of peace. The overture being accepted, the chiefs and principals of each band meet in council, sometimes in a wigwam, if there be a suitable one, else in the open air, taking their seats, as usual, upon their haunches in a circle proportioned to the number. If there be presents—and these are an indispensable earnest of friendship from the whites—the essence, the seal of the treaty, without which negotiation is vain—these are laid in the centre. A personage in the capacity of an orderly sergeant then lights the calumet, which he hands to a principal chief, who, before smoking, usually points the stem towards the four cardinal points, and towards the heavens and the earth—then takes a certain number of whiffs (generally about three), and passing it to the next, who draws an equal number of whiffs, it thus continues around the circle, in the direction of the sun, each sending fumid

it *the god of peace and war, and the arbiter of life and death.* One, with this calumet, may venture amongst his enemies, and in the hottest engagement they lay down their arms before this sacred pipe." The deference is perhaps not so great at the present day, though the ' pipe of peace' is still very much respected. Even the ashes from the calumet seem to be held sacred; for, usually after smoking, the pipe is emptied in some corner of the lodge specially allotted for the purpose. But as they have generally learned that smoking is not practised by the whites on these occasions, it is now not commonly held important for us to smoke with them; but presents are expected instead. Anciently, however, they were more strict; for, in another place, the same author (in 1673) relates :—
" As soon as we sat down, they presented us, according to custom, their *calumet,* which one must needs accept, for else he should be lookt upon as an enemy, or a meer brute; however, it is not necessary to smoak, and provided one puts it to his mouth, it is enough."

24*

currents upward from the nozzle. It seems
looked upon as sacrilege for a person to pass
before the pipe while the chiefs are smoking ;
and the heedless or impudent are sometimes
severely punished for the act. The 'big talk'
follows, and the presents are distributed by a
chief who exercises the office of commissary.
But in the petty truces among each other,
presents are scarcely expected, except they
be claimed by the more powerful party as a
matter of tribute.

Travellers and hunters are generally obliged
to hold a treaty or 'big talk' with every band
of prairie Indians they may encounter, if they
wish to maintain friendly relations with them.
Treaties have also been held, at different periods, with most of the wild tribes, by agents
of the U. S. Government, yet for the most part
with but very little effect—they generally forget or disregard them by the time the presents
they may have received are consumed.

These treaties, as well as other council de-
liberations, are generally promulgated by a
sort of public crier, who proclaims the stipulations and resolutions from lodge to lodge;
and the event is preserved in the memory of
the sages to future generations. Among some
of the tribes their memory is assisted by the
famous 'wampum belt,' which is a list or belt
made of wampum beads, so interwoven in
hieroglyphic figures as to form a record of important events. Others preserve the same by
hieroglyphic paintings on their buffalo rugs,
and the like.

The *arms* of the wild Indians are chiefly the bow and arrows, with the use of which they become remarkably expert. A dextrous savage will lay a wager, at short shots, against many riflemen. Indeed, there is hardly any more effective weapon than the bow and arrow in the hands of an expert archer. While the musketeer will load and fire once, the bowman will discharge a dozen arrows, and that, at distances under fifty yards, with an accuracy nearly equal to the rifle. In a charge, they are eminently serviceable; for the Indian seems to discharge his arrows with about as much certainty when running at full speed as when standing.

The usual length of the Indian bow is about three feet, though it is sometimes as much as four. It is generally made of elastic wood, yet elk's horn is occasionally used. Those of the latter are made of two of the longest and straightest shafts, which, being shaved down to the necessary proportions, are united by lapping their ends together and binding them firmly with sinew. Bows have also been made, in the same manner, of a pair of buffalo ribs; but as well these as those of elk-horn, are rather items of curiosity than of service: at least, they are not equal to bows of the bois-d'arc tree. Even the backs of the *wooden* bows are often lined the whole length with a broad strip of sinew, and the whole wrapped with shreds of the same. The arrows are generally about thirty inches long, and pointed with iron, though the primitive

flint points are still met with among some of
the wildest tribes.

Besides these, the lance or spear, the use
of which they may have learned from the
Mexicans, is an effective weapon in the charge
as well as the chase. Many are also provided
with the Northwestern fusil, and some have
rifles. Very few, however, have acquired the
dexterity of our frontier Indians with this
deadly weapon. But no Indian deems his
equipage complete without a 'scalping-knife;'
yet among the western prairie Indians the
tomahawk is but little known. These employ, in its stead, the war-club or 'war-
hawk,' which are bludgeons with an encased
stone for a head in the former, and with a
transverse blade or spike in its place in the
latter. Many are provided with shields of
raw buffalo or elk skin, upon which are frequently painted some rude hieroglyphical de-
vices representing the enemies they have
slain, as well as any other notable exploits of
which they can boast. Such as are without
these have their titles to renown recorded
commonly upon the handles of their hatchets,
their war-clubs, or perhaps tattooed upon their
breasts or arms.

Besides war, *hunting* seems the only creditable employment in which a warrior can engage. Every other labor is put upon the
squaws; and even when a party of hunters set out, they generally provide themselves
with enough of these 'menials' to take charge
of the meat: the Indian only deigns to shoot

down the game; the squaws not only have it to cure and pack, but to skin and dress.

Except such tribes as are expert with the rifle, very few of the prairie Indians hunt other game than the buffalo: not, as some have presumed, because they deem all small game too ignoble for them, but because the former is at once easiest taken, and affords the most bounteous supply of food. The antelope is too wild and fleet for their mode of hunting, and is only occasionally taken by stratagem; while the deer, as difficult to take in the chase, is less easily entrapped. But, mounted upon their trained steeds, and with the arrow or lance, they are not to be excelled in the chase. A few of them, let loose among a herd of buffalo, will soon have the plain strewed with their carcasses.

Among the amusements of the Indians generally, *dancing* is perhaps the most favorite. Besides a war accompaniment, it is practised as a recreation, and often connected with their worship. Their social frolics, in which the squaws are commonly permitted to join, are conducted with less ferocity of manner than their war dances; though even these are accompanied with the wildest and most comical gesticulations, and songs full at once of mirth and obscenity. In these, as well as in the war and scalp dances, a sort of little drum and a shrill squeaking pipe are their common instruments of music.

As so many tongues, entirely different, are spoken by the prairie Indians, a 'language of signs' has become the general medium of communication between the different nations. This system of signs has been brought to such perfection among them, that the most intricate correspondence seems to be intelligibly conducted by such as have acquired a proficiency in this 'dumb language.'

Their systems of telegraphs are very peculiar, and though they might seem impracticable at first, yet so thoroughly are they understood by the savages, that it is availed of frequently to immense advantage. The most remarkable is by raising smokes, by which many important facts are communicated to a considerable distance—and made intelligible by the manner, size, number or repetition of the smokes, which are commonly raised by firing spots of dry grass. When travelling, they will also pile heaps of stones upon mounds or conspicuous points, so arranged as to be understood by their passing comrades; and sometimes they set up the bleached buffalo heads, which are everywhere scattered over those plains, to indicate the direction of their march, and many other facts which may be communicated by those simple signs.

Almost every tribe has some peculiarity in the construction of their lodges or wigwams, in the manner of arranging their camps, and in the different items of dress, by any or all which peculiarities the experienced traveller is able to recognize the tribe of their owner. If a moccasin, or other article of apparel be found, he at once designates the nation to which it belongs—even a track is often sufficient to identify them.*　Also by the 'sign,' and especially the remains of fires, he determines the interval elapsed since their departure with remarkable accuracy.

The lodges are composed of a frame of small poles or rods, covered usually with buffalo skins, which receive but little further preparation than the currying off of the hair. Some give their lodges a round wagon-top shape, as those of the Osages, which commonly consist of a frame of bent rods, resembling wagon-bows, and covered with skins, the bark of trees, or, as is generally the case in their villages, with grass and earth.　Again, some dispose the poles in two parallel lines, and incline them against a ridge-pole, which gives the wigwam the shape of a house-roof: others, planting small rods in a circle, so twine the points together as to resemble, in some degree, when covered, a rounded hay-mow: but by far the most general style, among the wild tribes, of constructing their wigwams, is by planting the lodge-poles so as to enclose a circular area of from ten to twenty feet in diameter (the size depending upon the number of the family) ; and the tops being brought together, it forms a conical frame, which is closely covered with skins, except an aperture in the apex for the escape of the

* As many tribes make their moccasins of different shapes—some with hooked toes, others broad—some with the seam on the bottom, etc., there is always a palpable difference in the tracks.

smoke. This is the style of the Comanches and most other tribes of the great plains. The doors of the lodges being closed with a skin, they are kept very comfortable in winter with but little fire. This is kindled in the centre, and a hole is left in the vertex of the lodge, through which the smoke is discharged so freely, that the interior is but seldom infected by it.

These lodges are always pitched or set up by the squaws, and with such expedition, that, upon the stopping of an itinerant band, a town springs up in a desert valley in a few minutes, as if by enchantment. The lodge-poles are often neatly prepared, and carried along from camp to camp. In conveying them, one end frequently drags on the ground; whereby the trail is known to be that of a band with families, as war parties never carry lodge-poles. The Chayennes, Sioux and some other northern tribes, often employ dogs for carrying and dragging their lodge covers and poles; indeed for conveying most of their light baggage: but, for ordinary travelling purposes and packing their more weighty baggage, they use horses. So few navigable waters traverse the Prairies, that none of the Indians of the high plains have learned the use of canoes or water-craft of any kind.

There is some variety in the dress in vogue among the different tribes; though they all use moccasins, leggins, flap or breech-clout, and, when not in active pursuits, they generally wrap their bodies in buffalo rugs, blankets or

mantles of strouding, according to their wealth
or opportunities. Some of the northern tribes
display considerable ingenuity and taste in
the manufacture of moccasins. But this is
the work of the women, who often embroider
them with beads and colored porcupine quills,
in a most beautiful manner. The *leggin* is
a buckskin or cloth covering for the leg and
thigh, as of the pantaloon. A superfluous list
is usually left outside the seam, which, if of
skin, is slitted into long tassels, or if of cloth,
the wide border remains entire, to dangle and
flap upon the exterior of the legs. A strip of
strouding (that is, coarse broad-cloth) about a
foot in width and a yard or more long, constitutes the most usual flap; which being
passed betwixt the legs, the ends are secured
under the belt around the waist, whence the
leggins are suspended. As the flap is sometimes near two yards long, a surplusage of
half a yard or more at each end is sometimes
left dangling down before and behind.

The Indians use no head-dress, but support
the bleakest rains and hottest suns of those
bare plains with naked heads. Nevertheless,
their coarse black hair seems 'fertilized' by
exposure; for they rarely become gray till an
exceeding old age; and I do not recollect to
have ever seen a bald Indian. Their eye-
sight also, they retain in extraordinary vigor,
notwithstanding the want of protection even
of the eye-lashes and brows (which are plucked out), and in spite of the constant use of
apparently deleterious paints around the edges

of the lids. Though using no regular head-dress, they sometimes wear, as a temporary ornament, a fantastic cap of skins; and it is not unusual to see a brave with the entire shaggy frontlet of a buffalo, horns and all, set upon his head—which, with his painted face, imparts a diabolical ferocity to his aspect.

The Indians of the Plains, almost without exception, wear long hair, which dangles in clotted tresses over the shoulders—besmeared with gum, grease and paints, and ornamented with feathers and trinkets. But most of those intermediate tribes nearer our border, trim their hair in a peculiar manner.

Vermillion seems almost indispensable to the Indian's toilet; but in default of this they paint with colored earths. When going to war, they bedaub their bodies with something black—mud, charcoal or gunpowder, which gives them a frightful appearance. But 'ornamental' painting is much more gay and fanciful. The face, and sometimes arms and breast are oddly striped and chequered, interspersed with shades of yellow and white clay, as well as occasional black, though the latter is chiefly appropriated to war. Especial pains are taken to tip the eyelids most gaily with vermillion.

Besides painting, most of the tribes tattoo—some sparingly, while others make their faces, breasts, and particularly their arms, perfectly piebald. This seems practised to some extent by all the savages from the Atlantic to the Pacific. Figures are pierced in the skin with any sharp pointed instrument—often the keen prickles of the cactus—and pulverized charcoal or gunpowder, or sometimes the coloring juice of a plant, is rubbed into the fresh punctures, which leaves a lasting stain.

The most usual female dress is of the style worn by the Comanche squaws, which is described in speaking of that nation. With respect to dress and other ornaments, however, the order of the civilized world is reversed among the Indians. The 'fair sex' paint less than the men—use fewer ornaments generally, and particularly, wear no pendants in the ears. While a savage beauty pays but little attention to her person, a 'brave' will spend as much time at his toilet as a French belle, in the adjustment of his ornaments—his paint, trinkets, beads and other gewgaws. A mirror is his idol : no warrior is equipped without this indispensable toilet companion, which he very frequently consults. He usually takes it from its original case, and sets it in a large fancifully carved frame of wood, which is always carried about him. He is also rarely without his tweezers, whether of a fold of tin, of hardened wood, or of spirally twisted wire, with which he carefully eradicates, not only his beard, eye-lashes and brows, but every villous particle from his body, as fast as it appears; for they consider everything of the kind as extremely unbecoming a warrior. It is on this account that Indians have frequently been represented as naturally beardless.

All Indians are passionately fond of beads, trinkets and gewgaws of every kind. The men often cut up the rim of the ears in a frightful manner to admit their pendants of beads, plate, shells, etc.; and even strips of lead are sometimes twined around the separated rim, by the weight of which the detached portion of the ear is frequently swagged down some inches. It is not unusual to see near half a pound even of beads and 'jewelry' swung to each ear; and among some tribes, also a large quantity to the nose. The hair is likewise garnished with the same, and the neck with strings of beads, bear's claws, and the like; while the arms are profusely ornamented with bracelets of wire or plated metal. The 'braves' are those who commonly deck themselves with the most gaudy trappings, and would usually be taken by a stranger for the chiefs of the band, who, on the other hand, are often apparelled in the most ordinary manner.

The squaws are, in every sense of the word, the slaves of the men. They are called upon to perform every toilsome service—to carry wood and make fires—to skin and dress the meat and prepare the food—to herd, drive up, saddle and unsaddle their lords' horses—to pitch and strike the lodges—to pack up the baggage, and often indeed to carry heavy loads during travel—in short, everything else pretty much but fight and hunt, which the

Indian boasts of, as being his peculiar, if not his sole vocations.

What little of manufacturing is done among the Indians is also the work of the women. They prepare the different articles of apparel. In embroidering moccasins and their leathern petticoats, etc., their greatest skill, particularly among the northern tribes, is exhibited. But the most extensive article of their manufacture is the *buffalo rug*, which they not only prepare for their own use, but which constitutes the largest item of their traffic with the Indian traders. These are dressed and cured exclusively by the squaws.

To dress a buffalo rug, the first step is to 'flesh' the skin, or neatly scrape from the inner surface every carneous particle. This is generally done with an instrument of bone, cut something in the shape of a small adz, with a serrate edge. For this operation the skin is sometimes suspended in a frame upon the branch of a tree, or a fork of the lodge— though more commonly, perhaps, stretched with pegs upon the smooth ground, with the flesh-side up. After it dries, the spongy surface of the skin is neatly curried off with another adz-shaped bone or handle of wood, with a flat bit of iron transversely set for the blade, which is edged after the manner of a currier's instrument. The surface is then besmeared with brains (which the Canadians call *mettre à la cervelle*), and rolled up with the flesh-side in, in which condition it is left for two or three days. The brains of the same

25*

animals are generally used; those of a buffalo being more than sufficient to dress his own hide. The pores of the skin being fully penetrated by the brains, it is again wetted, and softened by continual working and rubbing till it dries. To facilitate this last operation, it is sometimes stretched in a frame and suspended before a fire, when the inner surface is scraped with the serrated adz before mentioned, and finished off by assiduous rubbing with a pumice-stone, if that article can be had; if not, by passing the skin by small sections rapidly back and forth over a slack cord.

Buffalo rugs are often observed with a seam in the middle. This is caused by cutting them in two, partly for convenience in dressing them, and partly to take out the hollow occasioned by the hump, particularly of the bulls. The hump of the cow being less, their skins generally bear dressing without being cut. The hide is frequently split in two, however, in skinning the animal, the Indians preferring to commence on the back.

The buffalo skin is often dressed without the wool. To this end the hide is soaked in water till the hair is loosened, when it is 'curried' and 'brained,' and softened as above. Of these dressed buffalo skins (known among Mexicans as *anta blanca*) is made a considerable portion of the Indian clothing for both sexes—even the petticoats of the females; though these prefer buckskin when they can procure it.

The chief aliment of the Prairie Indians is

flesh, though in default of this they often sustain themselves for weeks together upon roots, herbs and fruits. The buffalo are the common herds of these savages, affording them 'food, raiment and shelter.' It seems there were anciently occasional cannibal tribes* in those regions, but not a vestige of cannibalism, as I believe, now remains; except such an inhuman appetite may be ascribed to some of the more savage warriors, who, as I have heard, in the delirium of exultant victory, have been known to devour the hearts of their bravest victims, at once to satiate their bloodthirsty propensities, and to appropriate to themselves, as they fancy, the valor of the slain enemy.

However, they make food of nearly every animal of their country, and often of insects and even the filthiest vermin. By some tribes, grasshoppers, locusts and the like are collected and dried for future use. Among nearly all the northern tribes, the flesh of the dog† is considered as the greatest delicacy; so much so, indeed, that when a favorite visitor is expected to dine, they are sure to have served up for him the choicest pieces from some one of the many fat whelps which pertain to every lodge. In this way travellers have often been

---

* A diminutive tribe on the Texas border, called Tonkewas, made food of human flesh within the present century, and, it may be, of late years, though I have not heard it mentioned.

† Dogs seem always to have been a favorite article of food among the aborigines of different parts. Father Marquette, in his voyage down the Mississippi in 1673, remarks of an Indian feast, "The third service was a huge Dog, whom they killed on purpose," &c.

constrained to eat Indian dog-meat, and which, prejudice apart, is by no means an unsavory viand; but the flesh of the wolf, and even the American dog, is generally said to be ill-flavored and sometimes insupportable. The polecat is also a favorite food among the Indians; and though the celebrated Irving, during a "Tour on the Prairies," seems to claim a deal of credit for having "plumped into the river" a dressed polecat, whereby he prevented an Osage from "disgracing" their fire by the cooking of it, yet all travellers who have tasted the flesh of this animal have pronounced it fine, and of exquisite relish. "The flesh of the skunk," observes Dr. James, in his account of Maj. Long's Expedition, "we sometimes had dressed for dinner, and found it remarkably rich and delicate food."

These wild tribes are without other kitchen utensils than an occasional kettle. They sometimes broil their meats, but often eat them raw. A savage will feast upon the warm carcass of the buffalo; selecting bits of the tenderloin, liver, etc., and it is not uncommon to see him use the gall as sauce! Feasting is one of their favorite enjoyments; though their ability to endure hunger almost exceeds belief. They will fast a week and yet retain their strength and vigor: but then when they do procure food again, it seems as if they never would be satiated.

The Indians of the Prairies have become acquainted with the medical virtues of many of their indigenous plants, which are often used in connection with the vapor sweat, and cold bath: wherefore we may consider them as the primitive Thomsonians. After a profuse sweating, assisted by decoctions of sudorific herbs, in a tight lodge filled with vapor by pouring water over heated stones, and while still dripping, they will leap into a pool of cold water, and afterwards wrap themselves in a buffalo rug. This course has proved successful in some diseases, and extraordinary cures have thus been performed: but in other cases, and especially in the small-pox, it has been attended with horrible fatality. They frequently let blood for disease, which is oftenest performed with the keen edge of a flint: and though they sometimes open a vein, they more commonly make their incisions indiscriminately. They have great faith in their 'medicine men,' who pretend to cure the sick with conjurations and charms; and the Comanches and many others often keep up an irksome, monotonous singing over the diseased person, to frighten away the evil spirit which is supposed to torment him: all of which, from its effect upon the imagination, often tends, no doubt, to hasten recovery.

These Indians keep no domestic animals, except horses, mules, and dogs. With the latter every lodge is abundantly supplied; yet, as has already been shown, they are more useful appendages than the annoying packs which so often infest the country cabins, and frequently the villages, in the United States.

Horses, however, constitute the chief wealth of the prairie Indian. These are the incentives to most of their predatory excursions. The tribes of the north in particular, as well as the white trappers, frequently maintain their horses, during winter, upon the tender bark of the sweet cottonwood, the *populus angulata* of the Mississippi valley.

The western savages know nothing of the value of money. The wampum bead, it is true, among a few tribes, somewhat resembles a currency: for, being generally esteemed, it acquires a value in proportion to size, and sometimes passes from hand to hand, in exchange for necessaries. The legitimate wampum is only of shells, and was of aboriginal manufacture; being small long tubes with an ovate surface, or sometimes simply cylindrical; and handsomely polished: but imitations of glass or porcelain seem now the most common. The color is generally white, though sometimes blue or striped.

These Indians have no knowledge of the divisions of time, except by palpable distinctions; as days, moons and years; which last they commonly represent as so many springs, or falls of the leaves, or as often by winters, that is, frosts or snows. Distances are represented by days' journey, which are oftener designated by camps or 'sleeps.' When a day's journey is spoken of in general terms, it is meant that of a band in regular travel, which rarely exceeds twenty miles.

CHAPTER XV.

INDIANS OF THE PRAIRIES.

Intermediate Tribes—Their Wigwams and their Hunting Excursions—Dress and Cut of their Hair—The Pawnees—The Osages — Their Roguery — Matrimonial Customs — Accomplished Mourners—Their Superstitions—The Indian Figure—The 'Pawnee Picts'—Wild Tribes—Census—The Comanches—Their Range—Their Sobriety—Their Chiefs, etc.—Female Chastity—Comanche Marriage—Costumes—Horsemanship—Comanche Warfare—Predatory Forays—Martial Ceremonies—Treatment of Captives—Burial and Religious Rites.

THE tribes inhabiting near the borders of the frontier Indians differ from those that range the far-western prairies in several traits of general character. The former have their fixed villages, and, for the most part, combine the pursuits of agriculture and the chase. They form, indeed, a sort of intermediate class between the frontier and the wild tribes, resembling the one or the other in all important particulars. I will merely notice in this place a few of the characteristics by which the more conspicuous of these tribes are distinguished.

Their village wigwams differ from the lodges of the wilder tribes, in their being much more substantial, and usually covered with grass and earth instead of skins. The Indians commonly remain in their villages during the inclement portion of the winter; yet most of them spend the early spring upon the Prairies in buffalo-hunting; as well as such portions of the summer and autumn as are not occupied in the cultivation and gathering of their crops, which they secure in *caches* till their return.

In dress they differ but little from the wilder tribes, except that, having more communication with the whites, they make greater use of our fabrics—blankets, coarse cloths, calicoes and the like. Their most striking peculiarity consists in the cut of their hair. Most of them, instead, like the Indians of the Plains, of wearing the hair long, trim and arrange it in the most fantastic style. In the care bestowed upon this part of their toilet, they cannot be excelled by the most *soigneux* of civilized dandies. They shave a large portion of the head, but leave a fanciful lock upon the crown as a scalp-crest (an indispensable trophy for the enemy), which is in general gorgeously bedecked with painted feathers and gewgaws.

The *Pawnees*, who now have their principal village on the Loup Fork of the Platte river, are perhaps the most famous of these tribes. Small bands of their war-parties roam on foot through every portion of the Prairies, often to the Mexican frontier, though they generally contrive to return well mounted.

When upon these expeditions, they may properly enough be considered the Ishmaelites of the Prairies—their hands are against every man, and every man's hand is against them. They will skulk about in the vicinity of a prize of mules or horses for several days unsuspected, till a favorable opportunity offers to pounce upon them.

This nation is divided into four principal bands, the Grand Pawnees (or *Grand Pans*, as called by the Canadians), the Republics, the Mahas or Loups, and the Tapage or Noisy Pawnees. Their relatives, the Rickaras, are now considered a distinct tribe.

The *Osages* are at present the most important western branch of the Dahcotah stock, after the Sioux. There are two bands of them, the Big and Little Osages. Though the Pawnees stand most prominent as prairie marauders, these are unsurpassed in simple rogueries. Expertness at stealing appears indeed to constitute a part of their faith, and an all-important branch of education, in which degrees are conferred in true 'academic order;' for I have been assured, that, in their councils, the claims of the candidates to the honors of rogueship are duly considered, and to the most proficient is awarded an honorary badge —the right to wear a fancy feather stuck athwart his scalp-crest.

The habitudes of the Osages do not appear to have undergone any material change, notwithstanding the exertions of the government and the missionaries to civilize and to christianize them. Some of their matrimonial customs are very curious and rather peculiar. The eldest daughter seems not only 'heiress apparent,' but, when married, becomes absolute owner of the entire property and household of her parents—family and all. While single, however, she has no authority, but is herself held as a piece of merchantable property, estimated somewhat as in civilized life, in proportion to her 'charms,' and to the value of her 'hereditaments.' She is therefore kept under the strictest watch by her parents, that she may not diminish her worth by any improper conduct.

When some warrior 'beau' has taken a fancy to the heiress and wishes to possess her and her estate of sisters, dogs, rugs and household, he takes his finest horses, (and if she be a 'belle' he need not attempt it unless he have some of the noblest), and tying them at her lodge door departs without saying a word; leaving them, like a slow-match, silently to effect his purpose. After the 'pretender' has disappeared, the matron of the premises and her lord inspect the valuables, the 'demure damsel' barely venturing a sly peep through some crevice of the wigwam. If the offer be found unworthy, the horses are sent back to the owner as silently as they came, or maybe with some apology, provided he be a warrior whom they are afraid of offending. But if accepted, the father takes instead some of his own horses and ties them at the door of the proposer, as a token of admission. If the parties be without horses some other valuables are employed in lieu. After this the marriage is solemnized with a joyous fête and their primitive ceremonies.

But now the son-in-law is fully indemnified for his heavy 'disbursement' in the *purchase* of his bride; for he at once becomes possessor of the entire wealth of his father-in-law—master of the family-lodge and all the household: if there be a dozen younger daughters, they are all his *de droit*—his wives or slaves as we may choose to consider them: in fact, the 'heiress' herself seems in the same predicament, and the wife among them all who may have the tact to gain the husband's affections, generally becomes mistress of the 'harem.' From the refuse of this estate of 'fair ones' the indigent warriors and inferior Indians who are not able to purchase an 'heiress' are apt to supply themselves with wives upon a cheaper scale.*

The Osages bury their dead according to the usual Indian mode; and, though it seems always to have been the custom among most

* The custom of taking all the sisters of a family is also said to be common among the Kansas, Omahas and other kindred tribes; indeed it appears to have prevailed from the earliest ages among all the Dahcotah family as well as many Algonquins and most other tribes about the great Lakes. Mons. La Salle, in his trip from these to the Mississippi in 1763, remarks of the savages of those regions: "They marry several Wives, and commonly all Sisters, if they can, thinking they agree better in their Family." Hennepin, Charlevoix and others speak of the same custom. Murray also mentions something of the kind among the Pawnees. Forbes alludes to the same in California. But I am uninformed, whether, in these several instances, the husband's right was only *de facto*, or *de jure* as among the Osages, to all the younger sisters.

savage nations, to keep up a chorus of hideous
cries and yells for a long while after the death
of a relative, yet the Osages are by far the
most accomplished mourners of them all. Being once encamped near a party of them, I
was wakened at the dawn of day by the most
doleful, piteous, heart-rending howls and lamentations. The apparently distressed mourn-
er would cry with a protracted expiration till
completely out of breath. For some instants
he seemed to be in the very last agonies:
then he would recover breath with a smother-
ed, gurgling inspiration: and thus he continued for several minutes, giving vent to
every variety of hideous and terrific sounds.
Looking around, I perceived the weeper standing with his face towards the faint gleam
which flitted from the still obscured sun.
This was perhaps his idol; else he was standing
thus because his deceased relation lay in that
direction. A full 'choir' of these mourners
(which is always joined by the howls and
yelps of their myriads of dogs), imparts the
most frightful horror to a wilderness camp.

It is considered among these as well as
other 'crying' tribes, quite a merit to be a
graceful weeper: it becomes even a profitable
vocation to those whose eyes and lungs are
most capacious of such things. If you tell
an Osage that you have lost a kinsman or
friend for whom you wish him to mourn, he
will undertake the service for a trifling reward—and acquit himself with more 'credit'
—more to the spirit than the best tragic

actor.. He will mimic every exterior indication of grief and the most heart-felt wailing, till the tears trickle in torrents down his cheeks.

The Osages seem generally to worship a good and evil spirit, and to believe in the most usual Indian paradise. No people can have more implicit faith in witchcraft and all kinds of sorcery and superstitions—such as holding converse with deceased friends or relations—appointing a time to die, etc.: and instances are related of their fancying themselves thus called to the world of spirits, which would so powerfully affect the imagination as to cause them to pine away, and sometimes die even to the appointed day.

Owing partially, no doubt, to the burdensome life they lead, the squaws of all the tribes are, for the most part, much more inclined to corpulency than the men. They are generally chubby and ill-favored, while the males are usually tall, erect, well-turned and active. For their proverbial straightness, however, the Osages are perhaps more famous than any of the other prairie Indians.

The *Wacoes, Witchitas* and their kindred tribes on Red River, are, for the most part, a very indigent race. They are chiefly remarkable for their profuse tattooing, whereby they have sometimes acquired the title of ' Pawnee Picts:' the females particularly make a perfect calico of the whole under-jaw, breast and arms, and the mammæ are fancifully ornamented with rings and rays. The tattoo, in fact, seems to constitute the chief female or-

26*

nament of these tribes; for their only gown consists of about a yard and a half of strouding, or else a small dressed skin, suspended from the waist, and constituting a sort of primitive petticoat. The upper portion of the body remains uncovered, except by a blanket or small skin, thrown loosely over the shoulders. The men are often without any other vesture than the flap, and sometimes a buffalo rug or blanket.

As the remaining tribes of this intermediate class present few or no distinctive characteristics, we will pass at once to the consideration of the *wild tribes* proper of the Great Western Prairies.* These neither cultivate the soil nor live in fixed villages, but lead a roving life in pursuit of plunder and game, and without ever submitting themselves to that repose—to those fixed habits, which must always precede any progress in civilization. But as the *Comanches* are the only tribe of these 'wandering Arabs' of the Plains which

* The population of the intermediate tribes is estimated, according to the Report of the Commissioner of Indian Affairs, for 1842, as follows: Pawnees, 12,500 souls (though some experienced traders rate them at only about 5,000); Rickaras, 1,200; Chippewas, Potawatomies and Ottawas, 2,298; Sacs and Foxes, 2,348; Winnebagoes, 2,183; Iowas, 470; Poncas, 800; Omahas, 1,600; Otoes and Missouries, 931; Kansas, 1,588; Osages, 4,102;—besides of Caddoes and Inyes about 500; Wacoes, Witchitas, Towockanoes, Towyashes and Keechyes, 1,000; who maintain themselves chiefly in Northern Texas. The wild tribes proper of the Prairies, are, the Comanches, consisting of about 10,000 souls; Kiawas, 2,000; Apaches, 100; Arrapahoes, 2,000; Chayennes, 2,000; besides many others to the north and westward, who rarely descend within the regions to the notice of which these pages are confined. As these tribes would doubtless average at least three-fifths females, they could hardly turn out one-fifth of their numbers in warriors, though this is the usual rule of estimating them by men of Indian experience.

present any distinguishing features of interest—any prominent points of national character—the remarks that follow will be devoted almost exclusively to them.

The relationship of the Comanches to the Snakes or Shoshonies, shows them to have descended from the north: in fact, it is but half a century since their range was from the Arkansas river northward; but at present this stream is their *ultima Thule*. Yet they even now acknowledge no boundaries, but call themselves the lords of the entire Prairies—all others are but 'tenants at will.' They lead a wandering sort of life, betaking themselves whithersoever the seasons or the habits of the buffalo, their chief object of pursuit, may lead them. Although during summer they are not unfrequently found as far north as the Arkansas river, their winters they usually pass about the head branches of the Brazos and Colorado rivers of Texas.

In their domestic habits, these Indians, for the most part, resemble the other wild tribes; yet in some respects they differ materially. One of the most interesting traits of difference is to be found in their distaste for ardent spirits: but few of them can be induced to taste a drop of intoxicating liquors; thus forming an exception, I believe, to the entire race of the 'red man,' who appears to have a constitutional appetite for strong drinks. The frontier as well as the prairie tribes—the Mexican as well as the Mountain Indians—all are equally slaves to their use.

The Comanches are divided into numerous petty bands, each under the control of its own particular chief. When a chief becomes old and care-worn, he exercises but the 'civil authority' of his clan; while his son, if deemed worthy, otherwise some distinguished brave, assumes, by 'common consent,' the functions of war-chief. As is the case with all barbarous tribes, their chiefs assume every judicial and executive authority. Complaints are made to them and sentence summarily pronounced, and often as summarily executed. For most offences, the chief, if he considers his authority sufficiently well established, freely uses the rod upon his subjects. He rarely attempts this, however, upon noted warriors or 'braves,' whose influence and resentment he may have reason to fear. The punishment of murder among these, as among most of the savage nations, devolves upon the bereaved relatives, who are free to pursue and punish the perpetrators according to their own liking, which is seldom short of death. But the offended party, if disposed to compromise, has also the privilege of accepting a commutation and releasing the murderer.

The husband seems to have complete power over the destinies of his wife and children. For adultery, his punishment is most usually to cut off the nose or ears,* or

* This custom was perhaps once quite extensive. It prevails among the Creeks to the present day, and was anciently practised by other southern nations; and "Among the Miamis," says Father Charlevoix, "the Husband has a right to cut off his wife's nose if she runs away from him."

both; and he may even take the life of his
unfaithful wife with impunity.   The squaw
who has been mutilated for such a cause, is
ipso facto divorced, and, it is said, for ever pre-
cluded from marrying again.   The consequence is, that she becomes a confirmed har-
lot in the tribe.   Owing in part, no doubt, to
such severity in their customs, the Comanche
squaws have ever been noted for their chastity.
This may result also, in some degree, from the
circumstance, that the Comanche husbands,
fathers and brothers, seldom or never subject
their wives, daughters and sisters, to that de-
basing traffic practised among so many of the
northern nations.

Like the other wild tribes, the Comanches
tolerate polygamy, the chiefs and braves sometimes taking as many as eight or ten wives at a
time.   Three is considered the usual number,
however, for 'subjects' or common warriors,
and nine for the chiefs.   Their marriage ceremonies vary in different bands; but the following has been represented as the most
usual.   Unlike most other tribes, the consent
of the maiden has to be obtained.   This done,
the lover, from apparent delicacy, goes not
to the father of his intended, but, in accordance with a custom which prevails among
some other tribes, communicates his desire to
an uncle or other aged relative, who enters into
the marriage contract.   The parties, however,
are not yet fully betrothed; but, as a test of
the submission of the bride to the service of
her proposed lord, the latter ties his riding-

horse at her lodge door. If she turn him loose, she has resolved finally to reject him; but if she lead him to the *caballada*, it is an unequivocal agreement to take the charge of his horses and other property; and the marriage is soon concluded. The 'uncle' now communicates the engagement to the chief, who causes the 'bans' to be published, that no other wooer may interfere. As the horse is with them the type of every important interest, the bridegroom next proceeds to kill the least valuable one that he is possessed of; and, taking out the heart, hangs it at the door of his betrothed, who takes and roasts it, and then dividing it into two parts, each eats a half, which perfects the bond of wedlock. The heart of the buffalo or other animal may perhaps be substituted, if the bridegroom has not a superabundance of horses. Should the circumstances of the parties admit of it, the marriage is usually celebrated with feasting and dances; though, in general, the Comanches are less fond of dancing than most other Indians.

The Comanche dress consists of the usual leggins, moccasins, flap and blanket or robe. Many wear in addition a kind of leathern jerkin, or tight jacket closed before. Their moccasins differ from those of other tribes, by having a lengthy tassel of leathern fringes attached to the heels, which trail the ground as they walk. Instead of this fringe, the tassel sometimes consists of the tail of a polecat or some other animal. When he can procure it, the young warrior is wont to wear a mantle and leggins of strouding. Both of these articles, according to the 'latest fashions,' should be one-half red, the other blue. The bi-colored mantle, as well as the blanket or buffalo rug, is carelessly thrown over the shoulders, and must be long enough to drag the ground; for they seem to have an instinct for the 'regal grandeur of a sweeping gown.'

Though all the far-western Indians wear their hair long, the Comanche seems to take most pride in the voluminousness of his 'tresses,' and the length of his *queue*, which is sometimes eked out with buffalo or other hair, till its tip reaches the ground, and is bedaubed with gum, grease and paint, and decorated with beads and other gewgaws. We are not to think that foppery and coxcombry are generated exclusively in civilized life. I am sure I never saw a vainer creature than a Comanche brave in full costume, of dress, trinkets and paint. He steps as if he disdained the very ground upon which he walks.

The dress of the Comanche squaw is usually a kind of loose gown or tunic of leather, or cotton if it can be procured, which hangs from the shoulders and is bound around the waist with a girdle; thus presenting a resemblance in its appearance to our ordinary female costume. They wear moccasins, to which short leggins are attached, and which constitute a sort of leathern hose. They are not permitted to wear long hair: that 'manly' prerogative would be degraded by such an association. It is therefore kept docked so as scarcely to reach the shoulders.

A style of dress similar to that of the Comanche females, is worn by those of most of the erratic tribes. The squaws of the north usually embroider their leathern frocks in a fanciful manner with colored porcupine quills and beads, and bedeck the borders with rattling shells, tags, hawk-bells, and the like. Such as have the fortune to marry Canadian or American trappers, are those who usually dress most gaily.

The prairie Indians generally are an equestrian race; yet in horsemanship the Comanches stand decidedly pre-eminent; and can only be equalled by the Northern Mexicans, and perhaps the Arabs. Like the latter, they dote upon their steeds: one had as well undertake to purchase a Comanche's child as his favorite riding-horse. They have a peculiar mark for their animals: every one which has pertained to them may always be recognized by a slit in the tip of each ear; a practice apparently universal among all their tribe.

In their warlike expeditions they avail themselves of their equestrian skill with wonderful success. As they always fight on horseback, they depend chiefly upon the charge, at which they use their arrows and javelins* with wonderful efficacy. On such occasions a Comanche will often throw himself upon

---

* The Comanches employ usually short-handed javelins or lances, declaring, like the Spartan mother, that cowards only need long weapons.

the opposite side of his charger, so as to be protected from the darts of the enemy; and, while clinging there, he will discharge his arrows with extraordinary dexterity from underneath his horse's neck. Different from the 'prowling' tribes, they seldom attack at night, or in timbered or rough regions; for they would then be unable to manœuvre their coursers to advantage.

Although not meriting the title of brave Indians, they are held by the Mexicans as the most valiant of their border: but when they come in contact with Americans or any of our frontier tribes, they generally appear timid and cowardly. Their predatory forays are therefore directed mostly westward. They make continual inroads upon the whole eastern frontier of Mexico, from Chihuahua to the coast; driving off immense numbers of horses and mules, and killing the citizens they may encounter, or making them prisoners—particularly the females and boys. Of the latter they make slaves, to perform such menial service as usually pertains to the squaws, particularly the herding of the stock. It is perhaps this alleviation of their labor by slaves, that has contributed to elevate the Comanche women above those of many of the northern tribes. Of their female captives they often make wives; a fate which has befallen some of those taken from Texas.

Strange as it may appear, their captives frequently become attached to their masters and to the savage life, and with difficulty are induced to leave them after a few years' captivity. In fact, these prisoners, it is said, in time often turn out to be the most formidable savages. Combining the subtlety of the Mexican with the barbarity of the Indian, they sometimes pilot into their native frontier and instigate horrid outrages. The department of Chihuahua has been the greatest sufferer from their inroads.

But, though at continual war with the south of the republic, for many years the Comanches have cultivated peace with the New Mexicans—not only because the poverty of the country offers fewer inducements for their inroads, but because it is desirable, as with the interior Mexican tribes, to retain some friendly point with which to keep an amicable intercourse and traffic. Parties of them have therefore sometimes entered the settlements of New Mexico for trading purposes; while every season numerous bands of New Mexicans, known as *Comancheros*, supplied with arms, ammunitions, trinkets, provisions and other necessaries, launch upon the Prairies to barter for mules, and the different fruits of their ravages upon the South.

This powerful nation, combined with the petty southern tribes, has also waged an almost unceasing warfare upon Texas, ever since her independence. War-parties have frequently penetrated to the very heart of the settlements, perpetrating murderous outrages, and bearing away into captivity numerous women and children. They have entered the city of Austin, then the seat of government, in open day; and, at other times, have been known to descend to the very sea-coast, committing many frightful depredations. "On the 8th of August, 1840," writes a friend who resided at Linnville, on Matagorda Bay, "several hundred Comanches came down from the mountains, and charged upon us without the least notice. They burned and made a perfect destruction of the village and everything pertaining to it."

Besides continual hostilities with Mexico and Texas, the Comanches are at war with most of the Indians of the Mexican interior, as also with the tribes of the more northern prairies — and particularly the Arrapahoes and Chayennes, with whom they have many bloody rencounters. But they generally remain on friendly terms with the petty tribes of the south, whom, indeed, they seem to hold as their vassals.

As these Indians always go to war on horse-back, several days are often spent previous to a campaign in equestrian exercises and ceremonies, which seem partly to supply the place of the war-dance of other tribes; though they sometimes join in preparatory dances also. It is not an unusual custom, when a campaign is in agitation, for a band of about twenty Comanche maidens to chant, for three nights in succession, the victories of their ancestors, the valor of their brothers and cotemporaries, and the individual prowess of all such young warriors as they consider should engage in the contemplated enterprise: and all those designated by the serenading band are held as drafted for the campaign. Fired by the enco-miums and excitations of the 'fair *cantatrices*,' they fly at once to the standard of their favor-ite chief: and the ceremony is concluded by a war-dance.

Upon their return from a successful expe-dition, the 'war-worn corps' halts on some elevation at a distance from the village, and a herald is sent forward to announce their arri-val. Thereupon, one of their most respectable and aged matrons issues forth to receive them, carrying with her a very long-handled lance kept for the purpose. On the top of this the victorious Indians fasten all the scalps they may have taken, so arranged that each shall be conspicuous. The matron squaw then approaches the wigwams, holding her scalp-garnished lance high in the air, and chanting some favorite war-legend. She is soon joined by other squaws and Indian lasses, who dance around as the procession moves through the entire circuit of the village. If the victory has been brilliant, the dancing and feasting are apt to be kept up for several days, all parties joining in the general jubilee.

If the conquerors bring any prisoners with them, these have to encounter the scourg-ings and insults of the squaws and children. Each seems entitled to a blow, a kick, a pinch, a bite, or whatever simple punishment they may choose to inflict upon the unfortu-nate captives. This done, they are delivered over to the captors as slaves, and put to the service and drudgery of the camp.

After their first entrance it seems rare for them to treat their captives with much cruelty: though an instance was related to me by some Mexican prisoners, of a very barbarous massacre which they witnessed during their captivity. Two white men, supposed to be Texans, were tied to a stake, and a number of their marksmen, retiring to a distance and using the naked bodies of their victims as targets, began wantonly to fire at them, and continued their horrid sport, until some fatal balls put an end to their sufferings! The capture of these had probably been attended with some aggravating circumstances, which induced the savages to resort to this cruel method of satiating their revenge.

If a campaign has been unsuccessful, the warriors separate upon their return, and drop into the village one by one. Nothing is now heard for several days, but the wailings and howlings of the bereft relatives and friends. They will also scarify their arms and legs, and subject themselves to other carnal mortifications of the most powerful character. On these occasions their previous captives, and particularly such as may belong to the nation of their victorious enemy, are sure to be roughly treated, and sometimes massacred by the enraged relatives of the slain.

When a Comanche dies, a similar course of mourning is practised; and he is usually wrapped in his best blankets or robes, and interred with most of his 'jewelry' and other articles of esteem; accompanying which, it is said, an awl and some moccasin leather is generally added, as a provision, it would appear, for his use during his long journey to the 'happy hunting ground' beyond the grave. They also kill the favorite horses of the deceased, which are often buried by his side, doubtless with the same object.

The religious notions of the Comanches resemble, in most particulars, those of the other prairie tribes; yet they appear to have an occasional peculiarity. Some say the dry buffalo head or cranium is their idol. True it is that they show it great reverence, and use it in many of their mystic ceremonies. The Pawnees also hold these buffalo heads, with which the plains are strewed, in great reverence; and usually for many leagues around, these sculls are set up facing towards their villages, in the belief that the herds of buffalo will thus be conducted by them into their neighborhood. Of the Comanches the sun is no doubt the principal deity. When preparing for a campaign, it is said they do not fail to place their arms betimes every morning on the east side of their lodges, that they may receive the blessing of the fountain of light at his first appearance. This indeed seems the usual time for offering their devotions to the sun, of many tribes of the American aborigines.

THE END.

DATE DUE

GAYLORD   PRINTED IN U.S.A.